LEARNING TEXT

ENGLISH LEGAL METHOD

Rebecca Huxley-Binns, LLB
Lecturer in Law, Franklin College

 Blackstone Press

Published by
Blackstone Press Limited
Aldine Place
London W12 8AA
United Kingdom

Sales enquiries and orders
Telephone +44-(0)-20-8740-2277
Facsimile +44-(0)-20-8743-2292
e-mail: sales@blackstone.demon.co.uk
website: www.blackstonepress.com

ISBN 1-84174-277-5
© Nottingham Law School, Nottingham Trent University, 2001
First edition 1996
Second edition 1998
Third edition 2001

British Library Cataloguing in Publication Data
A catalogue record for this book is available from the British Library

Printed and bound in Great Britain by Watkiss Studios Limited, Biggleswade, Bedfordshire

LEARNING TEXT

ENGLISH LEGAL METHOD

FOREWORD

The Blackstone LLB series was designed for students studying law at undergraduate level and has become a firm favourite. A principal objective of the series was to make the law accessible by explaining it, as far as possible, in ordinary words. We also wanted to ensure that through Self Assessment questions and Activities students would be able to progress at their own pace, to support the learning process and to ensure they were in control of their own learning. We also tried to replicate in book form the kind of learning experience that students would receive when attending face-to-face classes at Law School.

The new series continues this approach through the combination of a *Learning Text* and *Cases & Materials*. However, we have made a significant change in the format of the series by carrying the *Cases & Materials* in electronic form in a CD inside the back cover of this book. This has enabled us to keep the *Learning Text* at a manageable length for undergraduate study while giving us the opportunity to widen and deepen the extracts from primary and secondary sources of law in the CD. As before, the *Cases & Materials* is fully cross-referenced from the *Learning Text*. In this single book you will find all you need to bring you understanding of the law.

The new series has been completely revised and aims to state the law as on 28 February 2001. Wherever possible, later developments have been incorporated.

CONTENTS

CONTENTS

CONTENTS

PREFACE

Learning the law is a lifelong process. The frequent changes in legal rules and the vast volume of legal material mean that it is impossible for any individual to be an expert in all areas of law. It is however perfectly possible for you to master the basic principles and skills which form the foundation of all legal study. It is also important for you to grasp the basic structures and processes of the legal system and for you to be able to build on that knowledge to become adept in your study of substantive areas of law. This *Learning Text* tries to help you to acquire legal skills within the context of the English Legal System, but it is not just a precursor for later study. The rules and concepts of the legal system are as complex and controversial as any you may find in other areas of the law. So, this text is designed with two main aims: first to provide you with legal skills as a means to an end, and secondly to allow you to acquire knowledge of the legal system as an end in itself.

You will have the opportunity as you work through the *Learning Text* to develop and practice the ability to analyse the raw material of the law, found in *Cases and Materials*. You will have to examine cases and statutes with which all lawyers engage whatever their chosen field of law. You will examine cases from the nineteenth century to statutes that may not yet be in force. You will have to examine the operation of existing law, suggest proposals for reform and predict the possible effect of future law.

The English Legal System is in a state of flux. The overhaul of the civil legal system in 1999, started by the Woolf Report, the Human Rights Act 1998 which came into force on 2 October 2000 and the Access to Justice Act 1999, to name but three, are changes that need to be considered in detail, but those details have not always been available from the Government, Parliament, or more commonly the Lord Chancellor, at the time of publication. What you will find is that the law has often been stated as correct at 1 January 2001, but beware some of it was already out of date by the date of publication. As frustrating as this is, this is the nature of the law. Provided you can master some of the key legal skills, it does not matter how the law changes in the future, you will be able to cope as you will use the same skills time after time.

I am very grateful to Erika Kirk, author of the first two editions of this book, for allowing me to use her thoughts, insights and material in the preparation of this edition. Thanks are also due to my colleagues at Nottingham Law School for their assistance, particularly to Juliette Grant, Jonathan Griffiths and Phil Huxley. Responsibility for the final product, however, rests firmly, with me.

This is for Gary.

Rebecca Huxley-Binns
January 2001

TABLE OF CASES

TABLE OF CASES

TABLE OF STATUTES

TABLE OF STATUTES

TABLE OF SECONDARY LEGISLATION

CHAPTER ONE

'DOING THE LAW': INTRODUCTION TO LEGAL SKILLS

1.1 Objectives

By the end of this chapter, you should be able to:

- identify the skills needed to 'do the law';

- identify some of the underlying principles of the English Legal System;

- develop the basic techniques of studying law;

- apply these skills to new situations.

1.2 Introduction

This **Learning Text**, and the **Cases and Materials**, is a tool to help you develop the skills you will need to become a good lawyer. A lawyer's role is to problem solve. There is a great deal of work to do to be able to solve a legal problem. There is a great deal of law. However, the skills used to solve legal problems are the same whatever type of law is involved. There are also a number of underlying principles and systems of which you must be aware that also form part of a lawyer's arsenal of skills and knowledge. These key areas are the subject of this chapter.

The main *legal skills* are:

1. understanding how you learn, when you learn best and how to increase your capacity for learning;
2. reading texts and abstracting key legal information;
3. researching the law by reading cases and Acts of Parliament;
4. applying this newly acquired knowledge to new situations.

The *underlying principles* of the English Legal System are the sources of law (courts and judges, parliament, Europe and so on); the relationship between these sources and the personnel and services involved in the administration of the system.

However, it is the process of APPLYING law to facts; applying knowledge to new situations, that is 'doing the law'.

Imagine you go to a solicitor for legal advice. You expect the solicitor to know the answer, or to be able to find out, and then tell you how the law applies to your particular circumstances.

The skill of application is vital to success in the law and it is a skill that most of us have, but rarely realise that we do.

ACTIVITY 1

Turn to *Cases and Materials* (1.1) and read the information given there.

Now read the following information and write brief notes on the advice you would give. This is a short exercise and should take no more than 10 minutes.

There is a wide ridge of very high pressure over the British Isles. Winds are very light near coasts but inland areas are calm. Daytime temperature will reach a maximum of 31° C. This anticyclone will persist for several days.

You have been asked to help organise an all-day picnic near an inland lake to go windsurfing followed by an evening barbecue. Your friends have asked if there may be any problems with travelling, what they should take and what they should wear.

You might have advised that fog could be a problem early in the morning, that they should take sunscreen, a sun hat or parasol, wear light clothes and may be a swimming costume and forget the windsurfing. This is because in anticyclonic conditions, winds are very light, so you can bathe in the lake, but you won't be able to surf on it. You might also have advised your friends to take warm clothes for the evening, as the temperature will go down with the sun. Of course, if the picnic was taking place in the winter (unlikely with temperatures of 31°)], you would advise them not to leave too early because of the fog, to wear wet suits, wrap up warm, or forget the idea and stay in some where with a real fire!

The process that you have just completed is the essence of legal skills. You were given new information (the definition and description of an anticyclone) and asked if you could apply it to a new situation.

Now try to do this in a legal context. This may be the first time you have completed a 'legal' task, but the skills you will use below are the same that you used in Activity 1 above. This may take up to 15 minutes, but try not to spend any longer as the exercise is quite straightforward.

ACTIVITY 2

The definition of murder is causing the death of another human being, intending to kill them or intending to cause them serious bodily harm.

Do you think the following people (defendants) are guilty of murder?

1. **Ann and Bob, married for 7 years, have had a row and Ann goes back to her mother's house for a while. After a couple of weeks, Bob goes round to visit her and to try to persuade her to go home. Bob is carrying a shotgun in his jacket and he has sawn the barrel off it. When Ann refuses to return home, Bob takes the gun out of his coat and threatens to kill himself unless she changes her mind. Bob becomes very agitated and the gun goes off, killing Ann.**

2. **Carol has been having an affair with David for six months. She finds out that David has been cheating on her with Elaine, a woman who lives near Carol. Carol buys some petrol and goes round to Elaine's house, when she knows David is not there, pours the petrol though the letterbox and sets it alight. Her motive was to frighten Elaine into staying away from David, but two of Elaine's children are killed in the blaze.**

You might have said 'I don't know', because you want more information. It may be that you have made provisional conclusions. This means you may have decided Bob may be guilty of murder _if_ it had crossed his mind that he might kill Ann if she refused him. You may feel that his intention was not to kill or cause serious bodily harm, but to commit suicide. You might therefore feel he is not guilty of murder.

Similarly, Carol's motive was clear, but if she knew Elaine and/or her children were home, you may feel that provides evidence that Carol intended to cause their death or, at least, serious injury. Of course, if you were a member of the jury, you may have heard the answers to these questions in the form of evidence. Your decision would then, perhaps, be easier.

The above examples are based on real cases which you will come across in the Criminal law and the law of Evidence; and there is no right or wrong answer to these questions at this stage because the two cases were decided many years ago when the law was different.

The purpose of setting this exercise was to introduce to you the idea of identifying the law (that was done for you here in the definition of murder) and applying the law to new situations. That's 'doing the law'.

1.3   Learning Skills

Your success in becoming a skilled law student will depend not only on the degree of motivation which you bring to it, but also on your ability to adapt your behaviour in order to learn most effectively. To some extent, the way in which you learn best will vary from the way in which others learn, so self-awareness is important here.

Research into how people learn has revealed that effective learners have a greater awareness of the techniques which they use in their studies, and adjust these techniques according to the type of task which they are undertaking. To improve your awareness of your own study methods, why not keep a journal or diary noting what, when, where and how you studied, and how effective you felt these study times were for you. Then compare your results with the responses which you give now to the questions set out below, and the advice which follows. You may be able to draw some useful conclusions about how to change your own study habits.

Your study journal can be in any form you like, but if you are not sure how to keep this sort of diary, turn to *Cases and Materials* (1.2) to see an example of an extract from a study diary.

SAQ 1

Based on your previous experience of learning situations, whether at school, college, or in the workplace, consider the following questions, and try to answer them as honestly as you can.

1. **At what time of day do you feel most alert and most able to solve problems or read complex texts?**

2. **For what length of time can you concentrate on the sort of activities referred to in question 1 without your mind wandering?**

3. **What sort of environment helps you to undertake serious study? For example, do you attempt this type of work with the television or radio on?**

The aim of this exercise is to help you become aware of your own behaviour when you are in a learning situation. If that behaviour is helping you to learn well, then it is important to work with it, rather than against it. But if you find that you are behaving in such a way that your learning is hindered, then it may be necessary to modify your behaviour if possible. The following suggestions are obviously based on generalisations about human behaviour, but nevertheless contain a great deal of truth.

For example, if you know that you study best in the morning, and that you need a quiet environment in which to read and think, you may find that getting up half an hour earlier each day in order to study the *Learning Text* enables you to make much greater progress than if you attempt to study for an hour in the evening when you are tired and there may be more to distract you.

Your study environment is important too. Although it can be helpful to make use of short periods of time on public transport and in work breaks for reviewing materials on which you are currently working, you will need a permanent base at home in which to study, with a desk or table, and somewhere to store your books and papers. It is particularly helpful if your family is able to respect this as 'your' space, so that you are able to leave work in progress on the desk without having to put everything away after each study session.

Tidiness is often a matter of personality: you may be the type of person who is not affected by an untidy working environment, and you may be able to work effectively in spite of a cluttered desk on which there are numerous books and papers not related to the task in hand. For a great many people, however, chaos is stressful! You may well feel more in control of the academic work if your study space is clean and tidy. Certainly you should try not to use your desk or table as storage space, but to have on it only those books and papers which are required for the current piece of work.

Try to ensure that you have a good light source over your desk, which does not shine directly in your face, and that the temperature in the room is neither too hot nor too cold. Experiment with the seating arrangements so that you can be relaxed but alert, and if bending your head over books causes your neck or shoulders to ache, try using a reading-stand which props your books open on the desk at an angle. It is worth taking the time to attend to these details, for you will find that you will concentrate much better if your environment is suitable for the task.

By the way, if you find that you can concentrate on your studies with the radio on, all well and good. But some people will find that music can be a distraction, and trying to watch the television whilst studying tends to spoil the enjoyment of both activities!

SAQ 2

Here are two more questions which may help you to identify your own preferred style of study.

1. **Do you plan ahead and set yourself goals when you have academic work to do? Do you find that the work often takes longer than you originally estimated that it would?**

2. **Do you prefer to work in a group, rather than on your own, and to exchange ideas with others before coming to your own conclusions?**

For most people, time spent thinking about what you are going to do before you actually start to do it will not be time wasted. Setting targets, both for the long and the short term, will help to ensure that you complete assignments on time, and allocate time to be spent on different topics more carefully. To set long term targets, you will probably want to take account of examination dates, coursework deadlines, and your own holidays or other special events, such as periods when you know that you will be very busy in your job and may have less time to spend on your studies.

Short term targets will help you to structure the week, the day, and even the next two hours ahead. But don't be surprised if you underestimate the amount of time which you need to allocate to a particular task. For example, if you plan to spend two hours working on a particular chapter from the *Learning Text* you may find on some occasions that you cannot complete the amount of reading which you have set for yourself in the time allowed. This is a very common occurrence in any situation, and you need to bear in mind when setting your targets that it is human nature to think (mistakenly!) that a task can be completed in less time than it actually takes. You may need to get into the habit of adding an 'extra time' allowance to your targets.

Finally, remember that your own personality type will affect the way you study. If you enjoy the company of other people, and prefer to work in a group rather than on your own, then you may occasionally find yourself feeling very alone with the work. The amount of written material which must be read in order to study law means that you will have to spend quite a lot of time working alone, and this may be hard for you. If there are other students in your geographical area who feel the same way as you do about this, then you may be able to set up an informal network so that you can have discussions with each other from time to time. But you will also have to come to terms with the fact that studying is often a solitary occupation.

1.4   Reading Skills

Just as there are many different styles of learning, so there are a number of different styles of reading which you may need to use according to the nature of the text with which you are working. Whether you spend a long period of time making a careful study of a piece of text, or whether you glance over it quickly, will depend on the type of material it is, and the reasons for which you are reading it.

SAQ 3

Consider the different types of text listed below. First ask yourself *why* you would read these items, and then think about *how* you would read them (i.e. quickly, slowly, carefully, selectively etc.). Write your answers in the space provided next to the list.

A newspaper

The index of a textbook

An advertisement in a magazine

A chapter of *Learning Text*

A novel

A train or bus timetable

The contents page of a textbook

You will have discovered from this exercise that your own method of reading already varies more than you may have realised. Some types of text, such as newspapers and advertisements, you probably read out of interest. If you are looking for particular items in the newspaper or advertisement, then it is likely that you will browse through the text first, then concentrate and read more thoroughly the parts that are of particular interest to you. The same may be true when you are seeking specific information from the bus or train timetable, as you will probably skim over the parts that are not relevant to you and study those sections which contain the details you need.

Reading a novel is a different matter. Presumably you are doing this for enjoyment and therefore you will be reading attentively, trying to absorb details about the plot and the characters in order to follow the story. Attentive reading will also be required when you study the *Learning Text*. Whether you are reading a chapter for the first time and trying to obtain mastery of the subject matter, or whether you are selecting information to use for an assessed piece of work, you will probably be employing a higher level of concentration than when reading the newspaper, and noticing more of the details of the text.

To aid your concentration when studying the *Learning Text* or any other legal textbook, you may find you wish to make notes. This is especially the case if you are gathering information for a piece of written work. In this situation it is most important to include in your notes exact details of the name, date, author, and page numbers of the book you have used. This information will be needed if you have to provide a bibliography to your essay, and in any event, you should always acknowledge the source of your information if you have taken a particular quotation or line of argument from a book. It is really frustrating if you take notes without recording these details, as you will have to search through the books all over again when you come to provide the references for your work.

Reading the contents page or index of a textbook requires a different technique again. In this case, you will probably be looking at the contents page to get an overall picture of what is in the book and whether it is useful to you, and at the index to help you find the answer to a specific question, and so you will probably browse these pages until you find what you are looking for. The point of all this is that you need to be aware of the way in which you read, so that you can use an appropriate technique according to the type of text and the reason why you are reading it.

1.4.1 READING TEXTBOOKS

When reading the *Learning Text* and extracts from the *Cases and Materials* or any other legal book, it is vitally important that you find some way of maintaining your interest in what you are reading. You will find that legal material is not always easy to read, and there is often a great deal of it! You need to find a way of engaging with the text, so that you think about what you are reading and why you are reading it as you go along, otherwise you will undoubtedly have the all too common experience of reading a paragraph of text without concentrating properly, and then realising that you have no idea what you have just read.

One way in which you can increase your awareness and concentration whilst reading is to set yourself tasks related to the reading, similar to the Self Assessment Questions which are set for you in this *Learning Text*. First, you need to be very clear about the reason why you are reading the text. Are you looking for a specific piece of information to answer a question? If you are, then you will need to have that question at the forefront of your mind, and keep reminding yourself not to get distracted from the specific search.

If you are reading for mastery of a legal topic, before you begin to read thoroughly, skim through the material, and then set yourself some questions which you hope to be able to answer when you have finished reading. For example, if you are learning about the doctrine of consideration in contract law, you might set yourself the task of being able to define consideration in two short sentences, to give three examples of something that constitutes consideration, to name four important cases on the subject, and to identify one area in which there has been debate amongst lawyers about the nature of consideration. This sounds like a lot to do, and you may think it will take a lot longer than simply reading the text in the normal way. But in fact it could save you time, as you will be less likely to have to keep re-reading the text because you did not concentrate on the first read through. It's worth a try anyway!

ACTIVITY 3

In *Cases and Materials* (1.3.1) you will find an extract from Elliott and Quinn, *English Legal System*, 3rd ed, London, Longman, 2000, pp. 148-172.

The extract concerns juries, that is a group of up to 12 people without legal expertise (lay people) who decide issues of fact in 'certain' legal cases.

Imagine you have been asked to read the extract in preparation for a tutorial, but you have not been told to research any particular aspect of the topic. Before you start, answer these questions:

1. Will you makes notes? If so, how detailed will they be? If not, will you be able to recall key issues you may wish to bring up in tutorial?

2. How long do you think reading the extract will take? It is 17 pages long.

Now read the chapter.

1. Did you plan to take notes? Did you take notes?

2. How long did it take? Reflect on this answer in your study diary.

The chapter you have read is very accessible in that it uses subheadings to guide you through the topic. Not all texts do this, so be prepared to ask yourself questions as you progress to keep an eye on the subject matter.

ACTIVITY 4

Two days before a tutorial, you are telephoned and asked to bring with you notes on the following:

1. Five cases that illustrate jury use in the English legal system (note: you may be asked to justify your choice).

2. A summary stating whether jury selection is truly random.

Please prepare these notes. This should take about 30 minutes.

A suggested answer to each of these tasks is in *Cases and Materials* (1.3.1), where you will also find advice on note-taking skills.

Whilst reading the extract, you may have noticed words which were unfamiliar to you. This will be a common occurrence once you begin to read legal books more frequently. It is therefore a good idea to have both a reliable English dictionary, and a specialist legal dictionary available, so that you can check the meanings of words which you have not encountered before.

There are an increasing number of legal dictionaries on the world wide web. Two that are reliable and quick are found at http://www.duhaime.org/diction.htm and at http://www.wld.com/conbus/orans/. Whilst both are U.S. sites, they do provide clear and accessible translations for often obscure legal terms. (Note: web addresses cannot be guaranteed. If these sites do not work, do a search for 'dictionary AND law'.)

Textbooks and dictionaries are not the only legal materials which you need to read however. Two of the primary sources of law which you will have to be able to handle are statutes (Acts of Parliament) and cases decided by the courts. Later in the *Learning Text* you will learn a lot more about how to analyse these sources, but you need to become familiar with the look of them now, so that you can feel comfortable using them.

1.4.2   READING CASES

Case law as decided by the various courts which constitute the English Legal System (together with case law from the European Courts) is vitally important to the development of the law. It is therefore necessary for you to become familiar with the conventions (or traditions) about the way in which reported cases are set out, and that you know how to identify important pieces of information which are provided in the report.

ACTIVITY 5

In *Cases and Materials* (1.3.2), you will find a typical report of a case decided by the courts, which you should read through carefully. You could try to ask yourself questions about the case as you read, as you may have done when reading the extract from the textbook in the previous Activity. When you read the case, there will undoubtedly be many words and concepts which you do not understand at present. Try not to let this worry you too much at the moment. The aim of this exercise is simply to introduce you to a case, and allow you to see for yourself what this important source of law looks like. After you have read the case, try to answer the questions set out below, using your common sense and powers of observation. You are allowed to refer back to the case to do this – you are not expected to do it from memory.

The following questions refer to the letters (A-Z) found in the right hand margin next to the case. The letters do not form part of the case; we have added them to guide you around it. The first question is answered for you to show what is being asked for.

A.　　How would you describe this?

It is the name by which the case is known. It is called the case citation. Different types of cases have different types of citations. (More information is given below.)

B.　　Is ..?

C.　　Is ..?

D.　　Why do you think there are two dates here?

E.　　What is this and what is it here for?
　　　　(This may be easier to describe when you have read the whole case.)

F.　　Describe what this is (don't repeat the content, but explain what it is).

G.　　Is ..?

H.　　Is ..?

I.　　Is ..?

J.　　Is ..?

K.   Is ..?

L.   Who are these people?

M.   What is *cur adv vult*?

N.   You may need to refer back to D to explain what this date signifies.

O.   What do you think the 'CJ' at the end of Lord Bingham's title might mean?

When you have read the next couple of paragraphs, write down a brief summary of the facts of the case.

P.   Why do you think the appellant (Comerford) thought the consequence of allowing police protection would be detrimental to his case?

Q.   What does '[sic]' mean?

R.   In this paragraph, Lord Bingham CJ defines jury nobbling. You should already have an understanding of what it is from the chapter you read for Activity 3, but precisely how does Lord Bingham CJ define it?

S. What is '*R* v *Dodd* (1981) 74 Cr App R 50'?

T. What is '*R* v *Ling* [1987] Crim LR 495'?

U. In this paragraph, Lord Bingham CJ clearly states what procedures should be followed in making an application for police protection of jurors during a trial. What are these procedures?

V. Can you guess what a '*venire de novo*' is from the context?

W. Why do you think Lord Bingham CJ refers to the three cases in this paragraph?

X. What 'Act' is Lord Bingham CJ referring to? Why?

Y. What do you think 'dismiss this appeal' means? (Who 'won' the case?)

Z. Can you describe what information is included in italics here? Who is NP Metcalf Esq Barrister?

The answers to these questions can be found in ***Cases and Materials*** **(1.3.2)**. As you can see from looking at the extract, there are a number of different sections in a law report. Fortunately, a standard format is usually adopted by the publishers of the reports, and this will make it easier for you to find your way round the sections.

1.4.2.1 Case Citations

A case citation is the name by which the case is known. In the above activity, the citation is **R v Comerford [1998] 1 All ER 823, CA**. Most case citations are abbreviated to just the surname(s) of the relevant party once they have been written in full, but the numbers and letters that follow are also important (see below).

The first thing to note is that *R* v *Comerford* is a criminal case. This means it is concerned with a <u>prosecution</u> brought in the name of and on behalf of the reigning monarch against a defendant.

Thus the '*R*' stands for *Rex* or, in this case, *Regina*, the Latin for King and Queen. Almost all cases that start with '*R*' are criminal cases.

A civil case has a different case citation. Civil law involves one party <u>suing</u> another (see **Chapter 2**). In civil cases, the surnames of the parties appear.

For example, if Smith wanted to sue Comerford for negligence, the name of the case would have appeared as *Smith* v *Comerford*. There is a convention amongst lawyers which it is important to remember when referring to cases by name. Although in the written reports, the names of the parties are divided by the letter 'v' meaning 'versus' or 'against', this is not the way in which the case is referred to in speech. When discussing the case verbally, it should be referred to as 'Crown *against* Comerford'. If this had been a civil case, it would be referred to as 'Smith *and* Comerford'.

Smith would be the *claimant* (this term used to be 'plaintiff'), and Comerford is the *defendant*. If Comerford lost this case and was able to appeal, Comerford would be referred to as the *appellant* (the party appealing), and Smith would be the *respondent* (the party defending the appeal). The case citation would also change to *Comerford* v *Smith*.

The numbers and letters that complete the citation are also important.

ACTIVITY 6

What are the <u>full</u> citations of:

R v *Comerford*?

R v *Dodd*?

R v *Ling*?

The citations refer to when the cases were reported and where the law report can be found. It is worth also noting that the year of the case is not when the case was heard but when it was reported and there may be some delay between the two. The very important case of *Central London Property Trust* v *High Trees House* occurred in 1947, but it was not reported until 1956 when the judge in the case (who later became Lord Denning) referred to his previous judgment and the reporters then understood the significance of the case. The reports have since been reprinted and the *High Trees* case can now be found in the 1947 reports.

R v *Comerford* was reported in 1998, in volume 1 of the All England Law Reports starting at page 823 and the report you have read was from the Court of Appeal (i.e. [1998] 1 All ER 823, CA).

R v *Dodd* was reported in 1981 in volume 74 of the Criminal Appeal Reports at page 50 ((1981) 74 Cr App R 50) and *R* v *Ling* was reported in 1987 in the Criminal Law Review at page 495 ([1987] Crim LR 495). There is only one volume of the Criminal Law review each year, so there is no need to state volume 1.

SAQ 4

Are these three cases civil or criminal?

Because they all start with '*R*', they are all criminal.

You may have noticed that in two of the case citations, the year is in square brackets ([. . .]), and in one, the year is in rounded brackets ((. . .)). Years in square brackets are vital to finding the correct report. For example, the All England Law Reports usually run to three or four volumes per year, numbered by year and volume. Finding volume 1 of the 1997 All ER will therefore not find you *R* v *Comerford*. Years in round brackets are not vital to the case citation. For example, the Criminal Appeal Reports (commonly and humorously referred to as the "cr'ap reps") are numbered by volume only and not broken into years. Volume 74 where *R* v *Dodd* is reported happens to include reports from 1981.

One further case citation needs to be explained here. These are judicial review cases and you will come across a number of these in Constitutional and Administrative Law. Very basically, judicial review is where an applicant asks the High Court to review the procedures employed and decisions reached by public bodies including the courts, local councils and even Government Ministers.

Judicial review citations often look like this:

R v *Secretary of State for Employment ex p Equal Opportunities Commission* [1995] 1 AC 1.

As this citation starts with '*R*', the case is shown to have been brought in the name of the reigning monarch. The respondent was the Secretary of State for Employment, but the case was brought on behalf of (*ex p*, or *ex parte*, pronounced 'partay') the Equal Opportunities Commission which was the applicant in the matter. The case was reported in 1995, in volume 1 of the Appeal Cases reports at page 1.

A new form of case citation was introduced on 11 January 2001. To reflect the increased availability and use of electronic case reports, a new Practice Direction was issued providing for a harmonised and neutral citation of judgments given in every division of the High Court and in the Court of Appeal. All judgments will be issued as approved with sequentially numbered paragraphs. The year is given in square brackets, e.g., [2000], followed by the identifier EWCA (the Court of Appeal) or EWHC (the High Court), the division (Civ or Crim) and the unique number of the case given by the court:

e.g. Smith v Jones [2001] EWCA Civ 10.

Paragraphs should be referred to at the end of the citation, also in square brackets.

e.g. Smith v Jones [2001] EWCA Civ 10 at [59].

SAQ 5

Read the following citations and identify whether they are civil, criminal or judicial review; and where and when they were reported. This should take about five minutes.

1. *Afzal* v *Ford Motor Co Ltd* **[1994] 4 All ER 720, CA**

2. *Black-Clawson International Ltd* v *Papierwerke AG* **[1975] AC 591**

3. *R* v *Inland Revenue Commissioners ex parte National Federation of Self-Employed and Small Businesses* **[1982] AC 617**

4. *R* v *Tisdall* **(1984) 6 Cr App R 155**

5. *R* v *Ponting* **[1985] Crim LR 318**

Refer to *Cases and Materials* (1.3.2.1) for the answers.

Note: some other common citations are:

WLR: Weekly Law Reports
QB: reports of the Queen's Bench (see **Chapter 2**)
Ch: reports of the Chancery Division (see **Chapter 2**)

Law libraries always contain a full explanation of case citations.

As you work through *Cases and Materials*, do take the trouble to read the cases which are extracted for you, and to ask questions about them as you go along, for this will enhance your ability to understand legal writing and will increase your legal knowledge.

1.4.3   READING STATUTES

Acts of Parliament (statutes) are written in a particular form which can make them difficult to understand, and there are certain prescribed rules which have developed over time which are designed to help you interpret them. These rules are explained later in the *Learning Text* but at this stage it is useful for you to see the format of a statute and to appreciate some of its main features.

ACTIVITY 7

Turn to *Cases and Materials* (1.3.3). There you will find the Confiscation of Alcohol (Young Persons) Act 1997. Study the Act, and answer the following questions. This Activity should take about 20 minutes.

(a)   How would you describe the purpose of the Act? What is it designed to do?

(b)   Describe how the Act is organised and laid out. Why do you think it is broken down into parts?

(c)   Do you know whether this Act is in force, simply from reading the text?

(d)   Why does s. 1 set out a number of alternative situations?

(e)   From the text of the Act, is it possible to define a 'reasonable excuse' for failing to comply with the Act? (s. 1(3)).

As you will realise, this Act is designed to allow the police to confiscate alcohol which is in the possession of a young person, or which any other person is holding for use by a young person in places prescribed by the Act. The Act is laid out in the standard format for a modern Act of Parliament, with the short title and reference, followed by the long title (beginning, 'An Act to . . .') and the date of Royal Assent. (For the significance of this date, see below.)

The text of the Act is divided into a number of sections and subsections. These provide convenient points of reference for those who have to read and interpret the Act. When referring to the provisions of the Act, the convention is to abbreviate the word 'section' to 's.' (as in s. 2, or s. 2(3)).

Although the date of Royal Assent is obvious from the face of the Act, the commencement date is not. Section 2(2) provides that the Act will not come into force until the Secretary of State makes an order to appoint a day for its commencement. There is no way of knowing when that date will be simply from looking at the face of the statute, and this can be a problem when trying to discover whether an Act is in force or not.

One of the difficulties which arises in the process of drafting an Act of Parliament is the tension which must be held between covering every eventuality by the words of the Act, and making the wording of the Act specific enough to exclude situations which were not intended to be covered by it. You can see this tension at work in s. 1(1) and (3). In s. 1(1) three alternative situations are envisaged which will be included within the scope of the Act. The drafting is quite specific at this point, in order that only the types of behaviour mentioned are caught by the Act. Contrast s. 1(3), which refers to a 'reasonable excuse' for failing to comply with the Act. No definition is given within the Act of what will be regarded as a reasonable excuse, so it will be up to the court to develop an interpretation of this phrase, which may come to encompass many different types of situation.

These are the important features of the Act to note for the present, but you will learn a good deal more about statute law as you work through *Cases and Materials*.

1.5 Legal Writing

This chapter would not be complete without some mention of the skills in the use of the written word which are expected of a potential lawyer.

English Legal Method is an academic rather than practical subject, so in this text, you will not learn how to complete court forms, write letters to clients, or draft legal documents. There are particular conventions associated with these tasks, which you will discover later if you decide to practice the law. As a learner, however, your task is to become proficient in writing clearly, grammatically and succinctly, in sentences that are not too long, and without making too many spelling mistakes.

Written work is a major component of an academic course of study. It is therefore vital that you learn quickly how to interpret the different requirements for written work which relate to the different modules. On being set a piece of written work, study the instructions carefully. If a word limit is imposed for the essay, you must adhere to it – part of the assessment may well be to test your ability to express yourself concisely.

In the first instance, practice writing full answers to short questions. If you practice writing paragraphs, the whole essay will be complete before you know it.

SAQ 6

The three questions below could easily be part of a much bigger assignment. Before trying to tackle a full essay (which you will do at the end of the chapter), write a paragraph answering each of the questions below. You will find a suggested answer in *Cases and Materials* (1.4), where you will also find advice on how to structure answers in an appropriate way.

1. You are the defence barrister acting for John who has been charged with rape. As the jury is being sworn in, you notice Julie who has been the subject of recent media attention due to her outspoken and strong views on women's rights.

    (i) Can you exclude Julie from the jury?
    (ii) Should she be excluded from the jury?

2. Can the use of a majority verdict in criminal proceedings be justified? Give reasons for your answer.

3. In the extract you read for Activity 3, the authors mentioned the secrecy surrounding jury deliberations. This is governed by s. 8 of the Contempt of Court Act 1981. Should s. 8 of the Contempt of Court Act 1981 be abolished? Give reasons for your answer.

When tackling full essays be sure that you do not jump to conclusions about the task you have been set. You must answer the question given, not the question you would prefer to have been set. Notice the subtle differences between the words used in essay questions, such as 'discuss', 'describe', 'evaluate' etc. It is relatively rare for you to be asked to describe something at degree level, as this is regarded as too simple a task. It is more common to be asked to evaluate critically, thus giving you the chance to show that you have not only understood the material, but can also weigh its value and make a critique of it.

SAQ 7

Consider the following terms (or instructing words) commonly used in essay titles and coursework titles. Try to define them so you know what you are being asked to do:

(a) analyse

(b) compare

(c) contrast

(d) criticise

(e) discuss

(f) evaluate

(g) explain.

Suggested answers:

(a) analyse

An analysis consists of breaking the subject matter down into its constituent parts, examining them and providing a result or conclusion according to the question asked.

(b) compare

A comparison is drawing out the similarities and differences between two or more things.

(c) contrast

Contrasting consists of examining the differences between two or more things.

(d) criticise

This is a very common instructing word to find in law essay titles. It does not mean to concentrate only on the negative aspects of the subject matter, but to provide an objective and balanced argument, examining the positive and negative points and perhaps offering a solution, or recommending a reform.

(e) discuss

A discussion is a debate. Debates are two sided, balanced arguments where each argument is based on evidence. Evidence in law essays may be cases, examples, statutes or other (e.g. statistics on appeal rates, conviction rates and so on.)

(f) evaluate

An evaluation is an objective assessment of the subject matter. A common essay title may commence 'Critically evaluate . . .'. In this event, you would provide an assessment, structured clearly so the marker or examiner understands the progression of your argument, of the positive and negative points of the subject.

(g) explain

An explanation is the process of making a topic clear to the reader.

Most importantly, try to express your ideas as simply and clearly as you can. To practise this skill, try writing instructions for an everyday task, like making the bed, or try writing in your own words the facts of one of the cases from the *Cases and Materials* section. Avoid lengthy introductions and conclusions, and try to stick to the point of what you are writing about. Then give your work to a friend who will be honest with you, and ask them to tell you how clearly they have understood your writing!

Because the requirements of the written work vary from module to module, it is difficult to give more specific advice at this stage, apart from emphasising that when you have completed your work *always* read it through carefully, checking for errors, and ensure that you have actually answered the question posed.

ACTIVITY 8

Read the essay in *Cases and Materials* (1.4)

As you have now read the chapter on juries from Elliott and Quinn; and you are aware of the issues that arose in *R* v *Comerford* [1998] 1 All ER 823, you have a good understanding of this area. The purpose of this activity is not to test your knowledge (yet!), but to start to develop legal writing skills.

Mark the essay as if you were a law tutor, annotating it as you go along. This should take you about 20 minutes.

(a) Tick any credit worthy points.

(b) Circle any spelling mistakes.

(c) Point out areas of 'waffle', where the author has strayed from the point or mentioned something that is irrelevant.

(d) Is the bibliography adequate? (If not, why not?)

(e) Add a paragraph at the end giving advice for improvement (write it below).

Decide what % to give the essay.

Advice for improvement:

% given:

Compare your marking with that in *Cases and Materials* (1.4).

The essay is not of a high standard. Seeing how not to do it is beneficial, but only so you can avoid making the same sort of mistakes. You will have the opportunity to practice what you have learned at the end of the chapter.

In the meantime, here is some basic advice on essay writing in law:

(a) Planning your essay
You should quickly plan any law essay before you start it and break the content into the following parts:

(b) The Introduction
This is a short paragraph which gives brief information leading to the main part of the essay. In law, it usually consists of a definition of the area of law to be examined (e.g. the CPS is . . . , or Legal Aid is . . . etc.). Do not over complicate the opening paragraph - keep it simple.

(c) The Argument
This consists a structured, ordered and logical presentation of the issues to be discussed.

A general rule of thumb is
one idea per sentence,
one topic per paragraph
and the grouping of related topics together.

It is good practice to:
- make a short statement
- explain what you mean
- find a case, statute or procedure to illustrate that point
- you may then want to evaluate what you have said

(d) The Evaluation of the Argument
There is no hard and fast rule about whether you should include evaluation as you go through your argument, or leave it all to be dealt with in one go. This will often depend on the subject matter of the essay. For example, it may be easier to evaluate the appeal process as you go from one court to another, whereas it may be easier to evaluate the whole of the CPS after you have stated the main points in the argument. What is certain, however, is that at degree level, some evaluation is always required.

(e) The Final Paragraph or Conclusion
This draws together all the main points of the essay and makes a concluding statement. It is vital to the success of any essay. Writing conclusions well takes time and practice, but one good way of getting started is to re-read the title and answer it in one sentence. Some students benefit from planning the conclusion before they start answering the question. This means they know where the argument is taking them and helps to avoid 'waffle'. In some ways, this method provides the 'light at the end of the tunnel'.

1.6 Summary

We are never too old or too knowledgeable to discover new methods of learning which will enhance both our enjoyment and our proficiency in studying an academic subject. I hope therefore that in the course of this chapter you will have encountered some techniques which will have helped you to do the following tasks:

- discover the environment in which you learn best;

- acquire basic skills in reading texts, cases and statutes;

- appreciate the need for careful analysis of the question when writing an essay on a legal topic.

In the chapters of the **Learning Text** which follow, you will have ample opportunity to test these skills.

Figure 1
An overview of Chapter 1

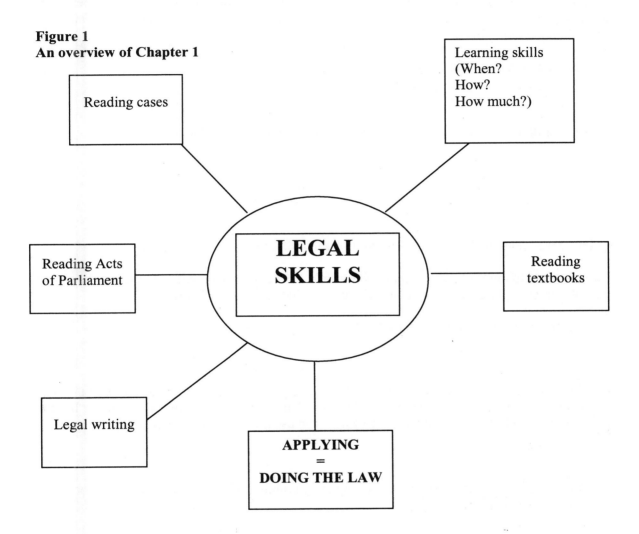

1.7   Further Reading

Rivlin, G., *First Steps in the Law*, London: Blackstone Press, 1999.

Bradney, A., Cownie, F., Masson, J., Newell, D., *How to Study Law*, 4th edn, London: Sweet and Maxwell, 2000.

1.8   End of Chapter Assessment Question One

Refer to the case of *Gregory* v *UK* (1998) 25 EHRR 577 in **Cases and Materials (1.5)**. This is a different style of report to *R* v *Comerford* [1998] 1 All ER 823 because *Gregory* is a European

Court of Human Rights case. We will look at the European Convention for the Protection of Human Rights and Fundamental Freedoms (the ECHR) in more detail later in this **Learning Text**.

Please note: the case refers regularly to 'counsel'. This is the term used to describe the legal representation of the parties at trial – in this context, the barristers for the prosecution and the defence. Further, the term *prima facie* is used. This Latin term means 'at first glance'. A *prima facie* case is a case that would appear to be made on the face of it or where sufficient evidence has to be or has been provided just to make the case out in the first instance. If and when more detailed examination is made of a *prima facie* case, it may be found to be otherwise. *Inter alia* means 'among other things'.

1. Briefly summarise why Gregory made this appeal.

2. Draw a flowchart, or briefly describe in words the chronological history of the case.

End the chronology with the following information (not given in the report itself):

It was referred to the European Commission in July 1993 and the Commission referred the case to the Court in December 1995. The court delivered its judgment on 25 February 1997.

3. Describe the role of an English trial judge.

4. The case report states that the Attorney-General's guidelines indicate *inter alia* that the right should be asserted only on the basis of clearly defined and restrictive criteria. Refer back to Activity 3 and describe when the prosecution <u>can</u> use the stand by challenge.

5. Can you explain what the law is regarding the possibility of bias on the part of a juror. What case is this law from?

6. The case was heard by the European Commission before it was referred to the Court. What was the decision of the Commission?

7. Why was it not possible for the trial judge to question the jury about the circumstances that gave rise to the note?

8. Can you briefly describe the two different types of law involved in this case? Hint: the first is English law.

9. Explain why there was felt to be no violation of Article 6 in this case. Compare this briefly to the *Remli* case.

10. What is a dissenting judgment? Briefly explain on what grounds Judge Foighel dissented.

Now you have finished reading the case and answering these questions, refer to the answers in *Cases and Materials* **(1.6)**.

1.9 End of Chapter Assessment Question Two

You should now feel confident about the topic of juries, legal skills and essay technique. As a result, it is now time to practice these new skills.

Write the following essay. Leave yourself 45 minutes for it. There is a suggested skeleton answer in *Cases and Materials* **(1.8)**; but you will benefit more if you read that after having at least tried the essay!

Judge Hiller Zobel, the judge in the Louise Woodward trial stated:

'Trial by jury is the worst method of trial I know . . . except for all the others.'

Discuss the extent to which this is true of the *English* legal system.

CHAPTER TWO

INTRODUCTION TO THE SOURCES OF LAW

2.1 Objectives

By the end of this chapter you should be able to:

- suggest at least one way of defining law;

- identify some of the ways in which law operates in relation to issues of morality;

- explain some of the different classifications of the law and then apply them to a fictitious case;

- give an account of the various sources of law;

- identify the basic workings of the court hierarchy.

2.2 Introduction

In this chapter you will learn about the ways in which lawyers define and classify the law, and the ways in which law is made. You will not find many legal rules in this chapter, nor will you find much case law. This part of the book may therefore seem to contain a great deal of theory, and you may be tempted to skip through it so that you can start work on the more practical areas such as the structure of the courts. Please try to resist this temptation! Although theories of law and methods of law-making may seem of less importance than the legal rules themselves, you will find as your studies progress that you will not be able to understand how legal rules evolve and operate in practice, unless you have a thorough knowledge of the ways in which these rules come into being and the ways in which lawyers categorise them.

As the different types of law are discussed you will need to refer to *Cases and Materials*. You will also find it useful to use a good English dictionary, for example *The Concise Oxford Dictionary*, and a good legal dictionary. As you work through this text, try to get into the habit of looking up unfamiliar words or phrases in your dictionaries.

2.3   Definitions of Law

SAQ 1

What do you think 'law' means? A very important legal skill is being able to define concepts and topics. To start with, you may wish to write down as many different examples or types of law that you can. Then reflect on that list and see if you can come up with a definition of 'law'.

The term 'law' is very difficult to define because it is used to mean different things in different contexts. A comprehensive definition is therefore hard to provide as it would have to be very wide.

The majority of people use the term 'law' to describe the criminal law. This may be because of the media coverage given to crimes, such as assault, murder, 'joyriding' etc. Some people use the word 'law' to describe the institutions of the legal system, such as the courts, the police, prisons and so on. Other people associate it with the processes of law, its rules and procedures, such as the steps that have to be followed when beginning a legal action.

Further, it may be used to describe the rules laid down by Parliament and/or the courts that govern our behaviour.

SAQ 2

Which of these options, in your opinion, is right?

None of the above can be said to be 'right' to the exclusion of the others. The better way of phrasing the answer would be to say that none of them is wrong.

ACTIVITY 1

Consult a good English dictionary, such as *The Concise Oxford Dictionary,* and notice the numerous different ways in which the word 'law' can be defined. You might like to note some of these below and refer to them as you progress through the *Learning Text.* You may find that your understanding of these definitions changes as your knowledge increases.

From this activity you will probably have realised that the word 'law' can be understood in many different ways, including those outlined above, but is very often defined in terms of rules. You are probably aware of many rules which people observe in their daily lives which regulate the way that they behave, and yet these are not necessarily referred to as law. Many people also live according to moral rules and abide by religious codes, and yet these are not laws either. So when is a rule regarded as part of the law? Rules are regarded as law when they originate from one of the recognised law-making institutions which you will learn about shortly (see **2.5**). But that is not the whole story, for where does the system of law and its processes fit into the picture?

One way of defining the law so as to take account of all three aspects mentioned above, i.e., the rules of law, the legal system and its processes, is to say that **law is a method of social control which maintains public order in society**. This definition is useful as a brief and simple way of explaining the concept of law.

SAQ 3

From your reading so far and from your general knowledge, which of the following statements are true and which are false?

1. There is no difference between moral rules and legal rules. TRUE/FALSE.

2. Procedural rules, for example, how to begin a breach of contract action in court, are not part of law. TRUE/FALSE.

3. The concept of law is not the same as the concept of justice. TRUE/FALSE.

4. Law is an instrument of social control, fostering social order. TRUE/FALSE.

These questions should have given you some food for thought! You will probably have realised that although many of the rules which we regard as laws are based on moral codes (for example, people must not commit murder), not every moral rule is part of the law of this country. For example, envy, though forbidden by moral codes, is not forbidden by law. Therefore the first statement in the exercise above is false, as law and morality are not the same, although they may overlap. (See **2.4** below.)

There is a great deal more to law than this, however, and you will probably realise by now that the law also comprises many procedural rules which must be followed in order for legal issues to be dealt with by the courts. The second statement in the self-assessment question is therefore false, as these procedural rules are also part of the law. (See **2.5** below.)

When legal issues are considered by the courts, or when Parliament creates law, one of the aims of those involved in the process is to do justice between people who are affected by the law. Sadly, we know that this aim is not always achieved, and therefore it has to be said that law and justice do not always coincide, and so the third statement in **SAQ 3** is true.

You should by now have a good idea of what law is, and what is not, and you should also have a good working definition of the law, which appears in the final statement in **SAQ 3**. This statement is true.

2.4   Law and Morals

ACTIVITY 2

Refer to *Cases and Materials* (2.1) where you will find the following:

(a)   **Article 8 of the Convention for the Protection of Human Rights and Fundamental Freedoms.**
(b)   **Section 1 of the Suicide Act 1961.**
(c)   **Sections 7 and 8 of the Education Act 1996.**

Read these provisions and answer the following questions.

What is the effect of each provision?
(a)

(b)

(c)

On whom (if anyone) does each provision confer legal rights?
(a)

(b)

(c)

On whom (if anyone) does each provision impose a legal duty?
(a)

(b)

(c)

Why do you think that each provision was passed into law?

(a)

(b)

(c)

What is the effect of each provision?
(a) To give people a right to privacy.
(b) To decriminalise suicide.
(c) Requires compulsory schooling to 16 years.

On whom (if anyone) does each provision confer legal rights?
(a) The individual.
(b) Probably no-one.
(c) Ditto.

On whom (if anyone) does each provision impose a legal duty?
(a) The State.
(b) No-one.
(c) Under s. 7, the parent; there is probably also a duty on an education authority to provide a school.

Why do you think that each provision was passed into law?
(a) To limit the power of the State to invade an individual's right to a zone of privacy.
(b) Because it was felt inappropriate for it to be criminal; or because there was no feeling of moral outrage; or because it was futile to criminalise it; or many other reasons.
(c) To provide an educated work force; to ensure that each individual is encouraged to maximise their own potential. Originally possibly to keep children out of child labour.

If we focus on the schooling provision, it is at least arguable that we are all better off if there is a literate, educated work force which can help us to compete as a nation in an ever increasingly competitive world market. This is then the overall objective. Compulsory schooling is one means of achieving that object. Law is the method by which that is brought about. Law is thus simply instrumental. It is used in this example to provide *the greatest good for the greatest number*. That is the principle of Utilitarianism and you should be able to think of plenty of other examples of it in our law. (Compulsory purchase, clean air, fluoride in water.)

On the other hand if we focus on the privacy provision we should be able to deduce something rather different. Here the law is being used not invasively (as with the schooling) but (and again instrumentally) as a protection. In other words it exists to protect rights. You should be able to see that there can be an inherent tension between the protection of such rights and the requirements of the state – say in the detection of serious crime. A balance is not always possible. Generally, Article 8 preserves the individual right at the expense of the interest of the State.

Between Utilitarianism and Rights there has been a long struggle and it is not only on-going but irreconcilable. You might care to think about this tension as your studies widen and deepen.

2.5 Classification of the Law

In order to study the law in more detail you need to be able to appreciate how it can be broken up into a number of different component parts. One method of dividing the law into different categories is to classify it as substantive law or as adjectival law. Substantive law is the term which is used to refer to the rules which govern our rights and duties under the law, for example the cases and statutes which create criminal offences, or the cases and statutes which define contractual obligations. Adjectival law prescribes how those substantive rules can be used within the legal system, for examples the rules of evidence, procedure and costs which are to be observed when bringing a case to court.

ACTIVITY 3

Look at the extract from the Civil Procedure Rules 1998 in *Cases and Materials* (2.2). What type of law is this?

Then look at the extract from the Bail Act 1976 in *Cases and Materials* (2.2). What type of law is this?

The Civil Procedure Rules 1998 contain the detailed procedural steps and guidance on commencing civil proceedings (e.g. suing another party). This should therefore be classified as adjectival law. By contrast, ss. 3 and 4 of the Bail Act 1976 describe the rights and duties of those involved in criminal proceedings and this is therefore substantive law.

An alternative way of classifying the law is by reference to its subject matter. From the point of view of lawyers and those involved in the legal system, this is the most useful way of dividing the law into categories.

The broadest distinction which can be drawn is between international law and domestic law. International law is concerned with the external relationships between different States and is based on treaties and conventions. A good example here is the Treaty of European Union (also known as the Maastricht Treaty). Domestic law comprises the laws of a particular State, that is the cases or statute law which govern relationships within that country and can be divided into public law and private law.

Public law cases are those cases in which one of the parties to the dispute is the Crown, usually acting through a government department. Public law can be further subdivided into the areas of criminal law and civil law.

Criminal law is concerned with conduct of which society disapproves so strongly that the State must punish the wrongdoer; for example, murder, theft, and driving offences. The major objective of criminal proceedings is to punish the perpetrator of the crime, not to compensate the victim. The Crown Prosecution Service, acting on behalf of the Crown, prosecutes the accused, who will be found guilty of the offence charged if the prosecutor can convince the court beyond reasonable doubt that the accused did commit that offence. Public civil law cases, by contrast, are concerned with problems in constitutional and administrative law. For example, these cases may challenge the legality of actions carried out by central or local government, or may bring test cases on individual freedoms which have been infringed by the government, such as telephone tapping.

As mentioned above, the other branch of domestic law is private law. This involves civil law and is concerned with the rights and duties which private individuals have in relation to each other. There are many different categories of civil law, for example the law of contract, the law of torts (wrongs such as negligence or slander), and the law of property.

The major objective of an action which involves private civil law is to compensate the person who has suffered the wrong, usually by payment of money (damages). A civil action is commenced by the victim, that is, the claimant, who sues the defendant in order to obtain a remedy. The claimant must prove his or her case on a balance of probabilities, in other words it must be more likely than not that the defendant harmed the claimant in the manner alleged.

ACTIVITY 4

On a separate piece of paper, draw a diagram which sets out the categories of law according to subject matter and which shows how these categories relate to each other.

After you have done this you may check your version against that given in *Cases and Materials* (2.2).

This system of classifying the law according to subject matter is not watertight however. One set of facts can have multiple legal consequences and can straddle the various categories outlined above. Road traffic accidents, for example, can result in infringement of rules of the criminal law and private civil law.

As you progress through your studies you will find that classifying the law in this way begins to be second nature to you. You will not normally need to spell out these classifications when dealing with a case, unless you are specifically asked to do so, as this knowledge is assumed on your part.

2.6 Sources of Law

Another way of dividing the law is into categories, as it can be classified according to the source of the legal rule.

The law of England and Wales has been shaped by many different influences, but a simple way to analyse these sources is to examine the institutions which have formed its rules. Four institutions in particular are relevant here, each one producing a distinctive type of law. They are the courts, Parliament, the European Union and the Council of Europe.

2.7 The Courts

The courts are responsible for the creation of two different types of law: common law and equity. The relationship between these two concepts will emerge through an explanation of the term 'common law', which like many other legal terms can be understood in a number of different ways.

2.7.1 A NATIONAL SYSTEM

First, the term common law can be taken to refer to the system of law which is common to the whole country. This has not always been in existence. Before the Norman Conquest of 1066, many different rules of law operated in different parts of the country. The Norman kings introduced a more centralised system so that common rules were administered by the royal judges through the common law courts in London and throughout the country by the Assize Courts.

2.7.2 COMMON LAW AND EQUITY

Secondly, the term common law is often used in contrast to the term equity. As early as 352 BC, Aristotle wrote of equity:

That which is equitable is just; not legally just, simply a correction of legal justice. This is so because the law is universal; but it is not possible to make universal statements about some things. When the law makes a universal statement and a case arises out of it that is not embraced in that statement, it becomes right (when the law-makers fall into error by oversimplifying) to correct the omission. This is the nature of the equitable - to correct the law where, because of its universality, it is defective.

ACTIVITY 5

Turn to *Cases and Materials* (2.3.1) and read the extract taken from Rivlin's *First Steps in the Law*. This extract deals with the development of the common law in more detail than above and it describes why the need for a further system (providing remedies where the common law did not) arose.

Keep in mind the quote by *Aristotle* above. Make brief notes on how equity was able to 'correct legal justice'.

It was never intended that the principles of equity would replace the common law rules, simply that they would fulfil it and make up for its defects. Having a dual system of courts administering different remedies did cause other problems, however, and by the Judicature Acts of 1873–1875, the court system was reformed. The result was that the administration of the common law courts and the courts of Chancery was merged, to create a unified system of courts and procedures. Thus all courts in the modern legal system can use both common law and equitable principles and give either type of remedy. But this does not mean that the common law and equitable rules have merged. These are still recognisably different.

One of the ways equity was able to plug the gaps of the common law was by using guidelines called *maxims of equity*. One of the better known maxims is 'He who comes to equity must come with clean hands'. This means that equity will not assist a party who has acted in bad conscience.

ACTIVITY 6

Refer to *Cases and Materials* (2.3) and read *D & C Builders* v *Rees* [1966] 2 QB 617, CA. Why was it decided that the Rees's had not *come to equity with clean hands?*

Lord Denning MR (denoting he was at the time of the judgment, the Master of the Rolls), was scathing of the conduct of Mr and Mrs Rees. He stated that Mrs Rees had 'held the creditor to ransom'. Danckwerts LJ found that the 'Rees's really behaved very badly'. A person who behaves 'rather badly' is unlikely to benefit from equity's protection, as the Rees's found to their cost. As equity would not intervene on behalf of the Rees's, the common law rules prevailed. One of these is that part payment of a debt does not satisfy the debt.

This shows that common law rules and equitable 'rules' have not merged.

For example, common law rules have a strong influence in contract, tort and criminal law, and common law remedies such as monetary damages are frequently used in the first two mentioned areas. By contrast, equitable principles are influential in land law and in trusts, where discretionary equitable remedies, such as the injunction, may be used.

You may have heard of the 'trust' mechanism before. It is regularly used when referring to financial investments (unit trusts), or when referring inheritance (trust finds). To understand how the trust was first established, read the fictitious story in the Activity below.

ACTIVITY 7

It is the time of the Crusades. Peter is 16 and an only child. Peter's father, Sir Ralph, wants to leave his mansion house to Peter and his mother in case he does not return from the Crusades, but <u>the common law</u> says he cannot do this as women and children cannot own land. Sir Ralph asks his brother, Sir John, to take care of Peter and his mother in the event of his death. Sir John agrees. Sir Ralph wills his property to Sir John on this understanding. Some months later, the family discover Sir Ralph has been killed. Sir John moves into the mansion and kicks Peter and his mother out.

In <u>law</u>, do you think Sir John can do this? Why?

What might <u>equity</u> have to say about this? Think particularly about the maxim above.

Unlike the common law, which recognises Sir John as the legal owner, equity will stop him from going back on his promise <u>and</u> it will recognise the interests of Peter and Peter's mother. These interests are not legal, but equitable and Peter and his mother are the beneficiaries of the estate (a beneficiary is an equitable owner). You will be able to develop your understanding of this topic in *Learning Text: Law of Trusts*.

2.7.3 CREATION OF LEGAL PRINCIPLES

The third way in which the term common law can be understood is in the sense of the creation of legal principles which evolve from cases decided by the courts. For example, in *Learning Text: Law of Torts*, you will encounter the famous case of *Donoghue* v *Stevenson* [1932] AC 562. In this case it was alleged that a woman had discovered the decomposed remains of a snail in a bottle of ginger beer, after she had consumed some of the contents. She became ill as a result of this, and wished to claim some legal redress. The judges developed a new common law rule, that a manufacturer of a product can be liable to the ultimate consumer, where the consumer is harmed by the manufacturer's negligence. This principle had not been recognised previously, and is a good example of the way in which the courts can create new law.

SAQ 4

Summarise in your own words the different ways in which the term 'common law' may be used in a legal context. You should try to be as concise as possible in your description.

One of the important skills which a lawyer must acquire is the ability to convey information accurately and succinctly. In making a summary of the different meanings which can be attached to the term 'common law', it would be important to include some reference to the early history of English law and the way in which the Norman kings developed a system common to all England. Secondly, the difference between common law rules and equitable principles must be established together with an explanation of the way in which all courts can now administer these rules. Lastly, some reference is necessary to the way in which the term is used to describe the rules created by the judges in the decisions made in court.

2.8   Parliament

2.8.1   LEGISLATION

Parliament (consisting of the Queen, the House of Lords and the House of Commons) is the originator of statute law (sometimes referred to as legislation). This consists of formally enacted rules dealing with a particular subject matter, produced in the form of an Act of Parliament. An Act of Parliament begins life in draft form as a Bill. This is debated by both Houses of Parliament and must undergo set procedures, until it is finally given the Royal Assent by the monarch. You should be aware that lawyers often use the terms Act, statute, and legislation interchangeably.

ACTIVITY 8

Refer to the flowchart of the legislative process in *Cases and Materials* at 2.4.1.

This is a simple flowchart of the process and gives no more than the basics.

To be able to comment on and evaluate the process, read the extract from Zander's *The Law Making Process* in *Cases and Materials* (2.4.1).

Annotate the flowchart with information from the extract.

Normally, Acts of Parliament are referred to by their short title and the year in which they were enacted, for example, the Bail Act 1976.

ACTIVITY 9

Look at the extract from an Act of Parliament in *Cases and Materials* (2.4.1). What is the short title of this Act, i.e., the name by which you would refer to it if you wished to cite it in an essay?

Acts of Parliament have both a short title, and what is known as the long title. You can see the long title of the Act which you have just looked at in *Cases and Materials*, beginning with the words 'An Act to'. The date which follows immediately after the long title is the date on which the Act received the Royal Assent. This Act is, of course, usually known by its short title as the Law of Property (Miscellaneous Provisions) Act 1989. Acts of Parliament are divided into numbered sections and subsections. In writing, these are abbreviated, and become for example s. 4 or s. 5(1).

However, just because a statute has been enacted and published (which lawyers refer to as 'being on the statute book') this does not necessarily mean that its provisions are in force. This is yet another source of confusion. There may be a lapse of time between the statute receiving the Royal Assent, and the whole statute, or sections of it, coming into force as binding law. The Law of Property (Miscellaneous Provisions) Act 1989 is a good example of this.

ACTIVITY 10

Look again at the Act referred to above in *Cases and Materials* (2.4.1).

1.   On what date did this Act receive the Royal Assent?

2.   Look at the provisions of s. 5: did all of the provisions of the Act come into force on the date of the Royal Assent?

3.   What other type of legislation is referred to in s. 5 of the Act?

As you will realise, not all of the provisions of the Act came into force on 27 July 1989, the date of the Royal Assent. Some sections of the Act became law immediately, but s. 5 provided that s. 2 and s. 3 and part of s. 4 would not come into force for two months. Certain other sections were not to come into force until the Lord Chancellor made an order by statutory instrument to that effect. This he duly did, and a statutory instrument was published in 1990, bringing these sections into effect as from 31 July 1990. (See below.)

Once in force, a statute remains operative until it is repealed by another statute. Alternatively, if there are a number of statutes, all of which deal with aspects of the same subject in law, Parliament may decide to repeal all of these statutes and re-enact them in one definitive Act. This is a process known as consolidation of statutes.

In this century, legislation has emerged as the most important source of law, as opposed to the law-making of judges through decisions in the courts. This is partly due to the fact that the social and economic problems of today require far more detailed regulation than can be provided by case law alone. In addition, legislation can be publicised and known in advance by those whom it affects, and it can be put in place quickly when this is necessary.

2.8.2   DELEGATED LEGISLATION

If the authority or power to do something is 'delegated', it is given or passed on to some one else. It is the function of Parliament to make the law (pass legislation) in England and Wales, but this power may be given by Parliament to someone else (i.e. delegated legislation). This may be done in one of three ways.

The power to make delegated law must be given under a statute (called the Parent or Enabling Act). Each type of delegated legislation will have a different Parent Act and it is the Parent Act that lays down the requirement and scope of the delegated legislation.

The three ways to make delegated legislation are:

Statutory Instruments

This is the most common way of passing delegated legislation. There are over 3,000 statutory instruments (S.I.s) passed every year (as opposed to approximately 80 statutes).

The process involves Parliament passing a very broadly drafted statute which delegates the law-making power upon a Government Department or Minister. The broadly drafted statute is the Enabling Act. The delegated legislation is called a statutory instrument because it carries out (is *instrumental* in giving effect to) the requirements of the statute.

ACTIVITY 11

See the legislation in *Cases and Materials* (2.4.2).

How and what does S.I. 1999 No. 5 bring into effect?

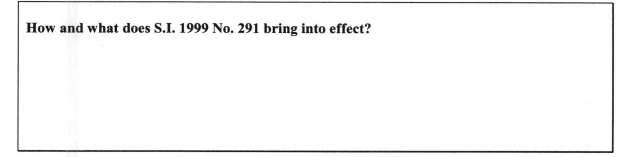

How and what does S.I. 1999 No. 291 bring into effect?

S.I. 1999 No. 5, is officially entitled The Knives Act 1997 (Commencement) (No. 2) Order 1999. It is an order made by Paul Boateng, a Minister of State for the Home Office, under the authority given to him under s. 11 of the Knives Act 1997, to bring s. 8 of the same statute into effect on 1 March 1999.

S.I 1999 No. 291 brings into effect new Codes of Practice under the Police and Criminal Evidence Act 1984, again, on 1 March 1999.

Byelaws

These are passed by local authorities, or e.g. the British Rail Board, who are subordinate to Parliament, for the *'regulation, administration or management of their district or property'*. The Parent Act is the Local Government Act 1972.

Orders of the Legislative Committee of the Privy Council

The Privy Council was originally established to advise the Crown (monarch) on the administration of Government. Its functions are now more concerned with the administration and supervision of the Commonwealth. In addition, it is used to pass domestic delegated legislation. Orders of the Legislative Committee of the Privy Council are either used only in emergency (for example, in wartime under the Emergency Powers Act 1920) or to give legal effect to European Directives (see below) under the European Communities Act 1972, s. 2(2).

2.9   The European Union

The third source of law of which you must be aware is the European Union. The United Kingdom became a part of the European Economic Community (the term in use at that time) on 1 January 1973. This has had a radical effect on the sources of English law.

When the United Kingdom signs an international treaty, the rights, duties and obligations imposed by the Treaty are imposed on the State itself. An individual or citizen of the UK, therefore, is not generally subject to the duties of an international Treaty signed by the UK, unless the Government has given direct enforcement of the rights etc. by passing a domestic statute. Similarly, a citizen will not generally be able to enforce any of the rights under the Treaty in the UK court systems without an 'entrenchment' of these rights in an Act of Parliament.

The UK joined the EEC by signing the Treaty of Rome (1957) in 1973, but to give individuals of the UK rights under the Treaty, Parliament enacted the European Communities Act 1972.

ACTIVITY 12

Turn to European Communities Act (ECA) 1972, s. 2 in *Cases and Materials* (2.5).

Under s 2(1), which three words assert the supremacy of European law?

Under s 2(2), reference is made to other sources of law. What are they?

The ECA 1972 recognises that European law can have effect in the UK **'without further enactment'** and where domestic law is to be used, delegated legislation in the form of Orders of the Legislative Committee of the Privy Council or statutory instruments ('regulations') can be used.

Whether or not European law is effective in the UK 'without further enactment' depends on how the particular European law is described in the Treaty of Rome.

The sources of English law are:

- Legislation.
- Delegated legislation.
- Decisions and judgments of the court system.

European law vaguely parallels this model:

- The primary sources of law (parallel to legislation) are the Treaties (of Rome, Maastricht and Amsterdam).
- The secondary sources (paralleling delegated legislation) are governed by Article 249 (ex. 189) (see below).
- Plus the decisions of the European Court of Justice form part of English law through the system of precedent (see **Chapter 3**).

ACTIVITY 13

Read Article 249 (ex. 189) of the Treaty of Rome (below) which describes the nature of the secondary laws of Europe. There is an important reason why two numbers are given in the reference here. Originally, under the 1957 Treaty, the article was number 189. The Treaty of Amsterdam re-numbered the Treaty of Rome. Article 189 became Article 249 i.e. Article 249 (*ex.* 189). You need to be aware of both numbers.

> *'In order to carry out their task and in accordance with the provisions of this Treaty, the European Parliament acting jointly with the Council, the Council and Commission shall make regulations and issue directives, take decisions, make recommendations or deliver opinions. A regulation shall have general application. It shall be binding in its entirety and directly applicable in all Member States. A directive shall be binding, as to the result to be achieved, upon each Member State to which it is addressed, but shall leave to the national authorities the choice of form and methods. A decision shall be binding in its entirety upon those to whom it is addressed. Recommendations and opinions shall have no binding force.'*

INTRODUCTION TO THE SOURCES OF LAW

(a) Which institutions of Europe are involved in making secondary laws?

(b) How many types of secondary laws are provided for in Article 249 (ex. 189)?

(c) Can you _briefly_ compare and contrast regulations and directives?

There are four main institutions of the European Union. The Council of Ministers is the decision-making body of the Union and is comprised of one representative per State (actual membership depends upon subject matter of law. For example, the Agriculture Ministers of each Member State would pass new laws on British beef). The second institution is the Commission, which must pass legislative proposals to the Council and each Commissioner must act in interests of the Union as a whole and not in interests of his or her own government. There is also the European Parliament which is the only directly elected body of the Union. Finally, there is the European Court of Justice which is not involved in passing primary or secondary legislation, but in interpreting and applying that legislation (see below). Your answer to (a) should therefore be the European Parliament, the Council and the Commission.

There are five types of secondary law, but only three have binding effect.

Regulations are said to have 'general application' which means that they are issued to all members of the Community. They are also 'directly applicable' meaning that regulations have legal force in all Member States as soon as they are made without the need for the Member State to enact domestic legislation. Individuals can invoke a directly applicable secondary law against anyone and rely on them before their national courts.

Directives operate to harmonise the civil law in each Member State. The relevant institutions will agree a standard to be set for the whole of Europe, and only those Member States who do not meet the required standard will have the directive issued to them. This means that they are not generally applicable. Directives are not directly applicable either as they invariably require the Member State to legislate within its own jurisdiction. The Member State may have a discretion as to how to implement the directive, but there are strict time restrictions (usually two years to implement).

Your answer to (c) should be that regulations have general and direct application, whereas directives are neither generally nor directly applicable. Do not think, though, that directives are 'inferior' in any way. The Member States are under an obligation to give effect to directives and this obligation cannot be ignored.

Decisions bind the Member State, company or institution to whom they are addressed, and are generally of an administrative nature.

Recommendations and opinions are not legally binding, but have persuasive authority if relied upon in a legal action.

ACTIVITY 14

Read *Commission* v *UK* **[1979] RTR 321 in *Cases and Materials* (2.5). The case illustrates the relationship between Article 249 (ex. 189) and regulations.**

How was the UK in breach of Article 249 (ex. 189) and Regulation 1463/70/EEC?

The UK Government had provided for optional and voluntary installation of tachographs in the relevant vehicles. The ECJ stated that 'it cannot be accepted that a Member State should apply in an incomplete or selective manner provisions of a Community regulation . . . [it] undermines Community solidarity . . .'.

In addition to the sources of law in Article 249 (ex. 189), the European Court Justice (the Court of Justice of the European Union; more commonly, the ECJ) has a very important role in European law. Its role is to ensure that the Member States fulfil their obligations under the Treaties, to decide disputes between Member States concerning the subject matter of the Treaties, and to ensure that the Institutions of the Union act legally within their powers.

ACTIVITY 15

Read Article 234 (ex. 177) of the Treaty of Rome below.

'The Court of Justice shall have jurisdiction to give preliminary rulings concerning:
(a)   the interpretation of this Treaty;
(b)   the validity and interpretation of the acts of the institutions of the Community . . . ;
(c)   the interpretation of the statutes of bodies established by an act of the Council, where those statutes so provide.
*   Where such a question is raised before any court or tribunal of a Member State, that court or tribunal may, if it considers that a decision on the question is necessary to enable it to give judgment, request the Court of Justice to give a ruling thereon.*
*   Where any such question is raised in a case pending before a court or tribunal of a Member State against whose decisions there is no judicial remedy under national law, that court or tribunal shall bring the matter before the Court of Justice.'*

Now refer to the extract from *Bulmer* v *Bollinger* [1974] 2 All ER 1226 in *Cases and Materials* (2.5) and answer the following questions.

(a) In which court was this case heard?

(b) Did either that court or the High Court <u>have to</u> refer the matter to the ECJ?

(c) Had the judge in the High Court acted correctly in failing to refer the question to the ECJ? If so, why?

(d) What watery analogy does Lord Denning MR use?

(e) Who has the final role of interpreting the Treaty of Rome?

(f) If this appeal had been heard at the House of Lords, would the outcome have necessarily been the same?

(g) What four guidelines does Lord Denning MR suggest should be followed as to whether a decision (to refer under Article 234 (ex. 177)) is necessary?

You will find suggested answers to these questions in *Cases and Materials* (2.5).

There is also a Court of First Instance of the European Communities. See *Learning Text: European Community Law*.

There is also an excellent source of information on the Internet. Access to the Internet is not compulsory to succeed in the law, but as legal websites improve, Internet access is beneficial. Web addresses do change, so no guarantees can be given that they will still work when you try them, but a number of suggested sites have been provided. For European law, try www.lib.gla.ac.uk/Docs/Research/europeanlaw.html.

2.10 The Council of Europe

It is easy to confuse the European Union (*née* the EEC) with the Council of Europe, but the two things are completely different. The Council of Europe was established in 1949 as one of many reactions to the Second World War (another is the North Atlantic Treaties Organisation, or NATO). The Council's first achievement was the ECHR. The European Union, on the other hand, was established in 1957 as an economic entity.

It may be interesting for you to know, however, that the European Union is a signatory in its own right to the European Convention.

ACTIVITY 16

Read the extract in *Cases and Materials* (2.6) adapted from Wadham and Mountfield's *Blackstone's Guide to the Human Rights Act 1998*.

Answer the following:

(a) What is the full title of the ECHR?

(b) What is the right of 'individual petition'?

(c) From your previous reading, give an example of where this right has been exercised.

(d) The ECHR has been incorporated into English law in the Human Rights Act 1998 (hereafter HRA). The HRA came into force in October 2000. Had Gregory brought his case after that date, how would the procedure be different?

More information about the ECHR and the HRA are to be found throughout this text. The importance of the HRA 1998 cannot be overstated, as you will be beginning to appreciate. Answers to the above questions can be found in *Cases and Materials* (2.6).

More information is available on-line at www.dhcour.coe.fr/eng/

SAQ 5

Place the sources of law about which you have been reading, in an order of importance which reflects the way in which they impinge on everyday life today.

This is not an easy task! In fact different lawyers might well give different answers to this question. Ignoring European law for the moment, most lawyers would agree that legislation has become the primary source of law in this country. There is a wealth of statute law which regulates almost every aspect of our lives, and it is a form of law which can be created to respond to situations when the need arises. By contrast, in order to develop the common law, it is necessary to wait for a case concerned with a particular issue to arise and for the parties involved to have the resources to test out the principles in court. Thus common law and equitable principles have become secondary in importance to statute law.

As between common law and equitable rules, in a conflict between these two sets of principles it is a long established rule that equity always prevails over the common law. However, in terms of impact on modern life, the rules of the common law are probably invoked more frequently.

This leaves the question of where the law emanating from the institutions of the European Union fits into this order of importance. European law can supersede our national law, and for that reason it could be regarded as superior to legislation created by Parliament, and to the rules of the common law and equity. However, there are still many areas of domestic law which are not affected by European law, and which will therefore seem more important to those who have to deal with the law of this country.

However, the incorporation of the ECHR by way of the HRA 1998 will have a unprecedented effect on English law. There is little doubt that the HRA 1998 will cause massive changes in the judiciary's approach to its task and in the workings of the courts and Parliament. You will have the opportunity to examine this in more detail elsewhere, but it is important that you become aware at this stage to keep an eye firmly placed on the HRA 1998 as you progress with your learning.

2.11 The Court Hierarchy

The court system is not, *per se*, a source of law, unlike the decisions and judgments of the courts. However, to complete this chapter, it is important for you to have an overview of the court structure in England and Wales. A more detailed examination of the procedures and workings of the individual courts is to be found in **Chapters 5**, **6** and **7**.

SAQ 6

From your work so far, your general knowledge and perhaps from what you have seen on the television or read in the papers, list the courts you have heard of in England. Try to decide which are more senior than the others.

2.11.1 TERMS AND DEFINITIONS

There are a number of different terms and ideas with which you need to be familiar before studying the individual courts in detail.

(a)   The system is based on the principle of a **hierarchy**, with courts higher up the hierarchy having greater authority than those lower down in the structure.

(b)   Certain courts are thus **superior** courts, for example the House of Lords, the Court of Appeal, the High Court and the Crown Court. Others, that is the magistrates' courts and the county courts, are **inferior** courts.

(c)   Certain courts are referred to as **courts of record**; this means that a record of all the business of that court is kept at the Public Record Office. With the exception of the magistrates' courts, all the courts mentioned immediately above are courts of record.

(d)   Some courts deal **only** with civil cases, some courts deal **only** with criminal cases, and some courts have jurisdiction to deal with **both** types of cases.

(e)   Some courts are limited with regard to the types of cases with which they can deal, according to the **amount** of money at stake, or the **seriousness** of the matter in hand.

(f)   Certain courts hear cases at **first instance**, whereas other courts are designated **appeal courts**. Cases are heard at **first instance** when they are heard for the first time and no previous decision has been made in any other court. Courts which hear first instance cases are said to have **original jurisdiction**. Contrary to what you might expect, the courts which hear cases on appeal from first instance courts are **not** referred to as courts of second instance; instead these courts are said to have **appellate jurisdiction**.

(g)   The Court of Appeal, the High Court and the Crown Court together make up the **Supreme Court of Judicature**. This was created by the Supreme Court of Judicature Acts 1873–1875 (known as the Judicature Acts) which were consolidated into the Supreme Court Act 1981.

ACTIVITY 17

Turn to *Cases and Materials* (2.7) where you will find two diagrams, one showing the courts which are capable of hearing civil cases and the other showing those courts which have jurisdiction in criminal cases. Using the information given above, you might find it helpful to note on the diagram the courts which are regarded as superior courts, the courts which are classed as courts of record, and those which form part of the Supreme Court. Later in your studies, when you have become more familiar with the names of the different courts, you could try to reproduce the two diagrams from memory, as this will help you to have an overview of the system.

2.12 Summary

By now you should have gained insight into some of the basic features of the legal system in this country. It should be possible for you to:

- discuss the ways in which law may be defined as a method of social control which fosters order in society;

- describe the way in which law may be classified according to the subject matter with which it deals;

- show how the classification of law into public and private law, civil and criminal law, can be used in analysing practical legal problems;

- classify the law according to its source, i.e., Parliament, the courts (common law and equity), the European Union, and the Council of Europe;

- begin to appreciate the interaction of different types of law.

2.12.1 OVERVIEW

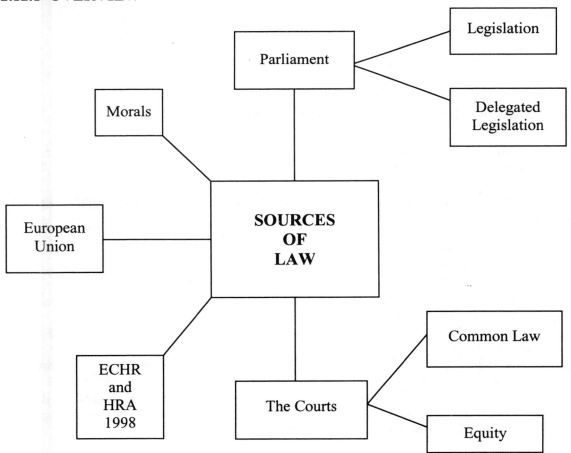

2.13 Further Reading

Slappper and Kelly, *The English Legal System*, 4th edn, London: Cavendish Publishing Limited, 1999, Chapters 1 and 2.

Ward, R., *Walker & Walker's English Legal System*, 8th edn, London: Butterworths, 1998, Chapters 1, 2, 5 and 6.

Zander, M., *The Law Making Process*, 5th edn, London: Butterworths, 1999, Chapters 1, 2 and 8.

2.14 End of Chapter Assessment Question One

Read carefully through the following story and then identify the different types of legal action which may result from it.

Albert is riding his pedal cycle along a country lane, when a car driven by Brenda hurtles past him and knocks him off his bike. Brenda has for many years harboured a grudge against Albert. Albert sustains serious injuries and is hospitalised for several months.

When he emerges from hospital, he discovers that the landlord of the flat which he was occupying before the accident has let the flat to another tenant. Albert applies to the local authority for accommodation, but he is told that he does not come within the statutory definition of 'homelessness'. Albert wishes to challenge the decision of the local authority.

See *Cases and Materials* (2.9) for a specimen answer.

2.15 End of Chapter Assessment Question Two

The following exercise is taken from Bradney, Fisher, Masson, Neal and Newell, *How to Study Law*, 2nd edn, London: Sweet & Maxwell, 1991.

Read the Human Organ Transplants Act 1989 (*Cases and Materials* (2.10)), and answer the following questions:

(a)   What is the short title of this Act?
(b)   Does this Act create civil or criminal liability?
(c)   When did the Act become binding law?
(d)   Ada pays Brian £20 for a pint of blood for use in a transplant operation. Does Ada commit an offence under the Act?
(e)   Fred buys a human kidney from Grace intending to dissect it. Has Fred committed an offence under the Act?
(f)   Henry agrees to donate a kidney for use in a transplant operation. He is given travelling expenses, hotel accommodation and £300. Is an offence under the Act committed?
(g)   June, a newsagent, puts a card in the window of her shop saying that Karl is willing to pay large sums of money to donors for organs which he intends to use in transplant operations. Has June committed an offence under the Act?

See *Cases and Materials* (2.11) for a specimen answer.

CHAPTER THREE

THE DOCTRINE OF PRECEDENT

3.1 Objectives

By the end of this chapter, you should be able to:

- define the doctrine of precedent;

- isolate fact from law and analyse the importance of the distinction;

- identify the *ratio decidendi* of a case;

- distinguish between *ratio decidendi* and *obiter dicta*; and between binding and persuasive precedent;

- advise on how to avoid a precedent;

- describe the operation of precedent in different courts;

- suggest reasons for and against the use of the doctrine.

3.2 Introduction

Imagine that you have developed a mysterious illness and that you visit your general medical practitioner. The doctor has never encountered this illness before, but remembers that a partner in the practice described something similar a while ago. Your doctor consults the other partner to find out what was prescribed.

Next, imagine that you are a solicitor in private practice. A wealthy client has asked you to draw up his will which is to contain an extremely complex trust. You have not drafted such a clause before, but you know that one of the partners has previously prepared this sort of will. You go in search of the file containing the clauses which you need.

What is happening in both of the above cases is that the professional who is faced with an unfamiliar problem seeks a **precedent** to help him or her in arriving at the best solution to that problem. Using previous decisions to help resolve a current problem is a technique employed in all walks of life, but particularly in the courts of most legal systems.

In the English legal system this is referred to as the principle of **stare decisis** (which means 'stand by cases already decided', pronounced 'star-ay de-sice-iss') or the **doctrine of precedent** and it is a concept which has a vital part to play in the day to day decision-making which takes place in our courts.

In this chapter, the operation of the doctrine of precedent *(stare decisis)* in the courts of the English legal system will be examined. The knowledge which you acquire in this chapter will develop your understanding of the way in which the courts and the judges work, and enable you to make some evaluation of the importance of decisions made in different courts. ***Cases and Materials*** will help you to recognise and apply the principles which you will encounter both as a learner of the law in an academic context, and as a practitioner.

3.3   What is the Doctrine of Precedent?

In very simple terms, the doctrine means that a judge who is hearing a particular type of court case does not have to make a decision using simply his or her own knowledge of the relevant legal rules, but that similar previous decisions can be consulted to guide and justify the conclusion reached in the instant case. In fact, where a judge in a lower court is aware of a decision of a higher court which sets a precedent in an analogous case, then this previous decision **must** be followed, and it is this element of **binding** precedent which is distinctive within the English system.

So, for example, imagine that a new statute has been created by Parliament, which regulates the activities of estate agents. A dispute arises concerning the interpretation of one of the sections of the Act, and a court case ensues. The case reaches the Court of Appeal, which makes a decision about the definition of 'an estate agent'. In all future cases in which the definition of an estate agent is in issue, lower courts must observe this binding precedent, and apply the decision from the previous case in these situations.

Clearly, if this system is to operate effectively, then it is essential that there is an efficient and reliable system of reporting court cases. This is achieved through the work of the Incorporated Council of Law Reporting for England and Wales, which produces the authoritative version of case reports (known as The Law Reports) and through the publication of alternative series of reports by private publishers such as Butterworths. Because of the vast number of cases decided every year, not every case from every court is published in this way, but the system does provide judges with access to decisions of the superior courts which will assist them in reaching a conclusion.

By consulting both the official and the privately published law reports, members of the legal profession and the judiciary are able to obtain valuable information about the way in which cases involving particular facts and legal principles have been decided on previous occasions. Because these precedents are regarded as binding, solicitors and barristers are thus able to give more accurate advice to their clients, and the judges are able to follow the reasoning of previous courts.

There are, however, both advantages and disadvantages in the operation of a system of binding precedent.

SAQ 1

From what you have learned of the operation of the doctrine of *stare decisis* so far, try to compile a list of advantages and disadvantages of the system of precedent as it is in England and Wales. Try to think of at least three points in favour of the doctrine and three against (although you may be able to think of more than this). Write them down below, and refer to them again when you have completed the work in this chapter. You may wish to add to or amend your list when you have learned more about the system.

At this stage, it is important to notice some of the basic arguments in favour of the doctrine as it is operated in the English legal system, and also to be aware of some of the drawbacks; not all lawyers (and not even all judges) agree with a strict application of the principle of *stare decisis*.

It is true that the doctrine enables judges to avoid having to solve the same legal problem more than once, and thus may save a considerable amount of judicial time and energy. A further advantage is that this system lends some degree of predictability to legal decision-making. This is of great importance to lawyers when attempting to advise their clients as to the likely outcome of litigation. When a particular factual situation or legal principle has featured in a previous court case, the lawyer is able to assess the case before him or her in the light of the previous decision, and guide the client according to whether the outcome is likely to be in the client's favour or not. Another argument in favour of a strict application of the doctrine is that use of previous precedents satisfies one of the requirements of justice, i.e., that people be treated alike in like circumstances. Thus, a case heard in the High Court in London, to which a precedent of the Court of Appeal is applicable, will, by the application of that precedent, be dealt with in the same way as a similar case being heard by the High Court in Nottingham.

Critics have however argued that this system leads to judicial laziness and discourages members of the judiciary from taking responsibility for thinking through solutions to legal problems. Certainly because the doctrine is essentially backward-looking, it may stifle creativity in decision-making, and may lead to stagnation in the law. Related to this latter point is the criticism that the law cannot develop and respond to changes in social circumstances, unless a case arises which allows a court the opportunity to amend a previous decision by not following the precedent. Legal change could therefore become dependent upon those who have the means to pursue litigation.

3.4 Law and Fact

In the paragraphs above, reference was made to 'similar previous decisions' and 'precedent in an analogous case'. These phrases need to be explained. The system of precedent is where a judge is bound by the LAW of a previous case, but the judge is not bound by the findings of FACT of that case. Thus, when we refer to 'similar previous decisions', as lawyers, we mean that the *law* applied in the cases was similar.

The distinction between law and fact is complex, but it is important that you can explain and illustrate the distinction because of the way the precedent system operates.

You will recall from the cases you have read in *Cases and Materials* so far that a reported case usually contains details of the facts which led to the legal dispute, statements of law relating to the dispute and reasoned discussion by the judges of the way in which the law applied to the facts. Most of the case reports you have read, however, concern appeals where (as you will see) the facts have been established. At first instance (trial), someone involved in the case has had to decide what the facts ARE.

Take the following example:

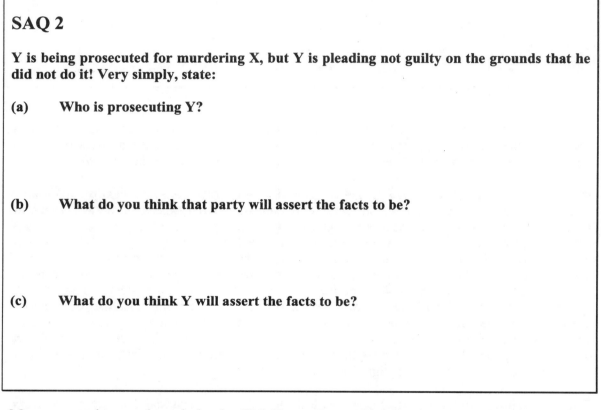

SAQ 2

Y is being prosecuted for murdering X, but Y is pleading not guilty on the grounds that he did not do it! Very simply, state:

(a)   Who is prosecuting Y?

(b)   What do you think that party will assert the facts to be?

(c)   What do you think Y will assert the facts to be?

Most prosecutions are brought by the CPS (Crown Prosecution Service). The CPS will be trying to establish that Y is guilty of murdering X beyond a reasonable doubt. Y, on the other hand, will assert that the facts are that Y did not murder X.

There are a number of different people involved in a court case. In a criminal case, there will be magistrates and there may be a judge and a jury. In a civil case, there will be a judge and possibly a jury. By the end of the hearing, some of these people have to decide <u>what the facts of the case are so that the relevant law can be applied</u>. (More information on the roles of magistrates, judges and the jury can be found elsewhere in this text.)

From the phrase underlined above, you can see that even though you know that it is the LAW that forms part of the system of precedent, it is the FACTS of the case that dictate the law that is relevant.

SAQ 3

What area of law do you think might be involved in the following?

(a)   A married couple wish to separate with a view to the final dissolution of their marriage.

(b)   A homosexual couple have just received a rejection letter on their application to adopt a second child, even though their first was approved.

(c)   An unmarried couple with children have separated and the father wishes to have regular contact with his children.

(a)   Family law; separation and divorce.

(b)   Family law; child law and adoption.

(d)   Family law; child law and parental responsibility.

You can see that even though each of the above examples involved questions of Family law, because the *facts* are different, the minutiae of the law is also different.

To enable us to get a clearer picture of the fact/law distinction, we need to have a clear understanding of what a 'fact' is.

3.4.1   WHAT ARE FACTS?

Most people would identify well known historical events as 'fact', for example, we would say that the outbreak of the First World War in 1914 is a 'fact'. But as you will have noticed in some of the cases which you have already read in *Cases and Materials*, it is not always so easy for the court to determine the 'facts' which have resulted in a legal dispute.

SAQ 4

How might you define a 'fact'? (You might want to consult a dictionary to help you answer this question.)

Give examples of three things which you would regard as facts. Show your examples to another person and ask if they agree that the things you have chosen are 'facts'.

If the other person does not agree about your 'facts', how else might you classify these items?

It is not too difficult to define the word 'fact'. If you consulted a dictionary you would probably find that it is usually referred to as something which is known to have occurred, or something which is known to be true. But once you begin to look for examples of things which people generally would agree to be facts, then problems can begin. For example, if you have stated some well known historical event as a fact, then other people will probably agree with you that this is indeed a fact which actually occurred. But if you present as one of your facts, the statement that 'England has an excellent football team', others might point out to you that this is not fact, but is merely an opinion. But what is the difference between the two types of statement? How do you know that one is fact and the other is opinion?

SAQ 5

How would you demonstrate to someone that your date of birth is a fact, and not simply your own opinion about the date when you were born?

In order to convince someone that you were born on a particular date, you would need to collect *evidence* which would provide sufficient proof to satisfy that person that your date of birth was a fact. Statements from your parents or other members of your family would be helpful, but might not be completely reliable. What if they are all mistaken, or are lying for some reason? Presumably the best form of proof would be your official birth certificate. This would provide documentary evidence that what you are claiming as a fact is true.

3.4.2 FACTS AND EVIDENCE

By now you should be realising that the simple definition of a 'fact' which the dictionary provides is not sufficient for all purposes. It now begins to appear that a fact is only a fact if it can be *proved* to have happened or *proved* to be true. This is particularly true of the facts which are alleged in legal disputes. As you read more and more case law, you may begin to see that what are initially referred to as the 'facts' of the case are merely propositions which the parties seek to prove. The material which they produce to support these propositions is the *evidence*.

ACTIVITY 1

Read the case of *R* v *Stratford-upon-Avon Council Housing Benefit Review Board and Another, ex parte White, The Time*s, **23 April 1998**, in *Cases and Materials* **(3.1.1)**, and answer the following questions:

(a)   From the information given in the report, what 'facts' do you think the Council would have had to establish in order to show that the applicant was not entitled to housing benefit?

(b)   What evidence would the court have accepted as proof of such facts?

(c)   Was such evidence available?

This case illustrates the way in which the facts of a case can be seen as propositions which must be proved by evidence of such weight that it will persuade the court to come to a particular conclusion. In order to convince the court that the applicant was not entitled to housing benefit, the Council would have had to establish as a fact that the applicant had contrived to place himself under a legal liability in order to take advantage of the housing benefit scheme.

The sort of evidence which would be taken to support this proposition might be, for example, that the applicant had entered into the arrangement to pay board and lodging for himself and his family with the sole purpose of making the claim for benefit, and would not otherwise have agreed to live in community in this way. Timing was evidently important to the court, so if the applicant had terminated the agreement after a successful application for housing benefit, this would have been evidence suggestive of bad faith on his part.

Another factor which the court took into account was the intention of the applicant and the landlord to create a legally binding relationship concerning the occupation of the property. Thus if the Council had been able to show that the agreement to live in the community house and pay board and lodging was not intended to create a legal obligation, then this also would have been evidence that the supposed legal liability was contrived with the intention of taking advantage of the system. In the event, the court could find no evidence of this nature, and therefore the facts which were required to be present in order to establish a breach of the law could not be made out.

The result in this case reveals another important feature about fact and evidence and the way in which the process of arguing a case works in practice. The aim of the parties involved in a legal case before a court is to persuade the court that there is sufficient evidence to support the facts which the parties seek to prove. The party that can provide the greater weight of evidence to support their argument will win the case. As a prospective lawyer, it is therefore vitally important that you become skilled in distinguishing fact from evidence and organising both in such a way that you will convince a court of the rightness of your case.

3.4.3   IDENTIFYING FACTS AND LAW

When analysing a reported case, you will sometimes find that not only do you have to try to distinguish facts from evidence, but you will also have to determine whether the issues raised by the case concern questions of fact or questions of law. You would think that this process would be fairly straightforward, but it is actually more difficult than it looks. This is because cases can raise questions which are a mixture of law and fact, and also because the way in which the factual issues are presented can affect the nature of the legal issues and vice versa.

ACTIVITY 2

Read the extract from Timothy Endicott's article *'Questions of Law'* (1998) 114 LQR 292 in *Cases and Materials* (3.1.2).

Why is the distinction between law and fact important? Be as specific as possible.

---

1.   The facts of the case dictate the law that is relevant.

2.   Appeals can generally be made on a point of law only, not on the facts of the case.

3.   The system of precedent is where a judge is bound by the law of a previous case, not bound by the findings of fact.

As a first step, in order for any court to resolve a legal dispute, it must investigate the facts of the case, and the evidence which is said to support those facts. The court cannot decide upon the legal rights and duties of the parties without establishing the order of events which led to the dispute, and testing the evidence adduced to prove the facts.

SAQ 6

Imagine that you are a judge in the High Court, and that you are hearing a case in which a worker in a textile factory has been injured whilst using a sewing machine provided by the owner of the factory. In order for you to decide the legal rights and liabilities of the parties involved, what findings of fact do you think you would need to make? (Remember you are not being asked about the law applicable to this situation – simply use your imagination to make a list of the sort of factual information which would be necessary in order for you to ascertain what has happened in this case.)

Obviously if you are going to come to some conclusion about how the accident occurred, you will want to establish a detailed account of the events surrounding the incident, and of the way in which the accident occurred. This will involve hearing the stories of the various witnesses involved and trying to form a composite history based on those stories which you believe to be accurate. You will probably also want to know about matters such as the condition of the machine, the training which the worker had been given, and whether the worker was using the machine in the appropriate fashion.

These findings of fact will help to define the legal issues involved and thus the rights and duties of the parties. For example, if it can be shown that the owner had provided a faulty sewing machine for the worker to use, and it was the defect in the machine which caused the accident, then a particular line of legal argument can be pursued by the injured worker. In this way, finding the facts concerning the condition and operation of the machine will be a necessary preliminary to identifying the legal rules which are applicable.

But it is also true that the legal issues which are selected for argument in court can determine which of the available facts are regarded as vital to the case. For example, if the facts show that the worker had been properly trained to use the machine in a certain way, but had chosen on this particular occasion to use it in a way which was dangerous and this led to the accident occurring, different legal considerations will apply. In this situation the owner of the factory may wish to put forward legal argument based on facts surrounding the behaviour of the worker, and this will need to be investigated by the court in greater detail.

When reading a case, you will therefore find that questions of fact (that is, questions as to what actually happened) are intertwined with questions of law (that is, what legal rules apply) but you will need to try to disentangle the two so that you can make a satisfactory analysis of the case.

ACTIVITY 3

In *Cases and Materials* (3.1.2) you will find the report of *Clarke* v *Kato and Others, The Times*, 11 December 1996. Read the report through carefully, and then answer the following questions:

(a)   What issues of fact were important in this case? Were there some facts which the court considered to be less important than others, and why?

(b)   What questions of law did this case raise? Were some of the legal questions more important than others in helping the court to reach a decision in this case?

This is a case in which the facts found and legal questions raised in the court below were narrowed down by the Court of Appeal in order for it to reach its judgment. The county court had established the facts concerning the layout of the premises at which the accident took place, the availability of access, the design and negotiability of the area, and the type of use of the car park which actually occurred. It had been established that there was regular and unrestricted pedestrian use of the car park, and the Court of Appeal considered that this was a sufficient ground on which to base the decision that the car park did come within the definition of a 'road'. As a result, it was unnecessary to make any specific finding of fact about the extent to which the area was used by prams and bicycles, because usage by prams and bicycles was not going to affect the decision on the legal issue. In answering question (a) it thus becomes apparent how the legal issues in the case can determine which of the factual issues are important.

A similar process can be seen at work in relation to the legal issues in question (b). Here, the central legal problem was that the Motor Insurers' Bureau would not compensate the victim of the uninsured driver unless it could be shown that the accident had occurred on a 'road', defined as 'any highway and any other road to which the public has access'. The county court had concentrated on the question as to whether the car park could be described as 'any other road to which the public has access'. The Court of Appeal pointed out that it was clear from the facts that the public did have access to the car park, so this meant that the legal argument could be narrowed down to the simple question of whether the car park came within the definition of the word 'road' at all. Question (b) thus shows how the identification of the relevant facts in a case can help to clarify the legal issues which must be decided.

ACTIVITY 4

Read the extract from *R* v *Feely* [1973] 1 All ER 341 in *Cases and Materials* (3.1.2). This is an important case in the Criminal law, but do note that it has been substantially overruled by the later case of *R* v *Ghosh* [1982] 2 QB 1053. We are examining that part of the case that has not been overruled, however. That part directs us as to what amounts to a question of LAW and what amounts to a question of FACT in the offence of theft.

(a) The trial judge's direction to the jury was correct. TRUE/FALSE.

(b) In deciding if a person acts dishonestly, the jury should apply standards of ordinary decent people. TRUE/FALSE.

(c) A judge should give the jury guidance on what amounts to dishonesty. TRUE/FALSE.

(d) The question of whether a defendant has acted dishonestly is a question of fact for the jury. TRUE/FALSE.

The trial judge directed the jury that *Feely* had no defence *in law*. He said 'if someone does something deliberately knowing his employers are not prepared to tolerate it, is that not dishonest?' The Court of Appeal disagreed with this direction. It held that the jury should have been left to decide whether Feely had acted dishonestly or not. The answer to (a) is therefore false. Your answer to (b) is true and your answer to (c) is false. Do note, however, that since the case of *R* v *Ghosh* (see above), trial judges <u>do</u> direct the jury on this question (this direction being a matter of law); but whether a defendant falls foul of the direction, is still a question of fact, as your answer to (d) should state.

It may be worth noting, just to add mud to clear waters, that a court makes an error of LAW when it makes a finding of FACT which there is no evidence to support (see *IRC* v *Scottish and Newcastle Breweries Ltd* [1982] 1 WLR 322 per Lord Lowry at p. 327).

The following quote is not designed to confuse you further, but it may put this topic in perspective:

'. . . there has been a very strong tendency, arising from the infirmities of human nature, in [an appeal] judge to say, if he agrees with the decision ... that the question is one of fact, and if he disagrees that it is one of law, in order that he may express his opinion the opposite way.'

(per Scrutton LJ, *Currie* v *Commissioners of Inland Revenue* [1921] 2 KB 332 at p. 339).

3.4.4   WHERE LAW IS ACADEMIC WITHOUT FACT

ACTIVITY 5

Read the extract from the case of *R* v *Secretary of State for the Home department ex parte Salem* **[1999] 2 WLR 483** in *Cases and Materials* **(3.1.3).**

Why did the House of Lords not proceed with the appeal?

If you had been a Law Lord in this case, would you have allowed the appeal to proceed? Give reasons.

The Supreme Court in the USA has a very strict rule that it will not hear appeals that are 'moot'; where the decision does not have a practical consequence or effect. The House of Lords has a discretionary power to do so, which it decided not to exercise in the above case because of the 'unusual facts'.

You may have decided that if you were, for example, Lord Slynn of Hadley, you would have allowed the appeal to proceed. It is sometimes regarded as human nature that we wish to know the outcome of events, even if it would not change anything. However, three points can be made in support of their Lordships' decision.

First, this was not a 'test' case. A test case is where the legal rights and duties of the parties are being 'tested' by the courts for the first time. An example of this could be the first case brought against the Chief Constable of South Yorkshire concerning the Hillsborough disaster. Secondly, the applicant received legal aid to bring the case and the House recognised the huge costs that would be incurred in this case where no practical solution could be achieved. Finally, the Government had published a White Paper in the previous year that might have rendered any decision of the House obsolete within months.

3.5   How does the Doctrine of Precedent operate?

The hierarchy of the courts, about which you have learned in the previous chapter, is an important factor in the operation of the doctrine in practice. A useful summary of this hierarchical approach has been made by the authors Twining and Miers in their book *How to do things with rules* (Weidenfeld and Nicholson, 1991) and it is worth learning these few simple principles, which apply whenever a court wishes to know whether or not to follow the decision of a previous case.

(a) If the precedent is a decision of a court superior to it in the hierarchy then it **must** follow that precedent in the present case (i.e., it is **bound** by the precedent).

(b) If the precedent is one of the court's own previous decisions, then subject to certain exceptions, it **must** follow the precedent.

(c) If the precedent is a decision of a court inferior to it in the hierarchy, then it is **not** bound to follow the precedent, but may do so if it chooses.

These statements provide a good rule of thumb and are therefore worth memorising, but like all rules of thumb they do not tell the whole story, and in practice the situation is rather more complicated. In order to obtain the full picture, it is necessary to examine the position of each individual court in turn, and so details about the way in which precedent is applied in the different courts can be found at **3.6**. Before that, however, it is important to appreciate two of the technical aspects of the doctrine.

3.5.1 AVOIDING PRECEDENTS

First, it may be that although a judge is bound by a precedent in a particular case, there are good reasons why the judge may wish **not** to follow it. In these circumstances it is likely that the judge will try to **distinguish** the precedent, that is to find some significant difference between the facts of the two cases, so as to avoid having to follow the previous decision. If the court can find sufficient difference between the material facts of the two cases, then it may feel it is justified in departing from the precedent. This process of distinguishing cases is extremely important in practice, because it enables judges to develop the law, rather than being bound by precedent in every situation.

It is also open to the superior courts in the hierarchy to **reverse** the decision of a court lower down in the hierarchy during the course of the **same** case. This will occur if, for example, the High Court has reached a particular decision in a particular case, but then the Court of Appeal reaches the opposite conclusion in the ensuing appeal in that case.

The Court of Appeal and House of Lords also have the power to **overrule** the decision of a lower court, in a later, **different** case. For example, the High Court may reach a decision in case X, and that decision becomes a precedent for the future. Some time later, a similar case, case Y, is heard by the High Court. Case X is used as a precedent, but the losing party appeals to the Court of Appeal. The Court of Appeal finds the original decision in case X to have been erroneous, and overrules it.

For the sake of accuracy, it is important to note that a judge DISTINGUISHES on the FACTS, but REVERSES OR OVERRULES the decision or judgment of LAW.

Distinguishing does not affect the validity of the precedent of the previous case. It is merely felt not to be relevant law on the given facts.

SAQ 7

It is important that you feel confident about the terminology associated with the doctrine of precedent, and that you can use it correctly. Consider the following (fictitious) scenario, and fill in the missing words. You will find the answers at 3.9.

(a)   In 1990, Betty Bloggs was convicted by the Crown Court of the murder of her husband Alf. In her defence, Betty claimed that Alf had treated her brutally throughout their 20 years of marriage, and that this constituted provocation, even though there had been no violence between them immediately prior to the murder. The Crown Court judge had been persuaded by this argument, and regarded Betty's defence as correct in law. On appeal by the prosecution, however, the Court of Appeal (Criminal Division) held that this extension of the defence of provocation was incorrect. The decision of the Crown Court on this point of law was . . . . by the Court of Appeal.

(b)   In 1993, a similar case arose. Carrie Careful was charged with the murder of her husband Denis. She pleaded a similar defence to that of Betty Bloggs. The Crown Court regarded itself as bound by the previous decision in the Court of Appeal. However, in Carrie's case, the court found that Denis had been violent towards her within an hour of the murder taking place. Because of this difference in the facts, the Crown Court was able to . . . . the case of Betty Bloggs, and did not follow it.

(c)   In 1994, Emily Earnest was charged with the murder of her husband Fred, in circumstances identical to those in the Betty Bloggs case. Both the Crown Court and the Court of Appeal followed the precedent set in the Betty Bloggs case, but on appeal to the House of Lords, it was decided that this interpretation of the law was completely incorrect, and the Betty Bloggs case was . . . .

ACTIVITY 6

Refer again to *R* v *Comerford* [1998] 1 All ER 823 (*Cases and Materials* (1.3.2)).

Lord Bingham of Cornhill CJ distinguishes *R* v *Williams* (1925) 19 Cr App R 67 in the *Comerford* case.
Write the definition of distinguishing here:

How was Lord Bingham CJ able to distinguish *Williams* in *Comerford*? (Remember that the process of learning a new aspect of law and applying it to a new situation is the essence of 'doing the law'.)

Does Lord Bingham CJ *use* the term 'distinguish'?

You should be able to see that the facts of *Comerford* and *Williams* are different. Even though they both concern the treatment of jurors and the right of the defendant to request a *venire de novo* when there has been an irregularity in the procedures adopted by the court, *Williams* deals with procedural irregularity on challenging the jury, whilst *Comerford* deals with alleged irregularity in granting police protection to the jury.

As Lord Bingham CJ has been able to find these 'material irregularities', the cases have been distinguished. Importantly, the effect of this, is that the law that governs these two cases are different, because the court has found the facts to be different.

Unfortunately, it is very rare for judges to state when they are distinguishing. It is left for law students, tutors, legal commentators and judges in later cases to decide that with hindsight. One judge, however, who did help to guide readers around his decisions, was the late Lord Denning.

ACTIVITY 7

Refer back to *D & C Builders v Rees* [1966] 2 QB 617 in *Cases and Materials* (2.3.1). Lord Denning specifically stated that he was distinguishing *Sibree* v *Tripp* (1846) 15 M & W 23 and he even admitted difficulty in distinguishing *Goddard* v *O'Brien* (1882) 9 QBD 37; which he also thought had been wrongly decided.
More on Lord Denning anon.

3.5.2 *RATIO DECIDENDI* AND *OBITER DICTA*

It is also important to be aware of which part of the decision of a previous case is to be regarded as binding. The decision itself, i.e., who wins and who loses, is only really of interest to the parties in the case. What really matters, from the point of view of lawyers who wish to apply the doctrine of precedent, is the abstract principle which can be drawn from the case by combining the relevant legal principles with the essential facts on which the decision is based. This principle is known as the *ratio decidendi* (literally, the reason for deciding, pronounced 'rayshio dess-i-dend-eye') and it is this part of the case which is absorbed into the general law, and which forms the basis of future legal reasoning. In discussion, lawyers generally abbreviate the term *ratio decidendi* to 'the *ratio*'.

The *ratio decidendi* is often contrasted with other parts of the judgment which are said to be *obiter dicta* (that is, sayings by the way, pronounced 'oh-bitt-er dicc ta'). These are remarks made by a judge which are less central to the decision, for example, hypothetical examples, statements of law which support dissenting judgments, and remarks concerned with broader principles of law which may not be directly in issue in the instant case.

The *ratio decidendi* is therefore that part of a previously decided case which later judges regard as binding on them, because it embodies the legal rule which justifies a particular decision. But how is it identified in any particular case? Discerning the *ratio* of a case requires a close analysis of the judgment or judgments in the case, and is made more difficult by the fact that the judges do not identify it for the benefit of later readers.

ACTIVITY 8

Carlill v *Carbolic Smoke Ball Company* [1892] All ER Rep 127, is one of the most famous cases in the English legal system. Although it belongs in a contract law text, the purpose for including it here is that it will illustrate the difference between *ratio* and *obiter*.

Refer to the case in *Cases and Materials* (3.2.1) and then answer the following questions. You will need to make notes on a separate piece of paper. Take an hour to complete this Activity.

(a) Briefly summarise the most important (i.e. the material) facts of the case.

(b) Summarise the Company's defence.

(c) Whilst the literal translation of the term *ratio decidendi* is 'the reason for the decision', it is better to think of it as the RULE OF LAW ON WHICH THE DECISION IS BASED ON THE FACTS AS THEY HAVE BEEN FOUND. What is the *ratio decidendi* of *Carlill* v *Carbolic Smoke Ball*?

(d) Give an example of *obiter dicta*.

Note: again, none of the judges use these terms, so find what fits into the definitions already given.

You will find suggested answers to these questions in *Cases and Materials* (3.2.1).

Academic writers such as Professor A. Goodhart have attempted to formulate methods of discerning the *ratio*. Goodhart's theory is that the *ratio* can be found by taking account of the facts treated by the judge as material, and the judge's decision as based on them. But it should be noted that this is only a theory and finding the *ratio* tends to be an intuitive process. Some help may be derived from the headnote in a reported case, that is the summary of the facts and the decision in each case, inserted by the editor of the reports, but it is unwise to rely on these as a method of ascertaining the *ratio*. There is, unfortunately, no substitute for reading carefully through all the judgments of the case under discussion. In fact this can reveal that a case may have more than one *ratio*, either because a judge has identified several reasons for a decision, providing several *rationes decidendi*, or because several members of either the Court of Appeal of House of Lords have given separate judgments with slightly different *rationes*.

From now on, every time you read a reported case, you should study the judgments provided with a view to identifying the *ratio* of the case. You will then be able to compare your assessment of the case with that provided in the learning texts or other books.

You should now have a reasonable grasp of the following elements of precedent:

- *stare decisis*
- *ratio decidendi*
- *obiter dicta*
- distinguishing
- reversing
- overruling
- how to read a case.

ACTIVITY 9

The following exercise should allow you to apply the above to a case that you may find interesting as you have already been directed to it. In *Gregory* v *UK* (1998) 25 EHRR 577, the European Court of Human Rights referred to the law from the case of *R* v *Gough* [1993] AC 646. You will find this case in *Cases and Materials* (3.2.1). Read it and answer the following questions. To complete this activity well, it should take up to an hour.

1.   What were the central facts of the case?

2.   What was the central legal issue in the case?

3.   From the information provided within the report, trace the chronological history of the case (so far as is possible) up to and including the House of Lords.

4.   How did the House of Lords distinguish between the present case and the earlier decision in *Dimes* v *Proprietors of Grand Junction Canal* (1852)? What principles of precedent are relevant here?

5.   In the case of *R* v *Gough,* the Court of Appeal followed the test laid down in *R* v *Spencer* [1987] AC 128. What principles of precedent are relevant here?

6.   What, in your opinion, is the *ratio decidendi* of *R* v *Gough*?

You will find an outline answer in *Cases and Materials* (3.2.1).

ACTIVITY 10

Read the case of *R* v *Bow Street Metropolitan Stipendiary Magistrate and Others, ex parte Pinochet Ugarte (No. 2)* [1999] 2 WLR 272, in *Cases and Material* (3.2.1).

1.   How does this case extend the *Dimes* case?

2.   Why wasn't *R* v *Gough* (Activity 9) followed?

Lord Browne-Wilkinson, in an interview with *The Times* (19 October 1999), whilst declining to comment on Lord Hoffman's lapse, made it clear he regarded the case as 'a unique first occasion concerning an interest which was not a financial interest.' It is in this way that the *Dimes ratio* was extended to include the promotion of a cause in which the judge was involved together with one of the parties. Accordingly, the *Gough* rules were not followed; they were clearly distinguished on the facts.

3.5.3 PERSUASIVE PRECEDENT

It is easy to focus on the binding nature and the binding element (*ratio decidendi*) of the system of precedent to the exclusion of all other factors. However, the final element to be examined before we look at how each court operates in the system is that of persuasive precedent.

SAQ 8

What do you understand by the word 'persuasive'?

You may have said that if something is persuasive it is 'influencing', 'inducing' or 'urging' you to go along with it or agree with it. A persuasive precedent is exactly that.

All previous decisions that are not binding are persuasive and all *obiter dicta* are persuasive. Some persuasive precedents are more persuasive than others. For example, the *obiter* of Bowen LJ in *Carlill* v *Carbolic Smoke Ball Co Ltd* [1892] All ER Rep 127, which is technically persuasive on a later decision in the High Court, will almost always be followed because of the seniority of the House of Lords.

3.6 The Doctrine as applied in Individual Courts

3.6.1 THE COURT OF JUSTICE OF THE EUROPEAN COMMUNITIES

The ECJ does not formally bind lower courts. Instead, the English courts regard themselves as bound. This distinction is because the ECJ does not deliver its judgments in the same way as an English Court (with *ratio decidendi* and *obiter dicta*). The ECJ adopts the same system as most of the continental European countries, that is, a *civil* system. This can be distinguished from the system in England and Wales which is a *common law* system. Within a civil system, courts do not operate *stare decisis* strictly. In common law systems, *stare decisis* rules. The ECJ does not therefore bind itself.

The European approach, there is no doubt, is influencing the courts of England and Wales. See in particular **Chapters 2** and **4**.

3.6.2 THE HOUSE OF LORDS

Decisions of the House of Lords bind all inferior courts in this country.

From the beginning of this century until 1966, the House also regarded itself as bound by its own previous decisions. This was because it was felt that there had be an end to litigation, i.e., it had to be possible for people to see that once a case had been to the House of Lords, then there would be no further debate on that legal point.

However, this approach proved to be unduly restrictive, in that it effectively prohibited any development in the law. Therefore in 1966, Lord Gardiner LC on behalf of himself and the other Law Lords issued a Practice Statement which declared that the House would feel free to depart from its own previous decisions 'when it appears right to do so'. The Statement acknowledged that the House of Lords regarded the doctrine of precedent as an 'indispensable foundation' upon which to decide the law, but that 'too rigid adherence to precedent may lead to injustice in a particular case and also unduly restrict the proper development of the law'.

ACTIVITY 11

In *Cases and Materials* (3.3.1) you will find reproduced the text of the House of Lords Practice Statement. (*Practice Statement (Judicial Precedent)* [1966] 3 All ER 77.) You will also see the text of the Press Release which was issued with the statement. From reading these extracts, what do you learn about the circumstances in which the House of Lords would be prepared to depart from its own previous decisions, and the accompanying pitfalls which the House wished to avoid?

As you will see from the Practice Statement itself, the House of Lords was very conscious of the need for caution in the exercise of its new power. This was felt to be especially important in cases where contracts, settlements, and financial arrangements had been made in reliance on previous House of Lords' decisions. The Law Lords also wished to avoid any reduction in the degree of certainty required for justice to be done in the sphere of criminal law. However, the House also recognised that there would be circumstances where modern conditions would require a change in the law, and that decisions which had been made in the past in response to factors which had since ceased to operate, could now be overruled by the use of the Practice Statement.

In practice, the Law Lords did indeed exercise caution in their use of this power, and following the publication of the Practice Statement in 1966, two years passed before the House of Lords departed from one of their own previous decisions. The first case in which the authority of the Statement was invoked was that of *Conway* v *Rimmer* [1968] AC 910, HL in which the case of *Duncan* v *Cammell Laird & Co.* [1942] AC 624, HL was overruled.

Both of these cases concerned the extent to which the Crown could claim the right not to disclose information during a court case. The earlier case of *Duncan* v *Cammell Laird & Co.* had been decided during the Second World War, and this had enabled the government to claim 'public interest immunity', and thus avoid the need to comply with an order of the court requiring disclosure of certain documents. The different circumstances under which the case of *Conway* v *Rimmer* arose meant that the House of Lords removed this immunity from the government. This case was therefore a good example of the way in which the Practice Statement could be used to adapt the law to changes in society.

This decision did not, however, mean that a judicial 'free-for-all' would ensue, and in the intervening years, the House of Lords has continued to use its power in a relatively small number of cases. For example, in *Herrington* v *British Railways Board* [1972] 1 All ER 749, a rule which had been propounded in the earlier House of Lords case of *Addie & Sons* v *Dumbreck* [1929] AC 358 HL *was* relaxed as a result of the Practice Statement. In *Addie,* the House had ruled that an occupier of property owed only a minimal duty of care to a trespasser, even where that trespasser happened to be a child. However, changes in society's opinion as to the appropriate duty owed in these circumstances led the Law Lords to formulate a duty on the part of an occupier to act humanely towards trespassers.

Similarly, in *Miliangos* v *George Frank (Textiles) Ltd* [1975] 1 All ER 1076, new developments in rules relating to the exchange rates for foreign currencies, and in particular the less favourable position of sterling, led the House of Lords to change its own earlier ruling in the case of *Re United Railways of Havana & Regla Warehouses Ltd* [1960] 2 All ER 332, that damages awarded by an English court could only be awarded in sterling. As a result of the *Miliangos* case, damages may be awarded by a court in England based on the currency specified in the contract which gave rise to the dispute.

Cases such as these, in which the Practice Statement has been used to positive effect, indicate that the House will expect to see that broad issues of justice and public policy are involved before altering a previous decision, and will not usually overturn a previous ruling simply because it is felt that the earlier decision was wrong. A good example of this line of reasoning can be seen in the case of *Jones* v *Secretary of State for Social Services* [1972] 1 All ER 145. This case concerned the interpretation of a statute, on which the House of Lords had previously given a ruling in the case of *Re Dowlin* [1967] 1 AC 725. Despite the fact that four of the seven Law Lords who heard the *Jones* case felt that *Re Dowling* was wrongly decided, the House declined to depart from its earlier decision. Some of the reasons offered as justification for this decision were that no broad issues of justice or public policy or legal principle were involved, the case involved the interpretation of a statute and therefore any harmful consequences of the interpretation could be cured by further statutory provisions, and the need for finality in litigation.

ACTIVITY 12

In *Cases and Materials* (3.3.1), you will find exrtacts from the cases of *Anderton* v *Ryan* [1985] 2 All ER 355 and *R* v *Shivpuri* [1986] 2 All ER 334.

(Note: prima facie, one of the cases above appears to be a civil case. Because *Anderton* v *Ryan* consists of two surnames, it would not seem to be a criminal case, but it is. This is an exception to the rules we looked at in Chapter 1. This is a prosecution appeal from the magistrates' court to the Divisional Court, using a process called 'case stated'. A case stated appeal does not start by way of summons, but by an information in the surname of the prosecutor and the defendant. See below.)

Explain the relationship between the two cases and the 1966 Practice Statement.

The case of *R* v *Shivpuri* [1986] 2 All ER 334 proved to be an exception to the principles set out in the *Jones* case above. Here, the Lords took the unusual step of overruling a previous decision of their own which had only been made one year before. The case of *Anderton* v *Ryan* [1985] 2 All ER 355 was felt to have been wrongly decided, and to contain an error which distorted the law. The Law Lords felt that this situation needed to be remedied as quickly as possible by overruling the previous decision, despite the fact that this was a case which affected the criminal law and the interpretation of a statute, both factors which were thought to militate against the use of the Practice Statement. The Lords emphasised however that this was an exceptional case, and that use of the Practice Statement generally would remain a rare occurrence.

You may have noticed from examining the text of the Practice Statement in *Cases and Materials* that the House of Lords emphasised that this change in practice was not intended to affect the use of precedent in any other court. However, when you reach the section on precedent in the Court of Appeal, you will find that Lord Denning, a former well-known Master of the Rolls, would have liked to extend the powers of the Court of Appeal in this direction, but was restrained by the House of Lords.

3.6.3 THE JUDICIAL COMMITTEE OF THE PRIVY COUNCIL

The Judicial Committee is not strictly bound by the decisions of the House of Lords, nor does it regard itself as bound by its own previous decisions.

Decisions of the Committee are not viewed as binding on other courts, but its advice is regarded as being of the strongest persuasive value. This means that a court lower down the hierarchy is not strictly obliged to follow decisions of the Committee, but will give weight to its opinions which are treated as highly influential.

SAQ 9

Why does the composition of the Committee mean that its decisions are treated with such respect? (You may need to refresh your memory from the previous chapter to answer this question.)

For judicial sittings, the Privy Council will normally consist of the Lord Chancellor, and the Lords of Appeal in Ordinary. Thus the composition of the Council is usually the same as that of the House of Lords. This accounts for the respect with which its opinions are regarded, and explains its influence as part of the system of precedent.

3.6.4 THE COURT OF APPEAL (CIVIL DIVISION)

The Court of Appeal is bound by decisions of the House of Lords.

The decisions of the Court of Appeal itself are binding on the inferior courts in the hierarchy.

The Court of Appeal is **normally** bound by its own previous decisions. This is known as the 'self-binding rule', and means that unless one of the established exceptions to this rule applies, then the Court of Appeal will always follow its own previous precedents. The classic statement of the exceptions to the self-binding rule can be found in the case of *Young* v *Bristol Aeroplane Co. Ltd*

[1944] 2 All ER 293. Here, Lord Greene MR identified three situations in which it would be possible for the Court of Appeal to depart from its own previous decisions:

(a)   Where previous decisions of the Court conflict with each other. In these circumstances the Court can decide which decision to follow and which to ignore.

(b)   Where a previous decision of the Court conflicts with a subsequent decision of the House of Lords. Here the Court of Appeal must follow the House of Lords ruling rather than its own even if it thinks the House of Lords ruling is wrong.

(c)   Where a previous decision of the Court appears to have been made **per incuriam**. This literally means 'through lack of care', which sounds as though it should enable later judges to ignore any previous precedent which seems to the later court to be wrong. The true position is not quite so simple however, as the technical application of the *per incuriam* rule is actually quite narrow.

According to the case of *Morelle* v *Wakeling* [1955] 1 All ER 708, a decision is regarded as having been made *per incuriam* if the Court of Appeal was in a state of ignorance or forgetfulness with regard to a relevant part of statute law or a binding precedent and, as a result, some part of the decision, or some step in the reasoning is found to be demonstrably wrong. The court did acknowledge the fact that in rare and exceptional cases, a decision might be held to be *per incuriam* where there was a 'manifest slip or error', and an illustration of this can be found in the case of *Williams* v *Fawcett* [1985] 1 All ER 787.

ACTIVITY 13

Read the extract from the case of *Williams* v *Fawcett* [1985] 1 All ER 787 in *Cases and Materials* (3.3.2) and try to identify the reasons for the application of the *per incuriam* rule in this case. You should be able to find three different factors which led the Court of Appeal to choose not to follow a precedent established by two of its own previous decisions.

As you will see from the extract, this was a case in which the Court of Appeal felt that there were special features justifying an extension of the traditionally accepted form of the *per incuriam* rule. Three of these features seem to be prominent in the judgment. They were first, the clarity with which the growth of the error could be detected if the previous decisions were read consecutively. Secondly, the fact that the cases were concerned with the liberty of the subject, and thirdly, that the cases were most unlikely to reach the House of Lords, which meant that there would be no further opportunity to correct the error which had crept into the law.

The *Young* rules above describe the currently accepted understanding of the doctrine of precedent as it relates to the Court of Appeal (Civil Division). You should, however, be aware of the fact that during the 1970s, the then Master of the Rolls, Lord Denning, challenged this accepted view of the role of the Court of Appeal. In a number of controversial cases he led a campaign, first, to establish that the Court of Appeal was not always strictly bound by House of Lords decisions, and could even declare them to be wrongly decided using the doctrine of *per incuriam*, and secondly, to adopt the philosophy of the 1966 House of Lords Practice Statement in the Court of Appeal, so that the Court could choose not to follow its own previous decisions in circumstances where it felt that it was right to do so, without having to bring the case within the exceptions outlined in the case of *Young* v *Bristol Aeroplane Co. Ltd.*

Lord Denning received a great deal of criticism from the House of Lords as a result of expressing these revolutionary views. In the case of *Broome* v *Cassell & Co. Ltd* [1971] 1 All ER 801, he had led the Court of Appeal to reject an earlier House of Lords case concerning the award of exemplary damages *(Rookes* v *Barnard* [1964] 1 All ER 367) on the grounds that it had been decided *per incuriam.* When *Broome* v *Cassell & Co. Ltd* reached the House of Lords ([1972] AC 1136) Lord Hailsham reminded Lord Denning that it was not open to the Court of Appeal 'to give gratuitous advice to judges of first instance to ignore decisions of the House of Lords in this way . . . it is necessary for each lower tier, including the Court of Appeal, to accept loyally the decisions of the higher tiers'.

Similarly, Lord Denning attacked the self-binding rule in the Court of Appeal in a number of cases, culminating in the case of *Davis* v *Johnson* [1978] 1 All ER 1132 which concerned the powers of the courts to provide protection to women who were subjected to violence by their cohabiting partners. Lord Denning had expressed the opinion that the Court of Appeal should be at liberty to depart from a previous decision of its own if convinced that the previous decision was wrong, in much the same way as the House of Lords had done since 1966. This view was again rejected by the House of Lords in no uncertain terms, and the principles set out in the case of *Young* v *Bristol Aeroplane Co. Ltd* were reaffirmed. It would seem therefore that the traditional view of precedent in the Court of Appeal now prevails.

SAQ 10

The Court of Appeal (Civil Division) is in the process of hearing appeals in the following three cases. Explain how the doctrine of precedent will apply in each case.

Case 1: There is a previous decision of the Court of Appeal (Case A) involving similar facts and legal issues, but the Court of Appeal hearing Case 1 thinks that whilst Case A was correctly decided, the decision is outdated in today's social climate.

Case 2: A previous case involving similar facts and legal issues was decided by the Court of Appeal in 1990 (Case B). The House of Lords has also made a ruling in a similar case (Case C) in 1993.

Case 3: There are two previous Court of Appeal precedents relevant to the point in issue. Both were decided on the same day, by differently constituted Courts of Appeal, and these two decisions conflict with each other.

In order to answer these questions, the traditional view of the doctrine of precedent must be adopted; Lord Denning's views having been rejected by the House of Lords.

In Case 1, the self-binding rule of the Court of Appeal is applicable. Where the facts and issues are covered by a previous precedent of the Court of Appeal, then unless one of the exceptions in *Young* v *Bristol Aeroplane Co. Ltd* applies, the Court is bound to follow it. The fact that it regards the previous precedent as outdated is irrelevant.

In Case 2, the self-binding rule would indicate that the Court should follow Case B. However, this is one of the exceptions from *Young's* case, i.e., that where there is a later House of Lords decision which conflicts with the earlier Court of Appeal decision, then the House of Lords case (Case C) prevails and must be followed.

Case 3 again concerns the rule in *Young's* case. Because of the volume of cases conducted in the Court of Appeal, it is possible that similar cases could be heard by differently constituted courts on the same day, and different decisions reached. In such cases, a later Court of Appeal may choose which of these decisions to follow, and decline to follow the other.

3.6.5   THE COURT OF APPEAL (CRIMINAL DIVISION)

The rules of precedent are in theory identical in the two divisions of the Court of Appeal, i.e., that the Court is bound by decisions of the House of Lords, and by its own previous decisions, subject to the exceptions outlined in the case of *Young* v *Bristol Aeroplane Co. Ltd*. Whilst the rule regarding House of Lords decisions remains the same, the self-binding rule is applied in a slightly different way in the criminal division. Case law indicates that the Court of Appeal (Criminal Division) may depart from its own previous decisions if it is satisfied that the law was misapplied or misunderstood, and that this power to deviate from the self-binding rule exists in addition to the exceptions set out in *Young's* case.

ACTIVITY 14

In *Cases and Materials* (3.3.3) there is a short extract from the case of *R* v *Taylor* [1950] 2 KB 368 which was decided by the Court of Criminal Appeal (which is the predecessor of the modern Court of Appeal (Criminal Division)). What does this case reveal about the justification for applying the self-binding rule in a different way in criminal matters?

As you will appreciate, the liberty of the individual is at stake in cases which are heard by the Court of Appeal (Criminal Division), and this is felt to be a more important factor than the consistency which is produced by rigid adherence to precedent. The danger of a wrongful conviction outweighs the need to follow the doctrine in its strict form. A slightly different view of precedent is therefore taken in such cases.

ACTIVITY 15

Refer to *R* v *Gould* [1968] 1 All ER 849 in *Cases and Materials* (3.3.3).

Can you explain how the Court of Appeal in *Gould* took advantage of the statement in *R* v *Taylor* (above)?

In *Gould*, the trial judge correctly regarded himself as bound by the previous Court of Appeal decision of *R* v *Wheat, R* v *Stocks* [1921] All ER Rep 602. When *Gould* appealed against conviction, the Court of Appeal (Criminal Division) agreed that the trial judge had been bound to follow *R* v *Wheat, R* v *Stocks*; but then it used the *Taylor* statement to avoid and then disprove it.

SAQ 11

Compare the approach of

(a) the House of Lords, and

(b) the Court of Appeal (Criminal Division)

in the operation of precedent in criminal cases.

The House of Lords in the 1966 Practice Statement specifically recognises the 'especial need for <u>certainty</u> as to the criminal law'. The Court of Appeal in *Taylor* and *Gould* adopt a more <u>flexible</u> approach. There would appear to be two approaches to precedent in criminal cases. The House of Lords takes one, the Court of Appeal, a different one. There is therefore an irony. In calling for certainty in criminal cases, the court system appears to operate uncertainly.

3.6.6 THE DIVISIONAL COURTS OF THE HIGH COURT

Divisional Courts of the High Court are bound by decisions of the House of Lords and the Court of Appeal.

Decisions of the Divisional Courts are binding on inferior courts.

The Divisional Courts are normally bound by their own previous decisions, unless one or more of the three exceptions enunciated in the case of *Young* v *Bristol Aeroplane Co. Ltd*, applies. As in the Court of Appeal, there may be a greater degree of flexibility in this rule when the Divisional Court of the Queen's Bench considers criminal cases.

SAQ 12

You will notice that the rule of precedent which applies to the Divisional Courts is the same as that applied in the Court of Appeal. Can you think what the reason for this might be? (Hint: look back to the earlier chapters on the jurisdiction of the courts and the system of appeals for help with this point.)

The similarity of the rules concerning precedent in the Court of Appeal and the Divisional Courts of the High Court can be explained in terms of function. The Divisional Courts are not generally courts of first instance: as with the Court of Appeal, they are appellate courts, and in certain circumstances they replace the Court of Appeal as the appropriate forum for appeal. In such cases, the next avenue of appeal is the House of Lords, which means that the Divisional Courts enjoy a great degree of authority and seniority. It is therefore logical for the same rules of precedent to be adopted here.

3.6.7 THE HIGH COURT

The High Court is bound by decisions of those courts which are superior to it in the hierarchy.

Decisions of the High Court are binding on courts which are inferior to it in the hierarchy.

The High Court does not regard itself as strictly bound by its own previous decisions, but they are of strongest persuasive value. Where previous High Court decisions conflict therefore, the judge will generally follow the later case, but is not empowered to overrule the case which is not preferred.

3.6.8 THE CROWN COURT

The Crown Court is bound by decisions of superior courts.

Its decisions are binding on those courts which are inferior to it in the hierarchy.

Decisions of the Crown Court are of persuasive, but not binding, authority for other judges in the Crown Court.

3.6.9 COUNTY COURTS AND MAGISTRATES' COURTS

These courts are bound by all superior courts. Their own decisions are not binding on any courts, not even on other courts at the same level in the hierarchy.

3.7 Summary

The doctrine of judicial precedent provides a necessary foundation for your study of the substantive law. By working through the previous chapter, you should have acquired the basic skills which you will need in order to analyse the primary sources of law, and understand how legal issues are dealt with by the different courts.

In particular you should be able to:

- identify, or at least describe, the difference between law and fact;

- describe the basic principles of the doctrine of *stare decisis*;

- apply these principles to different courts in the English legal system;

- discuss traditional and radical approaches to the doctrine;

- appreciate the significance of the doctrine for the development of the law.

At the end of this chapter you will find an exercise which will enable you to test your knowledge and skills in the areas covered by the Learning Text. You should then try to transfer these skills, and keep this knowledge in mind when you are analysing case and statute law in your further studies. I hope that you will want to return to this section of the textbook and ***Cases and Materials*** from time to time, so that you retain an interest in analysing the primary sources of law, and so that you do not forget the foundation principles which you will need as a lawyer.

3.8 Further Reading

Ingman, T., *The English Legal Process,* 8th edn, London: Blackstone Press, 2000, Chapter 9.

Anderson, T. and Twining, W., *Analysis of Evidence*, London: Weidenfeld and Nicolson, 1991, Chapters 1-3 and 5-6.

Bailey, S.H., and Gunn, M.J., *Smith and Bailey on The English Legal System*, 3rd edn, London: Sweet & Maxwell, 1996, Chapter 7.

Manchester, Salter & Moodie, *Exploring the Law*, 2nd edn, London: Sweet & Maxwell, 2000.

3.9 Answers to SAQ 20

(a)   Reversed.

(b)   Distinguished.

(c)   Overruled.

3.10 End of Chapter Assessment Question One

At the end of **Chapters 1** and **2**, you may have noticed the pictorial 'overviews' as summaries of the chapters.

Many students find it very useful using pictures, flowcharts and images rather than trying to memorise text. There are two main advantages to revising in the first way:

(a)   You can visualise images in your 'mind's eye' in examination conditions and the content is (you hope) easier to pluck from the depths of memory,

(b)   Learning text by rote (parrot fashion) can prevent you from properly <u>applying</u> your knowledge to the question set.

Instead of providing you with an overview for this topic, complete the following grids which you may find useful for revision purposes. You will find completed grids in *Cases and Materials* **(3.5)**.

Figure 1

Court	Is the court bound by a higher court?	Does the court bind any lower courts?	Is the court bound by its own previous decisions?
ECJ		Yes. The system of *stare decisis* means all courts are bound	
Privy Council	Strictly no, but it is rare for it to depart from a House of Lords decision		
House of Lords		Yes	
Court of Appeal (Civil Division)		Yes	
Court of Appeal (Criminal Division)	Yes	Yes	
Divisional Courts	Yes		
High Court			Previous decisions are strongly persuasive, but it may not overrule its own previous decisions
Crown Court		Yes	
County Court		n/a	
Magistrates' Court		n/a	

Figure 2

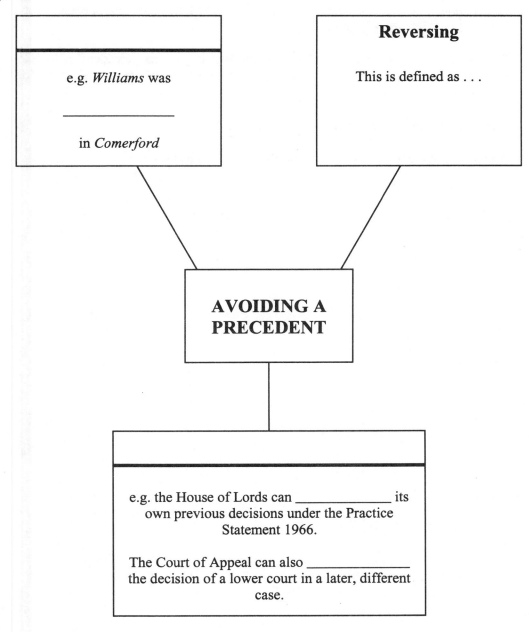

3.11   End of Chapter Assessment Question Two

Read the extracts from the case of *Davis* v *Johnson* [1978] 1 All ER 1132, in **Cases and Materials (3.6)**, or read the original report at the reference given, if you have access to a law library, and then answer the following questions. The answers can be found in **Cases and Materials (3.7)**.

1.   What were the central factual issues in the case?

2.   What preliminary question of law had to be determined?

3.   Explain the route through the court system by which the case reached the House of Lords.

4.   Did the House of Lords as a whole favour the narrower or the broader view of construction of s. 1 of the Domestic Violence and Matrimonial Proceedings Act 1976? Did Lord Diplock agree with this?

5.   According to Lord Diplock, what is the rule which governs precedent in the Court of Appeal, when that court is reviewing one of its own previous decisions? How does that rule operate?

6.   What are the reasons for the rule mentioned in question 5?

7.   How did Lord Denning attempt to alter that rule? Did he succeed?

CHAPTER FOUR

STATUTORY INTERPRETATION (OR STATUTORY CONSTRUCTION)

4.1 Objectives

By the end of this chapter you should be able to:

- identify the difficulties involved in understanding statute law;

- appreciate the differing roles of Parliament and the courts in this process;

- compare the different conventions used by the judiciary in the process of statutory interpretation or construction;

- identify the aids and presumptions used by the judiciary when considering the meaning of an Act of Parliament;

- analyse decided cases with a view to identifying the methods of interpretation or construction adopted by the judiciary.

4.2 Introduction

From your work on the previous chapters and the accompanying exercises in *Cases and Materials*, you will by now have formed a picture of the different sources of law and the different courts which deal with various types of cases. It is now time to make a closer study of the way in which statute law and case law are both applied and developed by the judges in the courts of England and Wales. In this chapter, we will analyse the methods by which judges interpret and give meaning to the complex words and phrases which can be found in Acts of Parliament. In order to obtain the most benefit from your study of this chapter, you will need to refer to *Cases and Materials* and a good quality dictionary.

Even though what we are going to discuss in this chapter has its basis in legislation, the emphasis will be less on the statute and more on case law. For example, a statute may refer to an item with 'four legs'. Whilst in one context, this could include chairs and tables, in another, it could include dogs, cats and elephants. The emphasis, therefore, is not on what words are used, but on how those words have been construed in cases. Judges have a complex role in this field.

4.3   Understanding Statutes: Interpretation and Construction

As the major source of law in England and Wales, statute law, in theory, ought to be easily understood by those to whom it is addressed. Nothing could be further from the truth. As anyone who has tried to read any sections of any statute will know, legislation is not easy to understand, and we require specialist help if we are to grasp its meaning. This specialist help is provided by solicitors (the 'front line' lawyers who provide advice on legal matters generally) and by barristers (the more specialist lawyers who represent clients in the higher courts and who provide legal opinions in complex cases). Ultimately, if the resolution of a legal dispute depends upon the meaning of a piece of statute law, then it may be necessary for the parties to commence court proceedings, and obtain a definitive interpretation from a judge, of the meaning of the words used in the legislation.

Over time, the judges have developed conventions (or traditions) which guide them in finding the meaning of the laws which Parliament and other rule-making bodies produce. It is these conventions which will be examined in this chapter.

In order to begin the process of understanding a piece of legislation, first of all the words used have to be given meaning, rather like interpreting a foreign language. This process of **interpretation** is one with which we are all familiar, as we constantly assign meaning to the words used in any document we read. But statute law may also be **construed**: this is the process whereby uncertainties and ambiguities in the application of the statute are resolved, otherwise known as **statutory construction**.

So, for example, if the word **credit** appears in a statute, first we need to **interpret** the word, i.e., give it meaning so that we can comprehend it, but secondly we may need to **construe** it, i.e., decide whether the word as used in the statute applies to a particular situation with which we are concerned, or whether the word should be understood in such a way that it does not have any relevance to the particular case we are considering. In practice, however, you may find that the two terms, interpretation and construction, are used interchangeably, and this technical distinction between the two becomes rather blurred.

But why is this process so complicated? There are a number of reasons why statute law presents such difficulties both to the ordinary individual in attempting to understand it, and to judges who have to make decisions as to its legal meaning, and apply it to particular cases.

4.3.1   THE GENERALITY OF STATUTE LAW

Case law is based on the facts of **particular** situations, but legislation is drafted in **general** terms. Rules which are set out in statutes have to be capable of application to different classes of people and situations. The draftsman has to create a rule which is general enough to cover all foreseeable circumstances which may fall within the scope of the rule. This is a difficult task, which is rendered even more complicated by the fact that the draftsmen and legislators may not be able to predict developments in society and in technology which ought to be covered by the scope of the statute in question, but do not fall within the wording used.

ACTIVITY 1

Turn to *Cases and Materials* (4.1.1), where you will find an extract from the Obscene Publications Act 1959. Section 2 of the Act creates the offence of publication of an obscene article, and s. 1 attempts to provide a definition of an 'article'.

What sort of articles do you think were in the draftsman's mind when these sections were prepared?

What developments in technology might not have been foreseen at the time?

Can you think of any items which were not mentioned in these sections but which ought to have been included?

At the time of its enactment, the sort of articles which were in the contemplation of the draftsman appeared to be items such as books, magazines, tape recordings and films. Apparently, the draftsman did not consider the problem of photographic negatives (which cannot be shown to the public without further processing), nor could the development of video cassettes, or access to pornographic material on the Internet have been foreseen.

The first of these problems (photographic negatives) had to be solved by additional legislation: the Obscene Publications Act 1964 was enacted to close this loophole in the law. The second problem was solved when the courts decided that the word 'article' could be interpreted in such a way as to include a video cassette.

The Court of Appeal had to decide recently in *R* v *Bowden* [2000] Crim LR 381 if downloading an indecent image of a young boy from the Internet and keeping the image on a disk, was 'making' a photograph, an offence under s. 1(1)(a) of the Protection of Children Act 1978. The Court of Appeal held that the word 'make' should be given its natural meaning and that in these circumstances an offence had been committed. The Court further stated that there was no ambiguity in s. 1, but it is clear that judges are having to interpret and construe statutes written before the advent of the Internet to include, where possible, unforeseen electronic and technological advancements.

From this example, you will appreciate the necessity for statute law to be drafted in wide, general terms; but there is a further problem in that if the language is too broad, then the Act may encompass people and situations which were not intended to be affected by this particular law. So in addition to trying to cover all possible circumstances, the draftsman must also include sufficient detail within the sections, so that the meaning is clear and unambiguous. It is difficult for the draftsman to meet both of these objectives.

SAQ 1

Although there are obvious drawbacks with legislation which is drafted in general terms, there are actually some advantages too. Can you think of at least two (possibly more) of these?

Although it is vital that every Act of Parliament should describe legal rules in clear and certain terms, there are some areas of law where clarity of drafting seems more important than it does in other areas. For example, in tax law and in criminal law, it is vital that the detailed provisions of the law be unambiguous in order to protect individuals from the serious consequences which flow from any breach of this type of law. However, in other areas of law, it may be beneficial for statute law to be drafted in much more general terms. This then allows the judge in an individual case a certain amount of discretion in the application of the rule which may lead to a more just outcome. A second advantage conferred by a more general style of drafting is that the legislation may encompass more cases, and so avoid litigation, as it will be apparent to the parties in dispute that their case falls within the terms of the statute, thus avoiding the need to test the matter in court. A third advantage is that legislation which is drafted in wide terms may not need to be amended with every new development in technology, as the words of the statute in its original form may be deemed to apply to new situations, thus saving valuable time in Parliament.

4.3.2   THE LIMITATIONS OF LANGUAGE

The second problem which may be encountered in dealing with statute law is the difficulty which has often been referred to as the limitations of language. All language is capable of ambiguity, and to a large extent our understanding of the language with which we communicate depends upon our having values and background in common. As the values and background of the people to whom the law is addressed vary greatly, then it becomes even more difficult to resolve these ambiguities.

One of the greatest problems which has been identified in the use of language in drafting statutes is that words do not always (if ever) have a fixed meaning, and may be understood in different ways according to the context in which they are used and the values and background of the audience to whom they are addressed. As a result, when judges are required to apply statute law, they have to make choices about how a particular word should be understood in a particular context.

ACTIVITY 2

Look up the word 'bar' in a good quality dictionary (for example *The Concise Oxford Dictionary*) and note the many different meanings of this word. A judge attempting to interpret a statute containing this word would assign a different meaning to it according to whether the context and subject matter of the statute was concerned with premises licensed to serve alcohol, the professional work of the barrister, or the provision of safety guards to protect people from dangerous machinery.

4.3.3 STYLE OF DRAFTING AND STRUCTURE OF STATUTES

Because of the difficulties of drafting mentioned in the previous sections, the language and sentence structure used in statute law tends to be very elaborate. Long sentences, with numerous sub-clauses, are often used, in a way which would not be acceptable to a teacher, marking a student's essay! The arrangement of sections in a statute is not usually designed in a way which is helpful to the reader.

As a result of these problems, the judges have, over the years, developed a number of presumptions which are used to assist in the task of providing an authoritative interpretation or construction of a particular statute. These are often referred to as the **rules** of statutory interpretation, although they are not binding rules in the true sense of the word. More properly they are referred to by writers as the **canons of construction** or **approaches to statutory interpretation**.

As Lord Reid explained in *Maundsell* v *Olins* [1975] AC 373:

'[The rules of interpretation] . . . are not rules in the ordinary sense of having some binding force. They are our servants, not our masters. They are aids to construction . . . Not infrequently one rule contradicts the other. In each case we must look at all the relevant circumstances and decide as a matter of judgment what weight to attach to any particular rule'.

4.3.4 THE JUDICIAL TASK

There is one further factor which must be borne in mind, as the approaches to statutory interpretation are studied: what **exactly** is the task of the judge when reading a statute? Is the judge's task merely to give meaning to the words which Parliament has used, i.e., to give the words their plain meaning regardless of what Parliament may have intended? Or should the judges be seeking for the meaning which Parliament **intended**, rather than relying simply on the words which have been used?

The answer to this question will depend to a great extent on the approach to interpretation which is adopted by a particular judge, and will therefore begin to emerge as the case law is analysed.

4.3.5 HUMAN RIGHTS ACT 1998

Following the coming into force of the **Human Rights Act 1998**, courts will be required to interpret legislation compatibly with the Convention (ECHR) where possible.

ACTIVITY 3

Read the extract from David Feldman's article *'The Human Rights Act 1998 and Constitutional Issues'* (19 L.S. 165) in *Cases and Materials* (4.1.2).

Now read the information below and tackle the 'conundrum'.

If a lower court was faced (after the HRA 1998 came into force) with a pre-HRA 1998 decision of the House of Lords which the lower court believes interprets a statute (or indeed the common law) in a way which is not compatible with the Convention, the lower court will be entitled not to follow the decision of the House of Lords. The statute (the HRA 1998) will take precedence. This is fairly straightforward, as legislation is the primary source of law. Where a previous court decision conflicts, the statute takes precedence.

Secondly, as with the ECJ, the European Court of Human Rights at Strasbourg does not operate the system of *stare decisis*. Thus, decisions of the Court are not binding on the courts in the English Legal System, but are highly persuasive. Indeed, in the past, the English Courts have operated as if they were bound (in the same way as they treat decisions of the ECJ). However, it is important to note that the European Court does not bind itself.

The Conundrum

1. Following the coming into force of the HRA 1998, the Court of Appeal decides that the Convention requires it to decide a case in a particular way. For example, it decides that it is unlawful under the Convention (Article 2) for a Health Authority to ration life-saving medicines.

2. After this decision, a similar case comes before the European Court of Human Rights. In that case, the European Court of Human Rights comes to a decision on the interpretation which is directly opposed to the earlier decision of the English Court of Appeal.

3. Subsequent to the decision of the European Court of Human Rights, the High Court in this jurisdiction is faced by a further application for judicial review, again on similar facts. What should it do?

Whilst the European Court of Human Rights is the highest court on matters of the ECHR, it is therefore an exceptionally important source of law on matters involving the HRA 1998.

The High Court is bound in the English legal system by decisions of superior courts and this includes the Court of Appeal. Further, English courts regard themselves as bound by decisions of the European Court of Human Rights, but strictly they are persuasive only.

Whilst it is surely logical for the High Court to follow the decision of the European Court of Human Rights, it is <u>bound</u> to follow decisions of the Court of Appeal.

The rules from *Young* v *Bristol Aeroplane* do not apply to the High Court (except the Divisional Courts) and would not help here anyway because we are not dealing with a later conflicting decision of the House of Lords which is part of *stare decisis*, but a later conflicting decision of the European Court of Human Rights, which is not.

It is probably unfair to set you an activity to which there is no answer (at least, yet), but as one eminent academic lawyer says; 'There are no answers, just a range of possibilities'!

4.4   The Approaches to Statutory Interpretation or Construction

4.4.1   THE LITERAL RULE — THE ORDINARY MEANING APPROACH

According to this approach, the words used by Parliament in a statute should be given their ordinary or usual meaning. Where this approach is adopted, the task of the judge is regarded as that of ascertaining the intention of Parliament (if Parliament can be said to have such a thing) by looking at the words which have actually been used. This approach emerged strongly in the nineteenth century, and is still widely used as the appropriate starting point in determining the meaning of a statute. The logical consequence of this rule, however, is that if the words used are clear, and the ordinary English meaning can be assigned to them, then that meaning must be applied however hard or unjust the result.

> 'The only rule for construction of Acts of Parliament is that they should be construed according to the intend of the Parliament which passed the Act. If the words of the statute are in themselves precise and unambiguous than no more can be necessary than to expound those words in that natural and ordinary sense. The words themselves alone do, in such a case, best declare the intention of the lawgiver.'

(Tindal CJ in the *Sussex Peerage Case* (1944) 11 CL and Fin 85.)

In the case of *Puhlhofer* v *Hillingdon London Borough Council* [1986] AC 484 the court was required to decide on the meaning of the word 'accommodation' in the Housing (Homeless Persons) Act 1977. This Act provides that a person is not homeless if he is occupying 'accommodation'. By using the literal or ordinary meaning approach, the House of Lords drew the conclusion that a person was occupying accommodation, even though the premises in question had no cooking or washing facilities, and he therefore had to eat out and to use a launderette to wash his clothes.

SAQ 2

Think, or refer, back to the discussion on fact and law in Chapter 3. In *Puhlhofer*, do you think the meaning of accommodation is one of fact or law?

The answer is not clear, even from the decision itself. First, Lord Brightman stated that:

'What is properly to be regarded as accommodation is a question of fact to be decided by the local authority. There are no rules.'

However, he then appeared to say that it was a matter of law, within the remit of the court to define:

'Clearly some places in which a person might choose or be constrained to live could not properly be regarded as accommodation at all; it would be a misuse of language to describe Diogenes as having occupied accommodation within the meaning of the Act.'

Endicott ('Questions of Law' (1998) 114 LQR 292) points out that if the local authority were to reject Diogenes' application for housing assistance on the grounds that he had a barrel available as accommodation, the court would reverse the local authority's decision as an error of *law*.

SAQ 3

Refer back to *R* v *Feely* [1973] 1 All ER 341 from Chapter 3. How did the Court of Appeal try to clarify the distinction between law and fact? How could you apply that distinction to *Puhlhofer*?

You might have decided that the interpretation (or the definition) of the words is a matter of law and the application of the word(s) to the law is one of fact. This is a common answer to the law *versus*. fact debate, but bear in mind the wide discretion judges have to decide these matters and do not forget Scrutton LJ in *Currie* v *Commissioners of Inland Revenue* [1921] 2 KB 332 at p. 339 (above).

The literal approach to interpretation can result in hardship, and has been criticised on the grounds that it is not always possible to ascertain the ordinary or natural meaning of a word. In addition the approach has been condemned for taking too narrow a view of the function of the judiciary.

ACTIVITY 4

For an explanation of this attitude to the respective roles of the judge and of Parliament, turn to *Cases and Materials* (4.2.1). There you will find an extract from the speech of Lord Diplock in the case of *Duport Steel Ltd* v *Sirs* [1980] 1 All ER 529 at page 541. Amongst judges who adopt the literal rule of statutory interpretation, how do the respective roles of the judges and Parliament in the law making process appear to be regarded?

As you will see from Lord Diplock's speech, those judges who adopt the literal rule appear to frown upon the use of creative thinking in judicial interpretation of statutes; Parliament and not the judiciary is regarded as the ultimate law-maker.

ACTIVITY 5

Read the extract from the case of *London and North Eastern Railway Company* v *Berriman* **[1946] AC 278** in *Cases and Materials* **(4.2.1).**

(a) What are the two key words to be found in both the Railway Employment (Prevention of Accidents) Act 1900 and the Prevention of Accidents Rules 1902?

(b) What was the deceased doing at the time of his death?

(c) How would you describe the purpose of the Act and the Rules (in (a) above)?

(d) Suggest two reasons why the respondent (the deceased's widow) was held not to be entitled to damages.

(e) Refer to the quote of Alderson B. and your answer to (c) above. Would you have decided the case in the same way?

You will find answers to these questions in *Cases and Materials* **(4.2.1).**

4.4.2   THE GOLDEN RULE — AN APPROACH TO INTERPRETATION TO AVOID ABSURDITY

As can be seen from the discussion above, the literal rule does not address the question of the problems which may arise as a result of the strict application of the plain meaning approach. The traditional response to this criticism has been that if the judicial interpretation of the words of a statute leads to undesirable consequences, then it is the task of Parliament to amend the law and remove the difficulties which have emerged. However, over time the judges developed a way of dealing with this problem without recourse to Parliament, and this strategy has become known as 'the golden rule'. The essence of this convention is that if the wording of the statute is ambiguous, and the application of the ordinary meaning or literal approach leads to some 'absurdity or inconvenience', then the ordinary meaning can be departed from, and another less usual meaning adopted in its place. The literal rule thus remains the starting point, but a secondary meaning can be assigned to the words in question where the use of the ordinary meaning will lead to some inconsistency or absurdity.

The golden rule may also be employed in cases where there may be only one possible interpretation which can be applied to the words of the Act under consideration, but public policy demands that an alternative interpretation is found.

A discussion of the use of the golden rule can be found in the case of *Adler* v *George* [1964] 1 All ER 628.

ACTIVITY 6

Read through the case of *Adler* v *George* [1964] 1 All ER 628 in *Cases and Materials* (4.2.2) and then consider whether the following statements are true or false:

(a) This case was decided on the basis of an ordinary, natural meaning approach to statutory interpretation. TRUE/FALSE.

(b) Lord Parker felt that the purpose of the Act and the context of the words were important factors in reaching a decision. TRUE/FALSE.

(c) Lord Parker felt that it would be wrong for the court to alter the language of the statute by reading words into the section. TRUE/FALSE.

As I hope you will have gathered from the judgment, in this case a literal interpretation of the words of the section would produce an absurd result. A natural meaning approach would mean that an offence would be committed if an obstruction took place outside the station, but not if it took place within it. The first statement above is therefore false, as the golden rule was applied in this case.

It is interesting to note that Lord Parker CJ, who delivered the judgment in this case, took what might be termed a liberal approach to the task of interpreting this statute, and was prepared to look at what conduct the statute was designed to prevent, and also at the context in which the meaning of the words should be ascertained. The statement at (b) above is therefore true.

Any judge who felt that the literal rule was the only appropriate method of statutory interpretation would be horrified to find that, in this case, Lord Parker actually altered the wording of the statute, by reading into it words which Parliament had not expressly included in that section. Thus the words 'in the vicinity of' were interpreted to mean 'in or in the vicinity of' in order to avoid the absurd result referred to above. This suggests that, in this case, the court took a much less restrictive view of the role of the judge, than would a judge who only approved of the ordinary meaning approach.

4.4.3 THE MISCHIEF RULE — THE RULE IN *HEYDON'S CASE*

It may seem from the previous paragraphs that members of the judiciary have a very limited role in terms of law-making, and that they are restricted to the task of declaring the meaning of the words which Parliament has used in the statutes which it has enacted. However, as long ago as the sixteenth century, the judges developed what is known as the mischief rule (*Heydon's Case* (1584) 3 Co Rep 7) which allowed them to look beyond what has been written to why it was written.

In this case, four questions were posed which have become the classic statements of the mischief approach. In using this approach, the court has to consider:

1.   What was the Common Law before making of the Act?
2.   What was the mischief and defect for which the Common Law did not provide?
3.   What remedy Parliament had resolved and appointed to cure the disease of the [Common Law]?
4.   The true reason for the remedy; and then the office of all the judges is to make such construction as shall suppress the mischief, and advance the remedy.

This rule therefore allows the court to look at the state of the law as it was before the statute was passed, in order to discover the mischief which the statute was designed to remedy.

An example of the use of the mischief rule can be found in the case of *Royal College of Nursing of the United Kingdom* v *DHSS* [1981] 1 All ER 545. This case involved the interpretation of the Abortion Act 1967. This Act requires termination of pregnancy to be carried out 'by a registered medical practitioner' in order for that termination to be lawful. The question arose as to whether a termination could be said to be carried out 'by a registered medical practitioner' in circumstances where the physical acts which caused the abortion were actually carried out by a nurse, acting on the instructions of a registered medical practitioner.

In order to construe the words of the statute, the court looked at the mischief which the Abortion Act 1967 was designed to remedy, and at the policy and purpose behind the Act. The court came to the conclusion that this statute was designed to ensure that abortions took place under qualified medical supervision and that this was indeed the case where a doctor took responsibility for the operation, even though the physical acts were performed by a nurse. The terminations were therefore lawful.

ACTIVITY 7

Extracts from the speeches of members of the House of Lords in the case of *Royal College of Nursing of the United Kingdom* v *DHSS* are provided at *Cases and Materials* (4.2.3). Read carefully through these extracts, taking your time, and then try to answer the following questions:

(a) Which approaches to statutory interpretation can you identify in the extracts set out?

(b) If an ordinary meaning approach to the words of the statute had been adopted by a majority of the judges, what would have been the outcome of this case?

(c) What does this case reveal about the way in which different approaches to statutory interpretation are based on different philosophies about the role of the judge?

This case established a number of important points about methods of statutory interpretation and about the role of the judge in the law-making process. These points emerge particularly clearly, because the members of the House of Lords who heard the appeal were sharply divided in their opinions. The first point to note is that the dissenting speech of Lord Wilberforce seems to be based on an ordinary meaning approach to the statute, and any liberal approaches to interpretation are rejected. Lord Diplock's speech, by contrast, contains clear reference to the mischief rule, and explores the history of the legislation relating to abortion. If you have been able to discern these approaches, then you have answered question (a) above, correctly.

Another important point to notice is that if the judges, in interpreting the words of the statute, had seen their role only in terms of giving meaning to what Parliament had actually said, then the ordinary meaning approach to the words used would have been regarded as conclusive. The result of this case would then have been very different. In answer to question (b) above, a literal interpretation of the words of the statute would have meant that, as the acts which induced the abortion were not carried out by a person with the qualifications specified in the statute, the abortions did not fall within the terms of the Abortion Act 1967, and were unlawful.

From your reading of the extracts in *Cases and Materials*, I hope you will have drawn the conclusion that the Law Lords who adopted the literal approach, did so as a result of their view that it is not for the courts to 'redraft' legislation to achieve a more acceptable outcome in a particular case, or fill in any gaps in the statutory provisions. Any such defects in the legislation must be corrected by Parliament itself according to this philosophy. This view of the judicial role was adopted by the dissenting minority in the *Royal College of Nursing* case. The majority of the Law Lords saw their role in a different, more interventionist, light however, and were prepared to take into account the history and policy of the statute, and to read the provisions in a wider sense, in order to achieve a just result in the case concerned. Members of the judiciary who adopt this philosophy regard themselves as having a law-making role alongside Parliament and would not see their task in purely mechanical terms, applying the words of a statute without question. Your answer to question (c) should reflect this divergence of opinion amongst the judiciary.

4.4.4 THE UNITARY (OR CONTEXTUAL) APPROACH

For many years, the three rules outlined above have been regarded as the classical theory of statutory interpretation. However, academic writers have identified the emergence of a fourth approach which Farrar and Dugdale in *Introduction to Legal Method* have called the unitary approach, or the contextual approach to the construction of statutes.

By examining the judgments of many cases, writers on statutory interpretation have observed that the three traditional approaches seem to be merging, and that greater emphasis is being placed on the importance of the context of the statute, in ascertaining its meaning. As a result, it is becoming even more difficult to identify which method of interpretation a particular judge may have used in arriving at a conclusion as to how the words of a statute should be construed.

4.4.5 THE PURPOSIVE APPROACH — THE MISCHIEF RULE EXPANDED

The restrictions of the mischief rule (that there should be an identifiable mischief in the common law before the enactment in question and so on) are now generally ignored in favour of a highly liberal approach referred to as the purposive approach.

Purposivism involves identifying the purpose of the statute and then using this as an indicator of the meaning of words.

ACTIVITY 8

Read *Smith* v *Hughes* [1960] 1 WLR 830 in *Cases and Materials* (4.2.4). Despite the fact that Lord Parker CJ uses the word 'mischief', is a defect of the common law (the alleged mischief) identified?

You would be correct in saying no, and to that extent, it is correct to regard *Smith* v *Hughes* as one of the first cases where the purposive approach was adopted. The purpose of the Street Offences Act 1959 was clearly stated:

'Everybody knows that this was an Act intended to clean up the streets, to enable people to walk along the streets without being molested or solicited by common prostitutes.'

SAQ 4

If *Smith* v *Hughes* [1960] 1 WLR 830 is an example of the purposive approach, how do the interpretation methods of the majority in the House of Lords in *RCN* v *DHSS* [1981] 1 All ER 545 and Lord Parker CJ's judgment in *Smith* v *Hughes* differ?

The *RCN* case specifically identifies the mischief of the previous law. Sections 58 and 59 of the Offences Against the Person Act 1861 are described there as an 'unsatisfactory and uncertain state of the law'. There is no 'unsatisfactory and uncertain state of the law' before the Street Offences Act 1959.

Identifying the Purpose
It is one thing to say that the purposive approach is more liberal, but quite another to demand of the judges to know the purpose of each new Act of Parliament and be able to apply it to each new case that arises therefrom. Some statutes are well covered by the media (and the law journals) during the enactment process for the judiciary to be aware of Parliament's stance, but there are many more Acts that do not court the same kind of controversy. Accordingly, if judges are to apply the purposive approach, where can they find the purpose of the Act?

ACTIVITY 9

Refer to any Act in *Cases and Materials*. Under the short title (the name of the Act) and the chapter number and so on, you will find the Long Title. For example, find the Law of Property (Miscellaneous Provisions) Act 1989 in Chapter 2. What is the long title?

STATUTORY INTERPRETATION (OR STATUTORY CONSTRUCTION)

The long title of a statute is a good starting point for deciding the purpose of an Act of Parliament. However, you may realise that even though we call it the long title, it is rarely more than a sentence and cannot cover in sufficient detail the purpose for each section. The judges may need just this type of detail of they are to interpret the intentions of Parliament and the words in question correctly.

Hansard is the official publication of all Parliamentary sessions in both Houses. It should be an accurate record of every debate, speech and question asked in Parliament on any given day. Where else could you find a better source to discover Parliament's intention?

Lord Scarman would, and did, argue that to look anywhere outside the statute itself was wrong.

ACTIVITY 10

Refer to *Cases and Materials* (4.2.4). Read the extract from Lord Scarman's speech in *Davis* v *Johnson* [1978] 1 All ER 1132, a case that you know well. What arguments does he put forward against the use of *Hansard* by the judiciary when interpreting statutes?

It is perhaps worthy of note that Lord Scarman is probably correct in both arguments. First, *Hansard* is long, can be tedious and rarely does the opportunity in Parliament arise for a person to state a single, clear, unambiguous statement of the purpose of legislation. Second, it is (or was, see below) an integral part of the Separation of Powers doctrine (see *Learning Text: Constitutional and Administrative Law*) that the judiciary should not have access to Parliamentary materials.

(As an aside, it is worth noting that their Lordships had no problem in consulting the historical development of the delegated legislation in question in *Pickstone* v *Freemans* [1988] 2 All ER 803 which you will examine in detail below.)

However, in *Davis* at the Court of Appeal ([1979] AC 264), Lord Denning stated:

> 'Some may say . . . that judges should not pay any attention to what is said in Parliament. They should grope about in the dark for the meaning of an Act without switching on the light. I do not accede to this view.'

You have already read Lord Scarman's response to this at the House of Lords.

Then, relatively recently, a special seven Law Lord committee convened to assist in the delivery of a five Law Lord judgment in *Pepper (Inspector of Taxes)* v *Hart* [1993] AC 593. This landmark case saw the relaxation of the so-called exclusionary rule about *Hansard*. You will have a chance to review this case in the End of Chapter Assessment Question One. It may be that, with time, when the House of Commons accepts as a regular occurrence their speeches being quoted by the judiciary, that *Hansard* will include clear statements as to the purpose of legislation. In fact, it is with gratitude that we should acknowledge Jack Straw, Home Secretary:

> 'I wish future Judicial Committees of the House of Lords luck in working through these debates. One sometimes wonders about the wisdom of the *Pepper* v *Hart* judgment in terms of the work it has given the higher judiciary.' (*Hansard HC 20 May 1998, col. 981*)

You can decide for yourselves whether the gratitude we show is for the Home Secretary acknowledging the judgment in *Pepper* v *Hart* or for lamenting it.

4.4.6   THE EUROPEAN DIMENSION — WHEN IN ROME . . .

The rules described above are those which apply to legislation which has been prepared and enacted in the Houses of Parliament and which forms part of English law. There is, however, a vast and constantly growing body of legislation which is being produced by the law-making bodies of the European Union. Different considerations and different procedures apply to the interpretation of legislation which emanates from the European Union, because this legislation is drafted in a very different way from the statutes produced by the UK Parliament. The legislation of the EU is based on the statement of broad general principles, which must then be interpreted and applied by the courts as appropriate. A literal approach to the interpretation of such material would not be helpful, as there may be insufficient detail to make this method meaningful. It is the practice of courts within the English legal system to adopt the purposive approach when interpreting treaties and conventions which have their origin outside this legal system, and similarly, the purposive approach is adopted when a court interprets legislation produced by the UK Parliament in response to initiatives from the European Union.

Manchester et al (*Exploring the Law*) define the ECJ interpretative techniques as 'techniques which focus on giving effect to the underlying aims of legislative provisions, rather than seeking to give a meaning to the particular words used, and, in doing so, adopting schematic and/or teleological approaches to interpretation, using general principle, . . . and engaging in "gap filling".' (page 70)

ACTIVITY 11

Refer to the extract in *Cases and Materials* (4.2.5) from *'Exploring the Law'* by Manchester, Salter, Moodie and Lynch about the case *Pickstone* v *Freemans* [1988] 2 All ER 803, the Equal Pay Act 1970 (EPA 1970) and Article 119 of the Treaty of Rome.

Do not spend too long on this Activity (half an hour maximum), but do consider how the Industrial Tribunal, the Employment Appeals Tribunal, the Court of Appeal and the House of Lords approached interpreting the words 'equal value'.

It is very important to be able to:

- identify the European approach as being a catalyst in the prolific use of the purposive approach in England and Wales, and

- illustrate this by case citation.

Therefore, you need to be able to examine the 'Ambiguity Interpretation Approach' which seemed to prevail at the Industrial Tribunal and which certainly prevailed at the Employment Appeals Tribunal, the 'Priority Approach' and 'General Interpretation Approach' at the Court of Appeal and how and why the Court of Appeal held that Article 119 prevailed over s. 1(2)(c); and then the judgment of the House of Lords. It is also important to be able to state how liberal the House's judgment was.

Of course, you must also be able to evaluate the importance of the ECHR and the HRA 1998.

ACTIVITY 12

Read the extract from David Feldman's article 'The Human Rights Act 1998 and Constitutional Issues' (19 L.S. 165) in *Cases and Materials* (4.1.2) again. What issues would you regard as important if you were a judge about to embark on a case involving (1) statutory interpretation and (2) aspects of the HRA 1998. Just to make this fun, consider yourself as a judge on the <u>day</u> the Act came into effect. You are the first judge to have to deal with this. You cannot back out and certify the issues as points of law to ensure an easy appeal either!

There are many issues to deal with here, but as Feldman points out:

- Strasbourg jurisprudence is persuasive (as if it were not already).

- What does s. 3's '[so] far as it is possible to do so' mean?

- It would appear that the literal rule, the golden rule and the mischief rule are not applicable as far as the 'compatibility' question goes; and further the purposive approach, as new as it may be, may already be dated. Section 3 requires the judges to go beyond the intentions of the official law makers in the UK (i.e. Parliament).

The only saving grace would appear to be that if Parliament intends to enact a statute that is incompatible with the Convention, it must be clear, unambiguous and unequivocal. The burden therefore falls upon the drafters of the Act.

4.5   Aids to Statutory Interpretation or Construction

To complete your understanding of the process of statutory interpretation and construction, it is necessary to examine briefly a number of assorted 'rules' or conventions which the judges employ in conjunction with the main approaches referred to above. These can be categorised under the general heading of internal and external aids.

4.5.1   INTERNAL AIDS

Sometimes referred to as intrinsic aids, these consist of material found within the printed copy of the Act itself, which may give clues as to the correct understanding of the law. Thus, the long title of the Act, whilst not to be used to contradict anything in the body of the Act itself, may be a useful indicator of the scope of the statute if there is a debate as to this. (Have you remembered the difference between the long title and the short title of an Act? If not, refresh your memory by referring back to **Chapter 2**.)

Similarly, the way in which the sections of an Act are punctuated will give clues as to how that section is to be understood. Perhaps most useful is the definition section of the Act, which is an increasingly common feature of modern legislation. This provides definitions of words used in the Act and their meaning in the particular context of the Act.

ACTIVITY 13

Refer to the extract of s. 205 of the Law of Property Act 1925 in *Cases and Materials* (4.3.1). What type of section does this appear to be?

As you will realise, this is the definition section for the Law of Property Act 1925, and contains numerous sub-sections which define words used in the Act, in order to clarify the interpretation of the statute.

A number of presumptions are also relied upon by the judiciary in construing legislation. Mostly these are of a general nature, for example, that a statute must be read as a whole, and that words take their meaning from the context in which they are used. (This is sometimes referred to as the *noscitur a sociis* rule, i.e., words are known by the company they keep!) Other important presumptions are that statute law does not make any fundamental change to the common law unless this is clearly intended, and that it does not have a retrospective effect unless this is expressly stated. A statute creating a criminal offence will normally require a guilty mind or criminal intent (known as *mens rea*) to be proved as an element of that offence, before any person can be convicted of the alleged crime. There are certain crimes (known as crimes of strict liability) which do not have this requirement of intent in order for a crime to be committed, but this must be clearly indicated in the words of the Act which creates the offence.

There are in addition some more specific rules of interpretation, for example, the *ejusdem generis* rule. This rule applies in situations where a section of a statute contains a list of particular words, which taken together might be said to form a class (a genus). If the list is followed by a general word, then that general word must be interpreted in such a way as to fall within the class created by the specific words. A famous example of this can be found in the case of *Powell* v *Kempton Park Racecourse Co.* [1899] AC 143, HL. This case concerned the interpretation to be applied to the Betting Act 1853 (since repealed). The Act prohibited the keeping of a 'house, office, room or other place' for the purpose of betting with others, and the question to be resolved was whether this could include an open air racecourse. By applying the *ejusdem generis* rule the court concluded that the genus or class created by the words was one which referred to indoor places. The words 'or other place' at the end of the list had to be construed in accordance with this and therefore an open air venue was not included in the scope of the Act.

The use of the *ejusdem generis* rule was debated in the recent case of *In Re Rhondda Waste Co Ltd* LTL 10/2/2000. The case involved a company in administration (an initial stage in the process of a company being would up). The Environment Agency wished to commence criminal proceedings against the company, but under ss. 10 and 11 of the Insolvency Act 1986 'no other proceedings' could be commenced against a company subject to administration. The EA argued that 'no other proceedings' should be limited to the genus of civil proceedings, as an administration order is civil, and that criminal proceedings would therefore fall outside the scope of ss. 10 and 11. Despite the fact that the Court of Appeal disagreed, holding that 'other proceedings' also included criminal proceedings, it did so on the basis of the literal rule and according to the purpose of the Act, rejected the need for the *ejusdem generis* rule in this context. This case should, however, illustrate how the different rules, approaches and aids can sometimes conflict.

4.5.2 EXTERNAL AIDS

Sometimes referred to as extrinsic aids, these are devices which assist in the interpretation of the statute concerned, but which are not contained within the printed copy of the Act. Examples of external aids are English dictionaries, which judges may use when seeking the ordinary meaning of the words used, and academic authorities in the form of textbooks, which may be consulted to help with an opinion on a particular point.

Two forms of external aid which have caused much debate are, first, the preparatory materials which precede legislation (e.g., Law Commission Reports, or reports of Royal Commissions, sometimes collectively referred to as *travaux préparatoires*) and, secondly, *Hansard*, the official report of the proceedings of the Houses of Parliament. There has been a good deal of discussion concerning the extent to which these materials should be consulted by the judiciary when considering the interpretation of legislation.

Before any major piece of legislation is put before Parliament, a group of eminent lawyers may be gathered together in the shape of a Royal Commission, or as members of the Law Commission, to consider how the law should be reformed. The report which is produced by this group may contain a draft bill, or other suggestions as to how a statute might be framed to create new law. The extent to which such materials can be consulted by the courts as part of the process of statutory interpretation was considered in the case of *Black-Clawson International Ltd* v *Papierwerke Waldhof-Aschaffenberg AG* [1975] 1 All ER 810. This case revealed quite wide differences of opinion amongst the members of the House of Lords but the outcome seems to be that it is legitimate for judges to consult this sort of material in order to establish the mischief which the legislation was intended to cure. The use of such reports to ascertain the meaning of legislation is not, however, regarded as permissible.

As far as the use of *Hansard* is concerned, the position has been clarified by the case of *Pepper (Inspector of Taxes)* v *Hart* [1993] 1 All ER 42, HL.

4.6 Summary

You will by now have realised that statutory interpretation is not an exact science. The judges vary considerably in their approach to this judicial task, and it is often difficult to discern from a judgment exactly which approach to the construction of the statute a particular judge has adopted. Unfortunately, the judges do not, as a rule, announce whether they are using one particular method of interpretation, or an amalgam of them all.

You should, however, feel able to:

- give an account of the different methods of statutory interpretation in use in this country;

- identify the different approaches to the law which underlie these different methods;

- give examples of cases in which these different methods have been used; and

- describe other aids to interpretation in common use and the historical background to these.

4.7   Further Reading

Ingman, T., *The English Legal Process,* 8th edn, London: Blackstone Press, 2000, Chapter 8.

Manchester, Salter and Moodie, *Exploring the Law*, 2nd edn, London: Sweet & Maxwell, 2000.

Slapper, G, and Kelly, D, *The English Legal System*, 4th edn, London: Cavendish, 1999, Chapter 5.

4.8   End of Chapter Assessment Question One

Refer to *Cases and Materials* **(4.4)**, where you will find extracts from the speeches of the House of Lords in *Pepper* v *Hart*.

(a) What reasons are given for the former rule which prohibited reference to *Hansard* as an aid to statutory interpretation?

(b) What conditions are imposed by the Law Lords on those who wish to consult *Hansard* as an aid to statutory interpretation?

(c) What implications does this have for modern methods of statutory interpretation?

See *Cases and Materials* **(4.5)** for a specimen answer.

4.9   End of Chapter Assessment Question Two

Read *R* v *Maginnis* [1987] 1 All ER 907 in *Cases and Materials* **(4.6)**, and answer the following questions:

(a)   What were the central factual issues in this case?

(b)   What were the central legal issues in this case?

(c)   From the information provided, trace the progress of the case through the courts.

(d)   How did Lord Keith of Kinkel define 'supply'?

(e)   How did the interpretation used by Lord Goff of Chieveley differ from that used by Lord Keith?

(f)   How did the interpretation of the Court of Appeal of the word supply as applied in *R* v *Delgado* differ from the interpretation applied in *R* v *Dempsey*?

(g)   How did Lord Keith distinguish between the cases of *R* v *Delgado* and *R* v *Dempsey*?

See *Cases and Materials* (4.7) for a specimen answer.

CHAPTER FIVE

THE STRUCTURE AND JURISDICTION OF THE COURTS: CIVIL CASES

5.1 Objectives

By the end of this chapter you should be able to:

- explain the structure of the court system in England and Wales;

- give an account of the jurisdiction of the courts which may hear civil cases;

- analyse the types of cases which can be dealt with by these courts;

- identify the personnel involved in the courts which have civil jurisdiction;

- cite the Woolf Report and comment on its recommendations.

5.2 Introduction

By now, you should be aware of the fact that there are a number of different ways of defining the word 'law' and that there are various ways of grouping together the different types of law that exist within the English legal system. The place where ordinary citizens will come face to face with the machinery of the law is the court system. It is therefore important for you as lawyers in the making (and as lay people) to have a thorough knowledge of the different types of courts which you will encounter in the English legal system.

In this chapter you will be guided through a summary of the functions and jurisdiction of the courts which are capable of dealing with **civil** cases, beginning at the top of the hierarchy and working downwards through the different levels. In **Chapter 6** you will find a similar outline of the courts which are capable of dealing with **criminal** cases. You should be aware, however, of the fact that some courts do not fit neatly into this classification, and may have to be mentioned twice as they have jurisdiction in respect of **both** civil and criminal cases. As usual you will need to refer to *Cases and Materials* to illustrate the points made in this chapter, and you will need to familiarise yourself with the introductory concepts which follow.

ACTIVITY 1

Refer to *Cases and Materials* (5.1) and look at the diagram of the civil court hierarchy. You will find it useful to keep this in front of you whilst you work through this chapter. You may find later that you may wish to annotate the diagram with the new procedures which we will examine below.

5.3 The Courts which Exercise Civil Jurisdiction

5.3.1 THE COURT OF JUSTICE OF THE EUROPEAN COMMUNITIES (COMMONLY KNOWN AS THE EUROPEAN COURT OF JUSTICE)

- **Sits in:** Luxembourg.

- **Personnel:** One judge from each Member State (drawn from those eligible for the highest judicial posts in their own country) and a President of the Court, together with the nine Advocates-General (with the same qualifications as the judges) whose task it is to advise the court on the relevant issues of fact and law and to make recommendations on cases referred to the court.

- **Jurisdiction:** Civil and criminal law.

The European Court of Justice was brought into being:

(a) to ensure that Member States fulfil their obligations under the Treaties of the European Communities;

(b) to decide disputes between Member States concerning the subject matter of the Treaties; and

(c) to ensure that the institutions of the Communities (i.e., the Council of Ministers and the Commission) act legally and within their powers.

The other aspect of the jurisdiction of this Court concerns the interpretation of Community legislation. Under Article 234 (ex. 177) of the EC Treaty, the court has the task of giving rulings on references made to it by Member States concerning the way in which Community law should be interpreted, and these rulings will then be binding on all Member States.

In *Learning Text: European Community Law* you will learn more about the work and status of this Court, but for now you should note that it appears above the House of Lords in the hierarchy because its rulings are capable of overriding decisions made by the Law Lords.

ACTIVITY 2

Turn to *Cases and Materials* (5.2.1) and look at the extract from the case of *Factortame Ltd and others* v *Secretary of State for Transport (No. 2)* [1991] 1 All ER 70 and then answer the following questions:

1. Which English court or courts referred this case to the European Court?

2. What procedure was used to obtain a decision from the European Court?

3. What effect did the ruling of the European Court have on the *Factortame* case?

The answers to these questions can also be found in *Cases and Materials* (5.2.1).

You should also be aware of the existence of the **Court of First Instance of the European Communities**, a separate court which was created to ease the workload of the European Court of Justice. The Court of First Instance deals with certain specialised cases, e.g., claims by employees of the Community institutions.

Remember there is yet another European institution which is often confused with the European Court of Justice, and which you must keep separate in your mind. This is the **European Court of Human Rights**, which sits in Strasbourg, and whose function is to interpret and apply the European Convention on Human Rights.

5.3.2 THE HOUSE OF LORDS

- **Sits in:** London.

- **Personnel:** The Lords of Appeal in Ordinary (usually referred to as the Law Lords, or simply the Lords.) Although these Lords are life peers, they are not the same people as the members of the House of Lords who are involved in creating statute law in Parliament. The Law Lords are usually drawn from members of the judiciary who have held 'high judicial office'. The House is presided over by the Lord Chancellor.

- **Jurisdiction:** Civil and criminal law.

The House of Lords has very little original jurisdiction, i.e., it hears very few first instance cases, for its power in this respect is limited to disputed peerage claims. Its main function is to hear appeals from courts lower down the hierarchy and most of its work therefore comes directly from the Court of Appeal. In cases **not** involving a European element, the House of Lords is the final court of appeal for England, Wales and Northern Ireland in both civil and criminal cases and for civil cases from Scotland. Its decisions are therefore binding on all other courts within the English legal system and its judgments can only be overruled either by legislation produced by Parliament, or by the Law Lords themselves choosing to revise their opinion of the law in a later case.

Appeals are usually heard by at least five of the Law Lords, the minimum being three. There is no rehearing of the parties' evidence on appeal; the case is dealt with on the basis of the documents relating to the case and the arguments of Counsel. Decisions made by the Lords are known as speeches or opinions: each judge may deliver a separate opinion, or one judge may speak for all where the decision is unanimous. Where opinion is divided about the outcome of a case, the majority view prevails.

ACTIVITY 3

If you have access to the Internet, go to **www.publications.parliament.uk** and select the Judicial Work page of the House of Lords. As web pages and addresses change regularly, this address and the information to be found there cannot be guaranteed, but web information on the English legal system is generally excellent and you may be able to while away many an hour surfing for relevant information. Any search engine should help you find your way, but remember to restrict your search to UK sites.

If you do not have Internet access, or even if you do but prefer hard copy research, the relevant pages of the site are reproduced for you in *Cases and Materials* (5.2.2).

> **Read and make notes on the judicial functions of the House. We will return to the appellate jurisdiction of the House in Chapter 7.**

Criticisms have been levelled at the House of Lords on numerous occasions. For example it has been argued that it adds an unnecessary top tier to the legal system, as final appeals could be dealt with by the Court of Appeal. This would have the advantage of saving time and money for litigants, and would mean that there would be less uncertainty and unpredictability about the eventual outcome of cases. To date however the House of Lords has successfully resisted any attempts to abolish it or to reduce its status.

5.3.3   THE JUDICIAL COMMITTEE OF THE PRIVY COUNCIL

- **Sits in:** London.

- **Personnel:** The Lord Chancellor and the Lords of Appeal in Ordinary usually constitute this court although other persons who have held high judicial office may be appointed to the Committee.

- **Jurisdiction:** Civil and criminal law.

As with the House of Lords, the jurisdiction of this court is almost completely appellate. The Committee hears appeals from:

(a) courts outside the United Kingdom, e.g., the Isle of Man, the Channel Islands and certain of the independent Commonwealth countries;

(b) prize courts, i.e., the Queen's Bench Division which has considered the ownership of a ship or aircraft captured by an enemy;

(c) ecclesiastical courts;

(d) medical tribunals.

The Committee may also have special cases referred to it by the Crown.

> # SAQ 1
>
> **What is the link between the House of Lords and the Judicial Committee? What effect do you think this link has on the status of decisions by the Committee?**

As you may have realised from the language used in the last few paragraphs, the Judicial Committee of the Privy Council is really a committee rather than a court in the true sense of the word. It therefore gives advice to the Crown rather than giving judgments, and its decisions are not binding on English courts as such. However, because the Committee is largely made up of members of the House of Lords, it is thus linked to the most influential court in the hierarchy and its decisions are treated as having great authority. Cases dealt with by the Judicial Committee are therefore said to be of 'persuasive' value when looking at the status of such decisions.

5.3.4 THE COURT OF APPEAL (CIVIL DIVISION)

- **Sits in:** London, usually, although technically it may sit anywhere in England and Wales.

- **Personnel:** The Lord Chancellor, the Lord Chief Justice, the Master of the Rolls (who is the President of the Civil Division of the Court of Appeal), the President of the Family Division of the High Court, the Vice President of the Chancery Division, the Lords of Appeal in Ordinary (if willing to sit), and most importantly, senior judges called Lords Justices of Appeal. Former Court of Appeal or High Court judges and present High Court judges may also be asked to sit.

- **Jurisdiction:** Civil cases on appeal; there is virtually no original jurisdiction.

When the Court of Appeal was created by the Judicature Act 1873, it was intended to be the final court of appeal, and the House of Lords was to have been abolished as an appellate court. Due to a change of government however, the abolition of the House of Lords did not take place, and so the two tier system of appeal courts remains today.

The Civil division hears appeals principally from the High Court, the county courts, the Employment Appeal Tribunal, and various other tribunals. Normally the appeal will be heard by at least three judges sitting together who rehear the case on the basis of the documents and the arguments of Counsel. The majority decision will prevail in cases where there is not a unanimous opinion. The Court of Appeal has a much heavier workload than the House of Lords, as many cases will not be taken further after the Court of Appeal stage. In order to deal with the volume of work, the Court of Appeal organises itself into divisions, and there may be four or five divisions sitting simultaneously on any one day. Even so there is usually a backlog of cases waiting to be heard, which leads to delay in individual cases.

SAQ 2

Think of three arguments that could be put forward for the abolition of the House of Lords (in its judicial, not its legislative capacity) and its replacement by the Court of Appeal as the most senior court. List them below.

As you may remember from the section on the House of Lords, various arguments have been put forward in favour of abolishing it as the final court of appeal in this country. Amongst the points which you might have mentioned above are the cost in terms of both time and money of taking a case right through the court system to the House of Lords, the argument that the Court of Appeal could act as the final appeal court thus making the existence of the House of Lords unnecessary, and the fact that the possibility of further appeal after the Court of Appeal adds a degree of uncertainty and unpredictability to legal proceedings.

5.3.5   THE HIGH COURT OF JUSTICE

- **Sits in:** London, and other provincial towns.

- **Personnel:** High Court judges, sometimes referred to as 'puisne' (pronounced puny) meaning lesser, or assistant, judges. Various senior members of the judiciary are also regarded as part of the High Court, e.g., the Lord Chief Justice, the President of the Family Division, the Vice-Chancellor, and a senior presiding judge appointed from the Lords Justices of Appeal.

- **Jurisdiction:** Mainly civil, with some criminal law. Certain divisions have both original and appellate jurisdiction.

The High Court is divided into divisions which deal with different types of work. Until 1880 there were five divisions but since that date there have only been three. Each division also has its own **Divisional Court** where a number of judges from that division sit together to hear appeal cases. Strictly speaking, these Divisional Courts are of superior status to the divisions themselves, but it is easier to explain the work of the divisions first, before looking at the work of the Divisional Courts.

An important point to note here is that students often find the distinction between the **divisions** of the High Court and the **Divisional Courts** confusing. It will help you to avoid these mistakes if you remember that on the whole, the three **divisions** of the High Court hear cases **at first instance,** with **one** judge sitting alone, whereas the **Divisional Courts** hear cases on **appeal** from other courts and **two** or **more** judges will deal with these cases.

It may help you to remember this by way of a diagram:

Figure 1

The High Court

THE DIVISIONS		
Chancery Division	Queen's Bench Division	Family Division
THE DIVISIONAL COURTS		
Chancery Divisional Court	Queen's Bench Divisional Court	Family Divisional Court

You may find it useful to annotate this with the information given in the paragraph above, and further as you progress through this part of the chapter.

5.3.5.1 Chancery Division

The nominal head of this division is the Lord Chancellor, but in reality the foremost judge is the Vice-Chancellor. The Chancery Division hears civil cases only, and most of its jurisdiction is original. It hears cases at first instance relating to matters such as:

- the sale of land

- redemption of mortgages

- trusts

- the administration of the estates of people who have died without leaving a will

- the granting of probate, i.e., the authority of the Court to administer the estates of people who have died and have left a will which names executors who will deal with the property

- disputes relating to wills and probate

- company and partnership matters

- patents and copyright.

Where two or more judges of the division sit together, this constitutes the **Divisional Court of the Chancery Division**. The work of this court is to hear appeals from the county court relating to bankruptcy and also registered land.

5.3.5.2 Queen's Bench Division

The Head of this division is the Lord Chief Justice. The bulk of the work of this court involves civil cases at first instance, e.g., disputes relating to contracts, and torts such as negligence and defamation. There are also two specialist courts: the Commercial Court which deals with business matters such as banking or insurance, and the Admiralty Court, which deals with various matters relating to ships.

The jurisdiction of the civil courts of first instance has recently been changed (see **5.4** below). It is important, however, that you have an understanding of the jurisdiction in existence before the changes came into effect so you can comment on and evaluate the need for them.

Under the previous rules (governed in the main by the Courts and Legal Services Act 1990), there was an overlap between the jurisdiction of the Queen's Bench Division and the county court in matters relating to contract and tort disputes. Technically, the High Court could deal with any claim of this type, worth any amount of money. In reality, however, there were procedural rules which required less complex cases, or those with a money claim of less than £50,000 to be dealt with at the county court.

A more detailed explanation of this can be found in the section on the county courts (see **5.3.6**).

Many cases which were commenced in the High Court were abandoned or settled out of court, and only a very small proportion of these cases ever came to trial. Despite this, there was often considerable delay involved in bringing cases to a hearing in the Queen's Bench Division, and considerable cost could be incurred.

Judicial Statistics (Annual Report 1998, The Stationery Office, Cm 4371, 1999), a report of the Lord Chancellor's Department, indicated that in 1998, the average waiting time between issue of writ and setting down in the Queen's Bench Division was 143 weeks, with a further 35-week wait until trial. In 1991, the average wait was 121 weeks with a similar wait to trial.

The Divisional Court of the Queen's Bench Division consists of two or more puisne judges sitting together to exercise an appellate and a supervisory jurisdiction. The Divisional Court will hear appeals on points of criminal law from the magistrates' courts and from the Crown Court where that court has heard a case on appeal from the magistrates. These appeals are dealt with by way of case stated, which means that one of the parties has identified a point of law which he or she wishes to dispute, and requires the court against whose decision the appeal is made to 'state a case' by providing all the necessary facts, arguments and decisions for consideration by the court dealing with the appeal.

The Divisional Court also acts as a supervisory court, and has the authority to examine decisions taken by inferior courts, public bodies and tribunals and assess whether the institution concerned has acted within its authority. This process is known as judicial review.

ACTIVITY 4

In *Cases and Materials* (5.2.3.1) you will find extracts from two reported cases which were heard by the Divisional Court of the Queen's Bench Division:

(a) *Tucker* v *DPP* [1992] 4 All ER 901; and

(b) *R* v *General Council of the Bar, ex parte Percival* [1990] 3 All ER 137.

Read the extracts from these two cases and then answer the following questions in respect of both cases.

1. What is the nature of the dispute in these cases?

2. In which courts did these cases begin?

3. Is the Divisional Court acting in its appellate or its supervisory capacity in these cases?

You will find the answers to these questions in *Cases and Materials* (5.2.3.1).

5.3.5.3 Family Division

The head of this court is the President of the division.

This court has both original and appellate jurisdiction in respect of all matrimonial matters and also matters relating to legitimacy, adoption, and proceedings under various Acts including the Family Law Act 1996 and the Children Act 1989. There is some overlap between the family matters dealt with by this court and the county courts and magistrates' courts. This is particularly so in relation to matters relating to children under the Children Act 1989. This Act governs the distribution of business between the three courts, which are regarded as one unified court for this purpose, and cases may be transferred between the three courts according to the complexity of the case and the interests of the child. The Family Division will thus deal with the more complex matrimonial and child cases, and in particular, divorce cases which are defended, i.e., where one party does not consent to the divorce being granted, or wishes to dispute some aspect of the divorce.

The Divisional Court of the Family Division has appellate jurisdiction over decisions made by the magistrates' courts in various types of family matters.

SAQ 3

In which divisions of the High Court would the following cases be heard?

(a) A dispute about contact with the children where one party to a marriage has left the other.

(b) A dispute about a large debt.

(c) A dispute about the sanity of a deceased lady who has left a will giving all her money to the Cats' Home.

(d) A dispute about a decision made by a local authority.

As you will have realised from the preceding paragraphs, the separate divisions of the High Court have distinct functions, and therefore it is not too difficult to allocate cases to the correct divisions. You are more likely to experience problems when trying to decide whether a case should be heard by the High Court, or in the county or magistrates' courts, because of the degree of overlap between these three courts.

As far as the High Court is concerned, disputes concerning contact with children in matrimonial cases (question (a)) will be heard in the Family Division, debts (question (b)) are dealt with in the Queen's Bench Division, matters of wills and probate where there is some dispute about the validity of the will (question (c)) come within the jurisdiction of the Chancery Division, and judicial review cases (question (d)) are heard in the Divisional Court of the Queen's Bench Division.

5.3.6 COUNTY COURTS

- **Sit in:** county court districts throughout England and Wales.

- **Personnel:** Circuit judges and also district judges (formerly known as Registrars). The district judges are also responsible for the administration of the county court, maintaining records, issuing summonses etc.

- **Jurisdiction:** Civil cases at first instance. There is no appellate work apart from the possibility of an appeal from the decision of a district judge to a circuit judge.

The county courts were originally created as local courts which were intended to deal with civil actions involving small amounts of money. Over time, however, the jurisdiction of the county court has been increased until much of its work overlaps with that of the High Court. Its work includes disputes relating to contract and tort, debts, personal injuries, faulty goods and services, bankruptcy, and family matters. The county court does not usually hear defamation actions, actions involving fraud, professional negligence or fatal accidents as these are normally dealt with by the High Court.

Under the High Court and County Courts Jurisdiction Order 1991 (S.I. 1991 No. 724), the business of the High Court and county courts was distributed as follows.

If the value of the claim (i.e., the amount the claimant expected to recover) was **less than £25,000**, then the case was tried in the **county court,** unless the court considered that it should be transferred to the High Court, according to the criteria set out below.

If the value of the claim was **£50,000 or more**, then the case was dealt with by the **High Court**, unless the court considered that the case should be dealt with by the county court, on the basis of the criteria given below.

Claims for amounts between the two sums mentioned were dealt with by either court as appropriate. The criteria which helped the court to determine where a particular case should be heard included factors such as the complexity of the facts or legal issues, the financial substance of the action, and whether the case raised questions which were of public interest.

The High Court and County Courts Jurisdiction (Amendment) Order 1999, came into effect on 26 April 1999. It gives effect to the changes introduced as a result of the Woolf Report. See **5.4** below.

ACTIVITY 5

Turn to *Cases and Materials* (5.2.4) where you will find an extract from the High Court and County Courts Jurisdiction (Amendment) Order 1999 setting out the current criteria for the allocation of cases between the two courts. What is the new financial limit on the two courts for contract and torts claims?

Certain county courts are designated as divorce county courts, and may deal with undefended divorces, i.e., where the divorce is by consent of the parties, certain matters relating to children, and applications for injunctions to prevent molestation. Again there is considerable overlap here between the work of the county courts, the High Court, and the magistrates' courts in respect of family matters, including adoption.

SAQ 4

The county courts were originally developed as a forum in which people who were not wealthy could pursue claims for small amounts of money. Given the current value limits for the jurisdiction of the county courts, do you think that this court can still be described as 'the people's court'?

Since the creation of the county courts, the number of cases and the value of the claims dealt with by these courts have increased greatly. During 1998, the average wait for trial at the county court was 85 weeks and the number of cases grew by over 2% on the previous year. It has also become apparent that the most frequent users of the county courts are not individuals trying to obtain justice in small claims, but firms who are suing consumers for non-payment for goods. In fact claims for small amounts of money are now dealt with in a different way from other legal issues in the county courts.

5.3.6.1 Small claims in the county court

Strictly speaking, the small claims court is not a separate court at all, but this is the term used to describe the way in which the county courts deal with claims for amounts of money of £5,000 or less.

Where such a claim is made, the case is not dealt with according to the usual county court procedure, but is automatically referred to the district judge to be dealt with by a process known as arbitration. In arbitration, the aim of the exercise is to settle the dispute in as informal and inexpensive a way as possible. The parties are invited to attend a private, informal hearing, in which the strict court rules of procedure and evidence are set aside in favour of a more 'user-friendly' approach. The parties are allowed to use lawyers if they wish, but this is discouraged by a rule which prevents the winning party from claiming the costs of a lawyer from the losing party.

It is possible for parties to a dispute to ask the court voluntarily to refer the case to arbitration even though the amount claimed is more than £5,000. Similarly, it is possible for a reference to arbitration to be rescinded by the district judge, if the case is more suitable for consideration in the county court, perhaps because it contains a difficult point of law. Certain cases, for example claims for the possession of land, and personal injury cases over £1,000 in value, are not deemed suitable for small claims jurisdiction, and are dealt with according to the usual county court procedures.

5.3.7 MAGISTRATES' COURTS

- **Sit in:** Local areas throughout England and Wales.

- **Personnel:** Lay magistrates (i.e., volunteers with no legal qualifications who sit on the bench part-time) sometimes referred to as justices of the peace; stipendiary magistrates (now called District Judge (Magistrates' Court), full-time, paid and legally qualified); and justices' clerks (one for each bench of magistrates) who are legally qualified and who are employed to advise the lay magistrates on the relevant law and procedure in each case.

- **Jurisdiction:** Civil and criminal law.

The magistrates' courts are local courts, hearing both civil and criminal cases at first instance. The civil cases that may be heard include the recovery of civil debts such as income tax, council tax, and gas and electricity charges, and the granting or renewing of liquor licences.

The most important part of the civil jurisdiction of the magistrates' courts is with regard to family law. When sitting to hear such cases, the court is termed the 'family proceedings court' and it may hear cases concerning financial provision for a spouse or children, personal protection or exclusion orders, and adoption, residence and contact matters. Once again there is quite a degree of overlap here with the work of the county courts and the High Court.

SAQ 5

Which of the following statements are true and which are false?

1 **The High Court (Family Division) is the only court which can authorise the adoption of a child. TRUE/FALSE.**

2 **A decree of divorce can be granted by the Family Division of the High Court, or by the county courts, or the magistrates' courts. TRUE/FALSE.**

3 **Where one party to a relationship is violent towards the other, this can be dealt with by the High Court, the county courts or the magistrates' courts. TRUE/FALSE.**

Jurisdiction in family cases is shared between the Family Division of the High Court, the county courts and the magistrates' courts. Many suggestions have been made as to how this overlap in jurisdiction might be rationalised, including the possibility of creating a separate, unified family court to deal with all family cases. One of the confusing aspects of the present arrangement is that although there is overlap between the three courts, the type of work they can do is not identical. This can be seen in the answers to the self-assessment questions.

Question 1 contains a false statement. The High Court, the county courts and the magistrates' courts all have power to deal with adoption cases.

Question 2 is definitely a false statement. The Family Division of the High Court has full power to grant a decree of divorce in any case, and certain county courts may also deal with undefended divorces. Magistrates' courts do **not** have power to grant decrees of divorce.

The answer to question 3 is true, in that all three courts have ways of providing protection to applicants who are involved in a violent relationship.

5.4 The Woolf Report

In June 1995, Lord Woolf, subsequently appointed Master of the Rolls and now Lord Chief Justice, presented an interim report entitled Access to Justice, to the then Lord Chancellor, Lord

Mackay. The final report was presented in July 1996 and was subsequently approved by the present Lord Chancellor, Lord Irvine of Lairg.

Lord Woolf was charged with the task of reviewing civil jurisdiction, litigation and procedure. His final report consists of an identification of the principles which should be met in any civil justice system, a statement of how our system fell foul of those principles and a set of general rules which formed the core of the new, combined (i.e. High Court and county court) code of rules for civil procedure.

ACTIVITY 6

Refer to *Cases and Materials* (5.3) and read paragraphs 1-3 and 7-9 inclusive of the final Access to Justice Report.

Can you summarise the following?

(a)   How would you describe the wording of the report (if you compare it to the High Court and County Court Jurisdiction Order above)?

(b)   How will the role of the judge change?

(c)   What effect do you think that rulings on procedure etc. before the new rules come into force will have on cases decided after that date?

Lord Woolf is an advocate of the use of 'plain English' in his report and this style has been adopted in the Civil Procedure Rules 1998 (CPR) which have been written following the report. The report called for proactive rather than reactive judges. A judge should be a case manager, overseeing a case from the beginning rather than allowing the parties to dictate the timescale of the case and the judge becoming involved only if it is not settled. Lord Woolf wanted a clear and unambiguous message to all courts and practitioners that there is a new culture in civil justice and as a result, earlier precedents should generally therefore not be referred to. See Activity 8 below.

The changes to be made were facilitated by an Enabling Act, the Civil Procedure Act 1997. It is under this Parent Act that the new Civil Procedure Rules and Practice Directions have been made. The CPR and some of the Practice Directions came into force on 26 April 1999. The CPR set out general principles. The Practice Directions fill in the details. For example, CPR, Part 28 provides for a new 30-week rule limiting the period between directions and the start of the trial. The whole of civil litigation procedure has been re-written. Extensive pre-trial disclosure has removed the secrecy involved in litigation.

THE STRUCTURE AND JURISDICTION OF THE COURTS: CIVIL CASES

There are now essentially three 'tracks' within the civil justice system:

1. The Small Claims Track generally dealing with cases with a claim for damages not exceeding £5,000 (the essence of a more informal court with straightforward procedure has not changed nor has the £1,000 limit for personal injury cases).

2. The Fast Track generally dealing with cases with a claim for damages not exceeding £15,000 (which is governed by standard directions and is dealt with in the county courts).

3. The Multi Track generally dealing with cases with a claim for damages exceeding £15,000 (where the proactive, case management judge will have the greatest impact). Cases up to £50,000 are generally dealt with on the multi track at the county court. Cases over £50,000 are dealt with on the multi track at the High Court, but the High Court has jurisdiction to hear any multi track case (i.e. over £15,000). A personal injury case may only be commenced in the High Court if the value of the claim exceeds £50,000. All cases on the multi track start with a case management conference. The financial limits in this list should answer Activity 5 above.

As a result of case-management and the new pre-trial disclosure rules, the role of the judge has changed. The judge has a far greater power to oversee the conduct of the case and make suggestions for how a case should be run.

As Turner, R.L., The Senior Master and Queen's Remembrancer, in his foreword to the new Civil Procedure Rules (London: Sweet and Maxwell, 1999) expresses (pages IX-X):

'And what will this new approach mean for practitioners? First, the profession is going to have to work much harder at the early stages of the case. Counsel and solicitors who come to the case management conference will have to . . . , wherever possible, reach agreement with their opponents on the approach to be taken. No longer will it be enough to agree not to use ADR because you "do not understand what it can achieve" as happens all too often at present. No more will you be able to go at your own speed, tackling one stage at a time and explaining to your client that that is how the courts work.

Now the client may have to attend the meetings in chambers. I see nothing wrong in the case management hearing being a five-party meeting between the judge, and the lawyers and the clients on both sides. Often it is not a bad thing for the opposing clients to meet on relatively neutral ground and to consider ways of settling their differences. Most clients usually want to get the litigation behind them and to get back into the marketplace and resume trading - litigation may be our chosen livelihood, but is it theirs?

But the key to making *any* case management conference effective is thorough preparation; it is a *conference* at which, allotted tasks already performed, decisions can be made about the next steps in the action . . .

Civil litigation will be trimmed of its inessential features in order to concentrate on the search for the true issues at stake. It is to this end, that the courts wish to see the parties being more open from the start with clear protocols before the litigation commences, with statements of case (especially defences) which do not try to fudge the true nature of the case and with the clients being properly advised as to the advantages of settling their differences by alternative means, if they can . . .

If, however, there has to be a trial, then the aim must be to restrict the amount of oral evidence, disclosure of documents, and reliance on experts to the right amount to ensure a fair and just trial.

But none of this can be achieved unless the courts and the judges realise that it is a partnership. The roles played by the profession - meaning the manner in which they co-operate and work with the courts - will be vital.' [*Emphasis original*]

(Note: ADR stands for 'alternative dispute resolution'. It is a collective noun used to describe any method of settling a dispute without going to court. It includes mechanisms such as negotiation between disagreeing parties, mediation, and arbitration. See **Chapter 8** for a more detailed analysis of ADR. Remember at this stage, though, that one of the stated claims of Woolf's 'New Landscape' is the use of ADR.)

The Civil Procedure Act 1997, s. 2 established the Civil Justice Council. Its remit is *inter alia* to keep the civil justice system under review; consider how to make the civil justice system more accessible, fair and efficient; and advise the Lord Chancellor and the judiciary on the development of the civil justice system.

It was reported in *The Lawyer* (8 November 1999) that there was a dramatic drop in the number of cases coming to the Commercial Court in the first six months following the Woolf Reforms according to Justice Rix, the judge in charge.

ACTIVITY 7

Read 'Woolf: euphoria or shambles?' by Brian McConnell [1999] NLJ 1886 in *Cases and Materials* (5.3). Which is it?

ACTIVITY 8

**Refer to Rule 1.1 of the Civil Procedure Rules in *Cases and Materials* (5.3).
What is the 'overriding objective'?**

This is a clear statement (in plain English) that the court must deal with cases *justly*. One of the ways in which this is to be achieved is to ensure the judges are active in case management.

ACTIVITY 9

Refer in *Cases and Materials* (5.3) to *Lombard Natwest Factors Ltd* v *Sebastian Arbis* (1999) LTL 1/11/99. If exactly the same wording is used in the old rules (Rules of the Supreme Court) and the new CPR, why would a court *not* interpret the rules in the same way?

It comes down to the overriding objective, which you can see from this case really is <u>overriding.</u>

Judicial Statistics for 1999 (HMSO) do show an improvement in waiting times in the county (except the small claims) and the High courts. Although the Woolf changes did not come into effect until April 1999, the average waiting time for that year in the county court was 79 weeks (85 weeks in 1998, 86 weeks in 1997) and in the High Court, 174 weeks, a four-week reduction on the 1997 and 1998 figures. The small claims court was, on average, slower in 1999, however. Parties waited for 26 weeks, as opposed to 24 weeks in 1998. It is hoped that *Judicial Statistics* 2000 (not available at 31/1/01) will show a greater improvement in delay as the Woolf reforms take greater effect.

However, a number of criticisms of the reforms have been made in advance of the publication of the official statistics ([2000] NLJ 1829). The front end loading of cases has in fact made cases more expensive. Although cases, once started, *are* dealt with quicker by the courts, there is no real decrease in delay or cost for the client. The legal representative has merely done much of the legal work earlier and has delayed the 'official' start of the case. Judicial case management is generally regarded as adding further expense and is seen as being bureaucratic. The courts are under-resourced in terms of staff, judges and the continued lack of IT facilities. There is no reduction in time wasting due to excessive pre-action protocols. The majority of cases are still settled at the door of the court just before the hearing is due to commence.

5.5   Summary

Now that you have read this chapter, you should have an overview of the various courts which have jurisdiction in civil cases. You will be able to identify the names of the courts and the personnel involved, and it should also be possible for you to:

- appreciate the significance of the Court of Justice of the European Communities and the relationship between this Court and the English legal system;

- compare the role of the Court of Appeal with that of the House of Lords and make a critical evaluation of the existence of these two appeal courts;

- identify the overlap in jurisdiction which exists between a number of courts and discuss the desirability of this.

In **Chapter 6** you will undertake a similar exercise in respect of the courts which exercise jurisdiction in criminal cases.

5.6   Further Reading

Ingman, T., *The English Legal Process,* 8th edn, London: Blackstone Press, 2000, Chapters 1, 2.

Slapper, G., and Kelly, D., *The English Legal System*, 4th edn, London: Cavendish, 1999, Chapters 2 and 3.

www.open.gov.uk/civjustice
www.open.gov.uk/lcd

5.7   End of Chapter Assessment Question

It has been said that the organisation of business between the High Court, county courts and magistrates' courts creates anomalies, inefficiencies, and confusion.

Critically examine this statement.

See *Cases and Materials* (5.5) for a specimen answer.

CHAPTER SIX

THE STRUCTURE AND JURISDICTION OF THE COURTS: CRIMINAL CASES

6.1 Objectives

On completion of this chapter you should be able to:

- give an account of the jurisdiction of the courts which may hear criminal cases;

- identify the impact of Article 6 of the European Convention on Human Rights;

- describe the way in which criminal offences are classified;

- identify the appropriate courts in which different types of cases will be heard;

- demonstrate knowledge of some of the personnel involved in criminal cases;

- evaluate whether a defendant should have the right to elect trial by jury in certain circumstances.

6.2 Introduction

The courts mentioned below exercise criminal jurisdiction. Some of the courts are also capable of exercising civil jurisdiction and have therefore already been mentioned in **Chapter 5** above. Where this is the case, the relevant information has not been repeated. The Woolf reforms do not apply to criminal cases.

ACTIVITY 1

Refer to *Cases and Materials* (6.1). There you will find the criminal court hierarchy. Again, you may find it useful to keep this in front of you during this chapter as you did with the civil court hierarchy in Chapter 5.

The *jurisdiction* of the criminal courts will not be changed by the incorporation of the European Convention on Human Rights, but Article 6 has an important effect on criminal *proceedings*.

SAQ 1

Article 6 provides:

1. In the determination of his civil rights and obligations or of any criminal charge against him, everyone is entitled to a fair and public hearing within reasonable time by an independent and impartial tribunal established by law. Judgment shall be pronounced publicly but the press and public may be excluded from all or part of the trial in the interests of morals, public order or national security in a democratic society, where the interests of juveniles or the protection of the private life of the parties so require, or to the extent strictly necessary in the opinion of the court in special circumstances where publicity would prejudice the interests of justice.

2. Everyone charged with a criminal offence shall be presumed innocent until proved guilty according to law.

3. Everyone charged with a criminal offence has the following minimum rights:
a. to be informed promptly, in a language he understands and in detail, of the nature and cause of the accusation against him;
b. to have adequate time and facilities for the preparation of his defence;
c. to defend himself in person or through legal assistance of his own choosing, or, if he has not sufficient means to pay for legal assistance, to be given it free when the interests of justice so require;
d. to examine or have examined witnesses against him and to obtain the attendance and examination of witnesses on his behalf under the same conditions as witnesses against him;
e. to have the free assistance of an interpreter if he cannot understand or speak the language used in court.

Under which part of Article 6 did Gregory (*Gregory* v *UK* (1998) 25 EHRR 577) bring his case?

You should remember it was under Article 6(1), alleging that he did not have a 'fair hearing'.

ACTIVITY 2

Read the extract in *Cases and Materials* (6.1) from Andrew Ashworth's 'Article 6 and the Fairness of Trials' [1999] Crim LR 261. Can you explain the effect of the decision in *Benham* v *UK* (1996) 22 EHRR 293?

It would appear that although civil and criminal courts have been dealt with separately in this book, the line that divides the two is becoming blurred. Articles 6(2) and 6(3) apply to cases that have been categorised as '*civil*' within our legal system, but are to be treated as *criminal* under the *Benham* rules. These afford citizens involved in such cases certain minimum rights that would not otherwise be available, in particular the right to be presumed innocent until proved guilty according to law. See further *Learning Text: Law of Evidence*.

6.3   The Courts which Exercise Criminal Jurisdiction

6.3.1   THE COURT OF JUSTICE OF THE EUROPEAN COMMUNITIES

In the same way that this Court may be asked to give rulings concerning civil law, so references may be made to it for the interpretation of European Community law, where this involves criminal law.

6.3.2   THE HOUSE OF LORDS

The House of Lords may hear appeals on matters of criminal law. These appeals may come either from the Court of Appeal (Criminal Division) or from the Divisional Court of the Queen's Bench Division. Certain conditions must be satisfied before the House of Lords can hear such appeals, and the details of this will be described in **Chapter 7**, which deals with the appeals system in greater depth.

6.3.3   THE JUDICIAL COMMITTEE OF THE PRIVY COUNCIL

In dealing with appeals from courts outside the United Kingdom, as already indicated, the business of this committee is mainly civil. The Committee will not grant special leave for an appeal to be heard in criminal cases, unless there are exceptional circumstances. Leave to appeal will only be granted if there has been a substantial injustice and the accused has been denied a fair trial.

ACTIVITY 3

For an example of an appeal to the Judicial Committee from Jamaica, see the extract from the case of *Pratt* v *Attorney-General for Jamaica* [1993] 4 All ER 769 in *Cases and Materials* (6.2.1).

Notice the names of the judges, which you may have come to recognise as you have encountered these names in cases decided by the House of Lords. Notice also (from the section headed 'Appeal') how special leave was required before an appeal could be made to the Judicial Committee from the Court of Appeal of Jamaica. You will appreciate, from reading the headnote and the first paragraph of the opinion of Lord Griffiths, why special leave was granted in this particular case.

ACTIVITY 4

Read 'The death penalty and the continuing role of the Privy Council' by Saul Lehrfreund [1999] NLJ 1299 in *Cases and Materials* (6.2.1).

The author presents a number of different points of view on the two subjects mentioned in the title. It is an important legal skill to present a BALANCED argument. It is a skill you will already be developing as you work through this text and you will have a further chance to practice it in the End of Chapter Assessment Question.

In the meantime, to focus on balancing arguments, can you identify points:

(a)   in favour of the death penalty,

(b)   against it,

(c)   in favour of the continued role of the Privy Council as the final appeal court for the Commonwealth Caribbean,

(d)   against it?

Lehrfreund recognises that set against a background of rising crime rates and criminal violence (supporting the rights of the States to have the death penalty), the relevant procedural laws of the countries in question are not able to provide safeguards to ensure a fair trial. He states 'the dice is firmly loaded against the accused person'. He supports the latter point by evidence of the 1995 Constitutional Court of South Africa. As you know, points of view are strengthened by such objective and reliable evidence. On the other hand, the evidence indicates that these States have the constitutional liberty to retain the death penalty and, as such, the Privy Council is 'a colonial anachronism'. Whilst 'every convicted murderer has used his right to appeal to escape the hangman's noose', it is conversely seen as important for the same people to ask for a review of their convictions by a higher tribunal, not on the basis that the death penalty is unconstitutional *per se*, but that a fair trial has not occurred.

In an interview with *The Times* (19 October 1999), Lord Browne-Wilkinson, the then senior law lord, said;

> 'I think the practice whereby a court in Downing Street seeks to decide what a country in the Caribbean should or should not do is not proving very satisfactory, and our decisions in death row cases are now not very well received. You can believe in the death penalty or you can not, but the problem I think - and this is just a personal view - is that to let those countries decide for themselves would be better for everybody.'

THE STRUCTURE AND JURISDICTION OF THE COURTS: CRIMINAL
CASES

It was reported in *The Times* ('Death Under the Sun', 18 January 2000) that Trinidad, Tobago, Barbados, Guyana and Jamaica have all signed up in principle to a new Court of Appeal to curtail the power of the Privy Council in criminal cases. It is reported that the opinion expressed in *Pratt* (above) may have made the Privy Council masters of its own destruction. Death row inmates who have been in prison for more than five years had, in the Council's opinion, suffered 'inhuman or degrading treatment' and accordingly their sentences would be commuted to life. *Pratt* is a very unpopular judgment in these countries where the death penalty is widely supported.

6.3.4 THE COURT OF APPEAL (CRIMINAL DIVISION)

Originally, the Court of Appeal was created to hear civil cases only, but the Court of Criminal Appeal, as it was then known, was created in 1907, to hear appeals in criminal cases only. This court was replaced in 1966 by the Court of Appeal (Criminal Division) the name by which it is now known. The head of this court is the Lord Chief Justice. It has jurisdiction to hear appeals against sentence or conviction by persons convicted of offences at the Crown Court, but it does not deal with cases which have been heard by the Divisional Court of the Queen's Bench Division; these cases go direct to the House of Lords. Again you will understand this point more thoroughly when you have read **Chapter 7** on the appeal procedures in the court system. The Attorney-General (the principal law officer of the Crown) may, on behalf of the Crown, also refer cases to the Criminal Division following a trial in the Crown Court, where the sentence appears to be unduly lenient, or where a person has been acquitted, but some clarification on a point of law is sought. See **Chapter 7**.

6.3.5 THE HIGH COURT OF JUSTICE

6.3.5.1 The Divisional Court of the Queen's Bench Division

You may find it odd to see the High Court mentioned here as it was dealt with in **Chapter 5** as a court which deals primarily with civil cases. However, as mentioned in **Chapter 5**, this court has jurisdiction in respect of offences which have been tried in the magistrates' courts, and an appeal has been made on a point of law by way of case stated.

ACTIVITY 5

Turn to *Cases and Materials* (6.2.2.1) and read the extract from the case of *Griffith* v *Jenkins* [1992] 1 All ER 65. As you will see, this was a relatively trivial case, which was considered by three different courts, the last of which was the House of Lords. From the initial hearing in the magistrates' court, an appeal was made by the prosecution to the Divisional Court of the Queen's Bench Division by way of case stated. Because of the difficulties which arose concerning the rehearing of the case, there was then an appeal to the House of Lords. Notice that in order to obtain a hearing before the House, it was necessary for leave (permission) to appeal to be obtained, and the court had to certify that a point of law of general public importance was involved in the case. You will find a further explanation of this in Chapter 7. Who 'won' the appeal?

It was the prosecutor who appealed and her appeal was dismissed, so in this sense, she did not 'win'. However, the points of law involved in the case were decided in agreement with her submission, so it is also clear that she did not 'lose'.

6.3.6   THE CROWN COURT

- Important note: Students often confuse the names and functions of the Crown Court and the county courts. Try to memorise now the fact that **the Crown Court** is a court which exercises **criminal jurisdiction**, whereas **the county courts** exercise **civil jurisdiction**.

- **Sits in:** Court centres throughout England and Wales. The Crown Court in London is referred to as the Central Criminal Court (known popularly as the Old Bailey).

- **Personnel:** All the judges of the High Court, circuit judges, recorders, and Justices of the Peace (who will sit with a judge drawn from one of the other categories).

A distinctive feature of the Crown Court is the use of the jury as part of the trial process. We have examined the role of the jury in **Chapter 1**.

- **Jurisdiction:** The Crown Court is regarded as one single court which sits in various parts of the country. It was created to replace the previous system of Assizes and Quarter Sessions.

The Crown Court is the only court which has jurisdiction to hear all **trials on indictment** for offences wherever committed. It also hears appeals from persons convicted by way of **summary trial** in the magistrates' courts. It has the power to sentence persons convicted by the magistrates, and it also has a small amount of civil jurisdiction, e.g., appeals in liquor licensing cases.

For a full explanation of the terms in bold in the paragraph above, see **6.4.1** below.

6.3.7   MAGISTRATES' COURT

In addition to their work in civil cases (described in **Chapter 5**), the magistrates' courts deal with a vast quantity of criminal cases; 98% of all criminal cases are tried summarily by these courts. Magistrates have jurisdiction in respect of **summary offences, either way offences**, and they also have the task of carrying out preliminary matters (bail, remand and related matters) in every case in which a person is accused of an **indictable** offence.

Before we examine these terms, we will briefly identify the personnel involved and the new system operating in this court.

- **Personnel:** Not surprisingly, the personnel of the magistrates' court consist of magistrates. There are two types:

1. Lay magistrates, or Justices of the Peace (JP). These are generally lay (not legally qualified, although a legal qualification is not a bar to becoming a JP), unpaid (expenses only), volunteers who live within 15 miles of the court area and have been nominated or have applied to be on the bench. Some training is provided, but a qualified Bench Legal Adviser (Court Clerk) advises them on legal matters.

2. Stipendiary Magistrates, or now referred to as District Judge (Magistrates' Court) (DJ(MC)) who have been solicitors or barristers for at least seven years (Courts and Legal Services Act 1990 and Access to Justice Act 1999, see **Chapter 9**).

There are approximately 30,000 JPs compared with approximately 100 District Judges (Magistrates' Court), plus Deputy DJ(MC)s. Justices of the Peace work part-time, sitting for 26 half days per annum. DJ(MC)s are full-time.

ACTIVITY 6

Read the article in *Cases and Materials* (6.2.3) from *The Times* (2 November 1999) by Frances Gibb. Note that the term 'fast-track' is now to be used both in civil proceedings (for cases at the county court) and in criminal proceedings at the magistrates' court.

Summarise the changes. Prepare a list of the potential (or actual) positives of the new system and the potential (or actual) negatives.

The Narey ('fast-track') system involves early hearings of criminal cases by using a lay prosecutor in cases of straightforward guilty pleas after the case list has been drawn up at the police station. The benefits (actual or potential) are an increase in the cases concluded at the first hearing, causing a reduction in time and expense from charge to disposal. This has/could lead to an increase in guilty pleas at the first hearing (further leading to a reduction in sentence). Closer co-operation between different criminal justice agencies cuts delays and inefficiencies. However, trained lay people are not legally qualified. A defendant who pleads guilty, for example, to shoplifting, but also wishes to state that he or she did not mean to forget to pay, is *in law* pleading *not guilty* (no intention permanently to deprive the owner of the goods or the payment therefore is in law a plea of not guilty). Half of the defendants dealt with by the lay prosecutor in the extract did not 'bother with a lawyer to represent them'. Added to the point made before, this could result in numerous miscarriages of justice occurring and then not being identified as the parties involved are not aware of the miscarriage themselves. This is/could be compounded by the fact that there are no defence representatives at the police station when the list is drawn up.

Lee Bridges, in 'Narey may not be a force for the good' (*The Times*, 9 November 1999) states:

> 'Recent pilots indicate that duty solicitor costs are likely to rise by 117 per cent, or nearly £18 million per annum. Is this not a case of "throwing money" at a problem in order to facilitate the Home Office's hasty and ill-thought-out reforms? In one case in the pilots, a solicitor advised his client to plead guilty at an EFH [early first hearing] because he felt pressurised to finish the case on the day.'

This was before the solicitor had had the chance to review the police tapes during which it was alleged that the defendant had made an admission in the absence of his solicitor.

SAQ 2

What human rights issue might arise in the above anecdote?

Article 6 may have been breached. The right to a fair trial must not be indirectly removed because there is time pressure on a defendant's legal representation.

There is evidence that the Narey pilots are working on one level however. The report by Ernst and Young, *Reducing Delay in the Criminal Justice System: Evaluation of the Pilot Schemes* (HMSO 1999), concludes that the average times between charge and disposal have been reduced from 85.5 to 30 days for adults and 89.5 to 37.9 days for youths. It accepts that during the six-month pilot schemes, the local Legal Aid Boards paid an additional £17.8 million, but there will be an off-set to the increase in the overall costs through a reduction in the number of cases getting full legal aid. There will be a further estimated saving of £14.6 million annually as a result of the increased speed of the cases.

6.4   Classification of Criminal Offences

6.4.1   DEFINITIONS

Criminal offences are divided into three categories:

(a)   **Offences triable only on indictment.** These are tried only in the Crown Court. These are the offences which are considered too serious to be dealt with by the magistrates' courts and must be heard by a judge and jury. Examples of indictable offences include murder, manslaughter and rape, serious offences against the person, e.g., causing grievous bodily harm with intent, and aggravated burglary. In the main, these are offences which were developed by the common law, rather than by statute. Indictable offences are themselves divided into four classes according to the gravity of the offence, and then matched to a judge of the appropriate status. Thus cases in classes 1 and 2 which include murder, treason and rape, are usually heard by a High Court judge with a jury. Cases in the other classes may be heard by a High Court judge, a circuit judge or a recorder, with a jury in every case.

(b)   **Summary offences.** These are dealt with summarily (literally briefly, without a jury) by the magistrates' courts. These are less serious offences including many motoring offences under the Road Traffic Acts, taking a motor vehicle without consent and many other offences created by statute.

(c)   **Offences triable either way.** These are crimes which can be tried **either** summarily by the magistrates, **or** on indictment, i.e., before a judge and jury in the Crown Court. They are often referred to as either way offences. They include less serious assaults, criminal damage in excess of £5,000, and many of the offences contained in the Theft Act 1968 but excluding, amongst other things, blackmail and certain burglaries.

6.4.2 INDICTABLE OFFENCES

It is worth remembering that ALL criminal offences start at the magistrates' court. The majority (98%) also finish there and will not 'move up' to the Crown Court. The remaining 2% therefore do go up to the Crown Court. This 2% is made up of indictable offences and either way offences to be tried on indictment.

Traditionally, when faced with an indictable offence, the magistrates undertook a preliminary hearing. These proceedings were known as committal proceedings in which the magistrates acted as examining justices. The aim of committal proceedings was for the magistrates to be satisfied on a preliminary examination of the evidence, there was a case for the accused to answer. Originally, committal proceedings involved the witnesses giving evidence in person before the court, i.e. an 'old style committal'. This proved costly, time consuming and traumatic for the witnesses however, so a new procedure (the 'paper committal') was developed as an alternative. This simply involved the magistrates making the decision to commit the case to the Crown Court or discharge it, on the basis of written witness statements. The Criminal Procedure and Investigations Act 1996 effectively abolished 'old-style' committals.

ACTIVITY 7

Read Crime and Disorder Act 1998, s. 51(1) in *Cases and Materials* **(6.3.1). What is the effect of this section?**

All offences start at the magistrates' court, but as s. 51(1) has abolished committals in indictable only offences, the role of the magistrates in such cases is to deal with legal aid (the Criminal Defence Service Fund, see **Chapter 8**), bail and remand.

6.4.3 SUMMARY OFFENCES

Summary offences are dealt with only by the magistrates' courts. Offenders are not entitled to trial by jury in respect of these offences. There are literally hundreds of offences which are triable summarily only, many of them being motoring offences under the Road Traffic Acts. To avoid the court system being totally overwhelmed by minor speeding or parking cases, it is possible for defendants to choose not to appear at court but to plead guilty by post.

Because of the less serious nature of these offences, the magistrates are restricted in the type of sentence which they can impose. Thus an offender can only be given a maximum of six months' imprisonment in respect of a summary offence. Similarly, the magistrates can only impose a fine of £1,000 in respect of summary offences, or such amount as is specified in the statute creating the offence, whichever is higher, up to an overall limit of £5,000.

The magistrates also have power to compensate victims of crime, by ordering a convicted person to pay an amount (again up to £5,000) to the victim of the crime.

6.4.4 OFFENCES TRIABLE EITHER WAY

The third category of offences with which magistrates may deal is the group of offences known as 'either way' offences. In very basic terms, summary offences 'live' at the magistrates' court, indictable offences 'visit' the magistrates' court but 'live' at the Crown; but either way offences are 'of no fixed abode'. The first thing that has to be done with an either way offence, therefore, is a 'home' has to be found according to plea.

All criminal offences start at the magistrates' court. Under s. 17A of the Magistrates' Courts Act 1980, a defendant charged with an either way offence will be asked to indicate his plea. An indication of 'guilty' leads the court to proceed with sentence at the magistrates' court or commit the defendant for sentence at the Crown Court. This procedure was introduced in 1996 (s. 49 of the Criminal Procedure and Investigations Act 1996 (CPIA), amended by s. 17 of the Magistrates' Courts Act 1980). Before the CPIA 1996, the magistrates made the decision as to *court of trial* without even knowing if the defendant intended to plead guilty. A guilty plea obviously means there is no need for a trial, as a trial is a hearing to determine guilt. The new system avoids unnecessary committals to the Crown Court unless the magistrates' sentencing powers are inadequate. It also provides the defendant with the earliest opportunity to plead guilty.

ACTIVITY 8

Read the article by Nicola Padfield [1997] NLJ 1396 in *Cases and Materials* (6.4.2). What two reasons does she suggest justify the introduction of s. 49 of the CPIA 1996? Can you explain the conflict between s. 49 of the CPIA 1996 and s. 22 of the Magistrates' Courts Act 1980?

The Government's Consultation Paper 1995 concluded that about three quarters of those committed for trial eventually pleaded guilty (and would not therefore have a jury trial) and secondly 80% of defendants who did elect for jury trial were convicted and received sentences that could have been passed by the magistrates' court. These are the two main reasons why it was felt important to increase the workload at the magistrates' court, rather than at the slower, more expensive Crown Court. The conflict between ss. 22 and 49 comes down to procedure. Whilst s. 22 lays down one procedure for certain either way offences (where the value is under £5000, the offence is to be treated as if it is a summary offence), s. 49 applies to all either way offences (i.e. there should be an indication of plea prior to a mode of trial decision being made).

ACTIVITY 9

Read ss. 3 and 5 of the Powers of Criminal Courts (Sentencing) Act 2000 in *Cases and Materials* (6.3). Explain the effect of these two sections.

If a defendant makes an indication of a guilty plea under s. 17A of the Magistrates' Courts Act 1980, the magistrates may decide to pass sentence in the magistrates' court. There is a general maximum of six months' imprisonment in this court. In the alternative, the magistrates may commit the case for sentence at the Crown Court where there is no general maximum sentence, other than that of the offence. For example, theft (an either way offence) is an offence with a maximum custodial sentence of seven years. A person convicted of theft and then sentenced in the magistrates' court could receive a maximum of six months. A person convicted of theft but sentenced at the Crown Court could receive seven years. The same procedure applies where a defendant pleads not guilty but is then convicted.

However, wherever a defendant charged with an either way offence indicates a not guilty plea, the magistrates proceed to a Mode of Trial Hearing. This is a pre-trial hearing, *not* a hearing to determine guilt. It is a hearing to decide which court an either way offence should be tried in, hence Mode of *Trial*.

ACTIVITY 10

Refer to the National Mode of Trial Guidelines issued by the Lord Chief Justice in 1995 in *Cases and Materials* **(6.3.2). All other factors being equal, at which court should trial be held?**

There are many 'other factors' to consider, but the starting point for the magistrates is to deal with the case summarily, but this is far from the end of the matter.

The next stage to consider is what the magistrates decide. If the decision is that the case should be committed to the Crown Court for trial, the case proceeds with a committal hearing and the defendant cannot request summary trial.

SAQ 3

Weren't <u>all</u> committals abolished by s. 51(1) of the CPIA 1996?

If you remember, the above section abolished only committals in indictable only offences. Committals should therefore be held in either way offences committed for trial. The committal is the 'new style' or 'paper' committal.

If, on the other hand, the magistrates' court decides that the case can be tried summarily, **the defendant must <u>consent</u> to be tried at the magistrates' court**. A defendant has the <u>right to elect trial by jury</u> and to be committed for trial at the Crown Court.

On 18 November 1999, the Criminal Justice (Mode of Trial) Bill was introduced in the House of Lords. This exceptionally controversial Bill would have given effect to the unanimous recommendations of the Royal Commission on Criminal Justice (Runciman) 1993 and the Review of Delay in the Criminal Justice System (Narey) 1997. Both reports stated that the decision on mode of trial is for the magistrates and not the defendant to make. Under the Bill, it would have allowed the court, for the first time, to have regard to previous convictions when deciding venue for trial.

SAQ 4

Can you reflect on how this change could have affected some defendants in the lights of s. 49 of the CPIA 1996?

Because of the early indication of plea procedure under s. 49 of the CPIA 1996, many more cases have been kept at the magistrates' court than were before. If the defendant indicated a not guilty plea but then lost the right to trial by jury, they could now be tried at the magistrates' court without a choice. You may feel that in certain cases (e.g. theft where the allegation is one of dishonesty), the consequences of such a change are undesired. However, you may also wish to bear in mind the number of defendants who plead guilty at the last moment, leading to cracked trials and a waste of administrative effort.

On 20 January 2000, the Criminal Justice (Mode of Trial) Bill was defeated in the House of Lords by a massive majority. On 22 February 2000, Jack Straw introduced the Criminal Justice (Mode of Trial) (No. 2) Bill in the House of Commons. The central proposal – that it is for the magistrates to determine venue of trial – remained unchanged, but it removed the power of the magistrates to make that decision taking any of the characteristics, including previous convictions, of the accused into account. The second Bill courted at least as much controversy as the first, despite or indeed because of this latter change. Professor Michael Zander, member of the Runciman Commission and outspoken supporter of the first Bill, quickly denounced the second. He believed the second Bill would leave magistrates to make a decision as to mode of trial where 'the most important question of all' could not be asked ([2000] NLJ 366):

> 'A case could ruin someone's reputation or result in him losing his livelihood is serious and the court should have the right to take that into account when deciding where he should be tried.'

The Criminal Justice (Mode of Trial) (No. 2) Bill was rejected by the House of Lords on 28 September 2000, but the Government has promised that a third Bill will be passed into law without the Lords' approval under the power of the Parliament Act 1911. This promise may not materialise, however, if Auld LJ's Review of Criminal Courts adopts a proposal mooted in his October 2000 Progress Reports. Probably the most controversial of the issues debated is to establish an 'intermediate' tier of criminal jurisdiction to deal with either way offences. It is suggested that this could take the form of a District Judge (Magistrates' Court) sitting with two lay magistrates.

It is clear that the criminal justice system is in a state of flux and is the current focus of legal, political and media attention. However, whilst it is important that you have a good understanding of the proposals for reform, you must be able to identify and describe the mechanisms of criminal court procedure. You should be able to practice this by completing SAQ's 5 and 6 below.

SAQ 5

Consider the story which follows, and the questions based on it. Mrs Smith claims that one day last year, she saw Dan point a gun in the direction of his girlfriend, and pull the trigger. The gun failed to fire because the mechanism was faulty, but Dan had not been aware of that until after he had pulled the trigger. Dan is now being tried for the attempted murder of his girlfriend, under the provisions of the Criminal Attempts Act 1981. He claims that he did not point the gun in his girlfriend's direction as alleged and that Mrs Smith was mistaken or is lying. Secondly, he claims that the act of pointing a gun in this way is not legally capable of falling within the relevant section of the Act.

(a)   Who decides whether Dan should be tried for this offence and by what procedure?

(b)   In which court would this case be tried and by whom?

(c)   Who will decide whether either Dan or Mrs Smith is lying about what happened?

(d)   Who will decide whether Dan's alleged actions are capable as a matter of law of being within the ambit of the Criminal Attempts Act 1981?

As you will realise from the preceding sections of the text, in order to answer the questions set out above, it is necessary to decide how to classify the offence concerned. As Dan has been charged with attempted murder, this is an offence which is triable on indictment.

The trial will take place in the Crown Court. As murder is a Class 1 offence, it will be heard by a High Court judge with a jury. It is the task of the jury to decide questions of fact, and it is therefore for the jury to determine whether the events really took place as the witness described, or whether Dan is to be believed in preference to Mrs Smith. The legal question, of whether the actions described can be regarded as falling within the wording of the legislation, is for the judge to resolve.

SAQ 6

Using the classification of criminal offences given in this chapter, identify the types of offences set out below, and state which of them will be tried by the Crown Court, and which by the magistrates' court:

(a) manslaughter;

(b) taking a motor vehicle without consent;

(c) taking goods from a supermarket without paying for them;

(a) deliberately causing damage to another person's property valued at £2,000.

You may have noticed in the text (see **6.3.7**) that it was said that the magistrates' courts deal with 98% of all criminal cases. This reflects the fact that the Crown Court could not possibly deal with all of the vast number of criminal prosecutions which arise every year, because of the time and expense involved in a full Crown Court trial with a jury. Only the more serious cases are therefore tried on indictment in the Crown Court. Manslaughter (question (a)) is one such offence and must be tried in the Crown Court.

Taking a motor vehicle without the owner's consent would appear to be a form of theft, and you might therefore expect it to be an either way offence along with most other thefts under the Theft Acts. However, this particular offence has, by statute, been designated a summary offence and is therefore dealt with by the magistrates' courts (question (b)). By contrast, shoplifting, even though it may seen a relatively minor offence, is an offence which is triable either way (question (c)).

Deliberately causing damage to another person's property is classed as criminal damage, and the way in which this offence is dealt with depends upon the monetary value involved. Where the sum of money concerned does not exceed £5,000, as in question (d), then the offence is treated as summary and is dealt with by the magistrates. Over that amount, the case is dealt with as an either way offence. However, if in any criminal damage case it is alleged that the accused had the intention to endanger life, then this will be treated as an offence triable on indictment.

6.5 Summary

By now you will have acquired a considerable amount of knowledge about the different courts which determine legal issues in this country. In particular you should now be able to:

- identify the courts which exercise criminal jurisdiction and distinguish these from the courts which exercise civil jurisdiction;

- identify the personnel involved in these courts;

- describe the classification of criminal offences into indictable, summary and either way offences and give examples of these;

- give an account of the way in which mode of trial is fixed for either way offences;

- match different types of offence to the appropriate court of trial.

There now remains only one piece of the jigsaw left to complete the picture of the court system in England and Wales and that is the way in which appeals are dealt with. This will be described in **Chapter 7**.

6.6   Further Reading

Ingman, T., *The English Legal Process,* 8th edn, London: Blackstone Press, 2000, Chapters 1, 2.

Ward, R., *Walker & Walker's English Legal System*, 8th edn, London: Butterworths, 1998, Chapters 21, 22.

Slapper, G. and Kelly, D., *The English Legal System*, 4th edn, London: Cavendish, 1999, Chapter 4.

Bailey, S. and Gunn, M., *Smith & Bailey on The English Legal System*, 3rd edn, London: Sweet & Maxwell, 1996, Chapters 13, 16.

6.7   End of Chapter Assessment Question

Baz has been charged with an either way offence. He has many previous convictions for minor offences. Explain and comment on the procedure for determining the trial venue.

See *Cases and Materials* (6.5) for a specimen answer.

CHAPTER SEVEN

APPEALS IN CIVIL AND CRIMINAL CASES

7.1   Objectives

By the end of this chapter you should be able to:

- describe the function of the appeal courts;

- identify the routes for civil and criminal appeals;

- compare the grounds for appeal in civil and criminal cases and compare the availability of appeals for those involved in legal disputes;

- evaluate the role of the Criminal Cases Review Commission.

7.2   Introduction

This is the last of the three chapters which together provide an analysis of the hierarchy of the courts.

By now, you should have a good working knowledge of the structure and jurisdiction of the court system as it applies to England and Wales. To complete your study of the system, it is necessary for you to be aware of the way in which appeals from the decisions of these courts are dealt with. Some of this information will be familiar to you, as you have already learned about the Court of Appeal and the House of Lords in the previous chapters. As you will have realised, both of these courts play a major role in the final determination of appeals from the decisions of the lower courts.

7.3   Appeals in Civil Proceedings

The Access to Justice Act 1999 has made it clear that appealing in civil cases is not an automatic right. This may strike you as harsh and restrictive, but it must be borne in mind that the rules have to strike a balance between the rights of the individual wishing to prove his or her case, and the pressure on the time and resources of the court system.

The Access to Justice Act (AJA) 1999 and a new CPR, Part 52 have provided a common and harmonised set of rules for all civil appeals (except, at the moment, public civil law and family cases). Since 2 October 2000 small claims cases have also been included. Section 54 of the AJA 1999 provides that before an appeal can be heard permission to appeal must be granted. Section

55 provides that there should generally be only one appeal in any case, rather than cases progressing, almost automatically, through the court hierarchy as occurred in the past. The Act also provides for a great deal of flexibility in deploying judges to hear appeals.

The new appeal regime has been subjected to detailed analysis in *Tanfern Limited* v *Gregor Cameron-Macdonald and Another* [2000] 2 All ER 801.

ACTIVITY 1

Read the extract from the case *of Tanfern Limited* v *Gregor Cameron-Macdonald and Another* **[2000] 2 All ER 801** in *Cases and Materials* **(7.1)** and answer the following questions.

(a)   Under the new rules, where will the following appeals be heard?

     (i)   An appeal from a district judge in a county court?

     (ii)   An appeal from a circuit judge in a county court?

     (iii)   An appeal from a High Court judge in the High Court?

     (iv)   An appeal from a district judge hearing a multi-track case at the county court?

(b)   When is permission to appeal required?

(c)   Under what circumstances will the appeal court allow an appeal?

(d)   What are the general rules concerning second appeals?

As you will see, unlike appeals in criminal cases (see below), where an appeal lies to the next *court* in the hierarchy, appeals in civil cases generally lie to the next *judge* in the hierarchy. As your answer to question (a)(i) above should show, however, the main exception to this is an appeal from a district judge hearing a multi-track case at the county court, which should be heard at the Court of Appeal. Permission is generally always required, which will be granted only where there is a '*real prospect of success or some other compelling reason*'. The appeal court's role is to review the decision of the lower court, it will not conduct a full re-hearing of the case. It will allow an appeal where the decision of the lower court was wrong or where it was unjust because of a serious procedural or other irregularity in the proceedings of the lower court. The appeal court also has all the power of the lower court; it may affirm, set aside or vary any order or judgment made or given by the lower court, may refer any claim or issue for determination by a lower court, may order a new trial or hearing and may make a costs order. Rules concerning second appeals may be seen as being harsh, but as Brooke LJ pointed out:

'All courts are familiar with the litigant, often an unrepresented litigant, who will never take "no" for an answer, however unpromising his/her cause.'

and accordingly:

'The decision of the first appeal court is now to be given primacy.'

Only the Court of Appeal can grant permission to appeal from a decision of a county court or the High Court if that decision is itself the determination of a matter forming the subject matter of an appeal.

The new appeal rules introduced in May 2000 did not affect civil appeals to the House of Lords.

ACTIVITY 2

In *Cases and Materials* (7.1) you will find ss. 12 and 13 of the Administration of Justice Act 1969 concerning leapfrog appeals. Make a list of the conditions which must be satisfied before this procedure can be used. You will find that it is quite complex. Check your list with that given in *Cases and Materials* (7.1).

Appeals from decisions of the Court of Appeal lie to the House of Lords, but in order to limit the workload of the Law Lords, permission to appeal must be given by one of these courts. There are also certain classes of cases in which any further appeal from the Court of Appeal is prohibited by statute, e.g., an appeal from a county court in probate proceedings. In all other cases, an appellant may seek permission to appeal from the Court of Appeal and if this is refused, he or she is free to apply to the Appeal Committee of the House of Lords for permission.

Appeals to the House of Lords in civil matters usually concern questions of law, although appeals on questions of fact are possible. Generally speaking the House of Lords will only hear appeals involving matters of general public importance, although this is not a statutory requirement, in contrast to criminal cases (see **7.4.2**). Where a case does involve an issue which is of general public importance, this will increase the likelihood of permission to appeal being granted.

7.4 Appeals in Criminal Proceedings

The system of appeals in criminal cases has been the subject of considerable discussion and criticism in recent years. One reason for this has been the emergence of cases where serious miscarriages of justice have occurred, resulting in the imprisonment of a number of people for crimes which they did not commit. Partly as a result of such cases, the criminal justice system has been the subject of a Royal Commission which reported in 1993 (the Runciman Commission) and which made a number of recommendations for improvement, some but not all of which have been adopted in the Criminal Justice and Public Order Act 1994. More far-reaching changes have been made by the Criminal Appeal Act 1995, which was enacted as a result of the recommendations of the Royal Commission on Criminal Justice.

More recent controversy surrounding appeals in criminal cases concerns the right of the prosecution to appeal against an acquittal. Generally, if the court (magistrates' or the jury in the Crown Court) has found the defendant not guilty, it is not possible (subject to one main exception dealt with below) for the prosecution to 'have another go'. However, in October 1999 and as a result of the MacPherson report concerning the Stephen Lawrence case, the Law Commission recommended a more flexible approach to this 'rule against double jeopardy', but without abolishing the rule.

ACTIVITY 3

Read 'Why the double jeopardy rule should be retained' by Stephen Silber QC in *Cases and Materials* (7.2) (*The Times*, 12 October 1999, Supplement page 9).

Do you think the rule should be retained?

What safeguards would you recommend to ensure both finality and justice?

The Law Commission's provisional view would be to include the following safeguards:

- new evidence (which would not have been available with due diligence at the first trial) would make the prosecution's case substantially stronger,
- overall, there should be a very high probability of a conviction at a retrial,
- a term of three years' sentence would be imposed on a not guilty plea,
- the interests of justice are satisfied,
- finally, the decision to allow a retrial would be taken by the High Court, with appeal to the Court of Appeal.

In November 1999, the Attorney-General, Lord Williams of Mostyn, suggested that the prosecution should have the right to appeal in limited circumstances against a judge's decision to direct a jury to acquit. A judge can never direct a jury to convict, but he or she has a discretion to direct a jury to acquit. Lord Williams said of prosecution appeals in these circumstances:

'If it cannot, are we not allowing in fact a system in which judges are unaccountable to the appeal courts as to a crucial aspect of their responsibilities, at the very time that we are providing them with greater powers through the implementation of the Human Rights Act 1998?' (*The Lawyer*, 6 December 1999, page 18)

However, critics believe that the plea before venue procedure introduced under the Criminal Procedure and Investigations Act 1996 (see **Chapter 6**) has already shifted the balance in favour of the prosecution and to provide an extra appeal route would be draconian, not *per se,* but in the wider context.

Lord Williams' reference to the Human Rights Act 1998 is pertinent to this debate.

Article 4 of Protocol 7 of the ECHR provides:

Article 4 – Right not to be tried or punished twice
1. No one shall be liable to be tried or punished again in criminal proceedings under the jurisdiction of the same State for an offence for which he has already been finally acquitted or convicted in accordance with the law and penal procedure of that State.
2. The provisions of the preceding paragraph shall not prevent the reopening of the case in accordance with the law and penal procedure of the State concerned, if there is evidence of

new or newly discovered facts, or if there has been a fundamental defect in the previous proceedings, which could affect the outcome of the case.

3. No derogation from this Article shall be made under Article 15 of the Convention.

ACTIVITY 4

Read 'Double Jeopardy: A Second Bite at the Cherry?' [1999] Crim LR 927 in *Cases and Materials* (7.2). Will the Commission's proposals be in line with Article 4 of Protocol 7 above?

The exceptions to the rules against double jeopardy under Article 4(2) go further than our existing law, so there is room for an expansion of the rule. The proposals appear to work within Article 4 as well in that they are limited to the discovery of new evidence which would not have been available with due diligence at the first trial. There are other concerns with the proposals, however, particularly in the proposal that a court, in deciding whether to allow a re-trial, has to use a crystal ball to predict likely sentencing on facts that may not yet be available.

There are various routes for appeal in criminal cases, but what must be borne in mind is that **the mode of appeal is always governed by the place of original trial**. This means that if a case was originally tried in the magistrates' court, then the route which an appeal will take will differ from that taken by a case which has been tried before judge and jury in the Crown Court.

7.4.1 APPEAL FOLLOWING SUMMARY TRIAL

The route for an appeal against a decision of the magistrates in a criminal case is initially **either** to the Crown Court **or** to the Divisional Court of the Queen's Bench Division of the High Court.

7.4.1.1 The Crown Court

The defendant may appeal to the Crown Court concerning a question of fact or law, i.e., he or she may dispute either the evidence or a decision on a point of law or both. The prosecution have a right of appeal from the magistrates' court to the Crown Court.

If the defendant pleaded not guilty before the magistrates, then there is a right of appeal against conviction or sentence or both. However, if the defendant originally pleaded guilty, then there is no appeal against conviction, only against sentence.

The appeal will take the form of a complete rehearing (called a 'trial *de novo*') with witnesses but without a jury, and the Crown Court may vary the original decision, or confirm it, and has the power to increase the sentence given by the magistrates, but it cannot exceed the magistrates' court's sentencing limits.

By way of further appeal, either the prosecution or the defence may require the Crown Court to state a case for the opinion of the High Court as described in **7.4.1.2**.

7.4.1.2 The Divisional Court of the Queen's Bench Division

Both prosecution and defence have the right to appeal from the magistrates' court to the Divisional Court, but only on the grounds that the magistrates' decision was wrong in law or that they exceeded their jurisdiction by making an order which was outside their powers. This is not a rehearing of the case with witnesses; instead, the magistrates 'state the case' in writing and the court works from these written documents. This procedure is known as an appeal 'by way of case stated'. The Divisional Court may confirm or alter the magistrates' decision. If the prosecution wins the case at this stage, the Divisional Court can direct the magistrates to convict and pass sentence on the defendant. Further appeal by either party is possible, from the Divisional Court direct to the House of Lords. However, before the House of Lords will hear such an appeal, the Divisional Court must certify that a point of law of general public importance is involved, **and** leave to appeal must be obtained from either court, as required by s. 1 of the Administration of Justice Act 1960.

SAQ 1

Look carefully at the respective rights of the prosecution and the defence to appeal in criminal cases which have been tried summarily, and notice how these vary. Which of the parties has the greater opportunity to challenge decisions of the lower courts?

As you may have gathered, the prosecution and the defence do not have equal rights to appeal against decisions which are adverse to them, in cases which are triable summarily. The defendant is permitted to appeal from a decision of the magistrates' court to the Crown Court, but no such possibility exists for the prosecution. With regard to the other avenues of appeal described above, the parties have the same opportunities as each other, but it does mean that if the prosecution wishes to dispute a decision of the magistrates, then this can only be done by the case stated procedure, on a point of law.

7.4.2 APPEAL FOLLOWING TRIAL ON INDICTMENT

From decisions of the Crown Court, appeal lies to the Court of Appeal (Criminal Division).

Under the Criminal Appeal Act 1968, when a person had been convicted of an offence by a judge and jury in the Crown Court, then there were important differences between the rules concerning appeal against sentence and appeal against conviction, and between appeals based on questions of law, and those based on questions of fact. The defendant had the *right* to appeal against *conviction* where the ground for appeal was a *question of law*. But if the defendant wished to appeal against conviction on a *question of fact* (or mixed law and fact), then *leave* to appeal had to be obtained, or a certificate had to be supplied by the trial judge stating that the case was fit for appeal. It was therefore much easier for a defendant to appeal against a conviction on a point of law, than if the ground of appeal was a question of fact.

This difference between the two types of appeal has been abolished by the Criminal Appeal Act 1995. The requirement of leave to appeal (or a certificate by the trial judge) will apply to all appeals against conviction.

The rules concerning appeal against sentence remain the same following the Criminal Appeal Act 1995. If the defendant accepts the fact of conviction, but wishes to appeal against *sentence*, then *leave* to appeal, or the certificate of the trial judge, must be obtained in every case. When appeal against sentence is made to the Court of Appeal (Criminal Division), the court can vary the sentence, although it cannot increase it. (But see below on the court's power to increase sentence on an appeal by the prosecution.)

There are a number of reasons for these restrictions on the defendant's right to appeal against the outcome of a trial. You will recall that, on a number of occasions in the text, your attention has been drawn to the fact that a balance has to be struck between ensuring that the liberty of the individual is protected and that people are not wrongly convicted of offences, and ensuring that the appeal system is not so overloaded that injustice results from the long waiting period for appeals to be heard.

Probably most of the defendants who are convicted of indictable offences would wish to argue that the jury's finding of fact was wrong and appeal on this basis. But there is a reluctance on the part of the Court of Appeal to question the facts as found by the jury, and so this avenue of appeal is restricted by the requirement of leave. Similarly, many defendants would probably wish to argue that their sentence should not be so severe, and so the possibility of appeal against sentence is limited, in order to ensure that only meritorious appeals reach the Court of Appeal.

From the Court of Appeal, further appeal by the defendant to the House of Lords is possible, but again there are statutory requirements which must be met before the House of Lords will hear such appeals. These are contained in the Criminal Appeal Act 1968. Section 33 of that Act stipulates that an appeal will only lie to the House of Lords if the Court of Appeal certifies that the case involves a point of law of general public importance **and** it appears that the point is one which ought to be considered by the House of Lords **and** either the Court of Appeal or House of Lords gives leave for the appeal to proceed.

SAQ 2

Compare the rules concerning appeals from the Court of Appeal to the House of Lords in civil cases with the rules which apply in criminal cases. What significant difference do you see between the two sets of rules?

There is what may seem to be a rather anomalous difference between appeals in these cases, in that in civil cases, there is no statutory requirement that the case involve a question of general public importance, whereas this is a prerequisite for criminal cases. In practice, it is likely that only those civil cases which do contain a point of law of general public importance will be heard by the House of Lords, but the technical difference is still there. The prosecution has limited rights to dispute the outcome of a case.

ACTIVITY 5

In *Cases and Materials* (7.2.3) read:

(a) s. 36 of the Criminal Justice Act 1972,
(b) s. 36 of the Criminal Justice Act 1988, and
(c) ss. 54 and 55 of the Criminal Procedure and Investigations Act 1996.

Summarise the three powers of the prosecution to appeal. Note that only one of these powers can have an effect on an acquittal - which one? Compare your answers to those in *Cases and Materials* at (7.2.1).

7.4.3   POWERS OF THE COURT OF APPEAL (CRIMINAL DIVISION)

The powers of the Court of Appeal are carefully prescribed by statute. The Criminal Appeal Act 1968 provided three different categories of cases in which the court must allow an appeal against conviction, as follows:

(a)   where the Court of Appeal thinks that the decision of the jury was unsafe or unsatisfactory, for example, if fabricated evidence was produced in court or if the trial judge had misdirected the jury;

(b)   where there was a wrong decision on a question of law, that is where the trial judge made an error on a point of law;

(c)   where there was a material irregularity in the course of the trial, for example, if the trial judge exercised his or her discretion wrongly in discharging a juror for insufficient reason.

In cases which came within these three categories, the Court of Appeal was bound to allow the appeal and quash the conviction.

The Royal Commission on Criminal Justice was of the opinion that these three categories were unsatisfactory. The wording was imprecise, and there seemed to be some overlap between them. The Criminal Appeal Act 1995 therefore abolished these three categories and replaces them with one ground only. Section 2 (1) provides that the Court of Appeal shall allow an appeal against conviction if it feels that the conviction is unsafe, and in all other cases, the appeal must be dismissed.

The meaning of unsafe.
A starting point of the meaning of 'unsafe' is the case of *R* v *Cooper* [1969] 1 QB 267:

'. . . the court must in the end ask itself a subjective question, whether we are content to let the matter stand as it is, or whether there is not some lurking doubt in our minds which makes us wonder whether an injustice has been done. This is a reaction which may not be based strictly on the evidence as such: it is a reaction which can be produced by the general feel of the case as the court experiences it.'

The Criminal Appeal Act 1968 used the terms 'unsafe or unsatisfactory'. The 1995 Act uses the term 'unsafe' only. The Court of Appeal has recently considered the difference between 'unsafe' and 'unsatisfactory' first in *R* v *Chalkley and Jeffries* [1998] 2 All ER 155 and then in *R* v *Mullen* [1999] 2 Cr App R 143.

Activities 6-8 and SAQ 3 should make you consider your own opinions on some controversial matters. Leave yourself plenty of time to read the following sources in *Cases and Materials*. Do not regard this exercise as a routine task, but as a serious, detailed exercise on moralistic, philosophical and legal matters. But don't forget to enjoy it too!

Before you start, please note that s. 78(1) of the Police and Criminal Evidence Act 1984 provides:

> In any proceedings the court may refuse to allow evidence on which the prosecution proposes to rely to be given if it appears to the court that, having regard to all the circumstances, including the circumstances in which the evidence was obtained, the admission of the evidence would have such an adverse effect on the fairness of the proceedings that the court ought not to admit it.

Activity 6 should make you consider the following.

SAQ 3

What is worse, in your opinion:

(a)   **for a guilty person to be released because the evidence against him was obtained improperly, or**

(b)   **for a guilty person's appeal to be dismissed despite the fact that the prosecution evidence against him was improperly obtained?**

ACTIVITY 6

Now read Clarke's 'Safety or Supervision? The Unified Ground of Appeal and its Consequences in the Law of Abuse of Process and Exclusion of Evidence' [1999] Crim LR 108 in *Cases and Materials* (7.2.2).

Is an *unsafe* conviction, in your opinion, the same as an *unsatisfactory* conviction?

Consider these questions, and finish Clarke's article, before moving on to the next activity. You may find it useful to make a list, containing a brief account of the facts in some of the cases mentioned and whether you agree with the judgments made, either by the relevant trial judge or the appeal court in question. Pay special attention to *R* v *Chalkley* [1998] 2 All ER 155.

In *R* v *Chalkley* [1998] 2 All ER 155, despite disapproving the trial judge's decision to allow the relevant evidence to be admitted (*i.e.* this was *unsatisfactory*), the Court of Appeal held that it did not have the power to quash the conviction unless that conviction was *unsafe*. It would appear that a conviction is unsafe where the person convicted was actually not guilty. The Court of Appeal, although specifically dealing with a s. 78 of the Police and Criminal Evidence Act 1984 matter, did not feel able to continue in a 'supervisory role', but Auld LJ did consider whether such a role would have to continue when the Human Rights Act 1998 came into force.

What sometimes worries students doing exercises like this, is the lack of clear answers forthcoming from the tutor. There is no definitive answer to the questions posed at SAQ 3 above. Different people (academics, practitioners, lawyers, lay and so on) have different perspectives on both the question and answer. Try to be clear on what *you* think, but also keep an open mind while you continue. There is still a source to go and it is the current authority.

In Clarke's last paragraph, he mentions 'invest[ing the safety test] with an element of due process'. Now read *R* v *Mullen* [1999] 2 Cr App R 143. You will now be asked to consider if the decision in *Mullen* such a 'linguistic fix'.

ACTIVITY 7

We will treat *R* v *Mullen* [1999] 2 Cr App R 143 as a case reading exercise just as you have in previous chapters. If you are working on a source material in search of the current authority or if you are investigating how a particular case has changed or developed the law, this is a good way to focus your mind on the points.

Read *R* v *Mullen* [1999] 2 Cr App R 143 in *Cases and Materials* (7.2.2).

1.   What are the central facts of the case?

2.   What was the central legal issue in the case?

3.   From the information provided within the report, trace the chronological history of the case.

4.   How did the Court of Appeal distinguish between the present case and the earlier decision of *Chalkley*? What other principles of precedent are relevant here?

5.   What issues of statutory interpretation arise in the present case?

6.   What in your opinion is the *ratio decidendi* of *Mullen*? Please restrict your answer here to the topic of appeals (the legality of the extradition is not part of the consideration here).

Compare your answers with those in *Cases and Materials* (7.2.2).

Following the decision in *R* v *Mullen* [1999] 2 Cr App Rep 143, Professor Sir John Smith stated ([1999] Crim LR 562):

> 'The word "unsafe" seems highly inappropriate for this situation. "Unsatisfactory" would be much more appropriate and it is a great pity that the word was omitted in such a short-sighted and unnecessary way. But we seem now to be close to achieving the result intended by Parliament - i.e. no change in the effect of the Criminal Appeal Act in this respect.'

He does further state, however, that: 'The dust has not completely settled'.

ACTIVITY 8

Refer back to *R* v *Mullen* **[1999] 2 Cr App R 143**. Professor Smith has identified three questions not answered by *Mullen*. Can you find them? Refer to *Cases and Materials* **(7.2.2)** for his answer.

For an excellent summary of s. 2(1) of the Criminal Appeal Act 1968, as amended, see (1999) 27 SLR 24, 'What makes the Court of Appeal think that a conviction is unsafe?' by Colin Bobb-Semple.

7.4.4   THE CRIMINAL CASES REVIEW COMMISSION

Section 17 of the Criminal Appeal Act 1968 empowered the Home Secretary to refer any case tried <u>on indictment</u> to the Court of Appeal "if he thinks fit". In 1993, the Royal Commission on Criminal Justice, the Runciman Commission, recommended:

'the responsibility for reopening cases [should be] removed from the Home Secretary and transferred to a body independent of the Government'.

At Chapter 11, para 5, the Commission stated:

'The available figures for the number of cases referred by the Home Secretary to the Court of Appeal under section 17 of the Criminal Appeal Act 1968 show that the power is not often exercised. From 1981 to the end of 1988, 36 cases involving 48 appellants were referred to the Court of Appeal as a result of the doubts raised about the safety of the convictions concerned. This represents an average of between 4 and 5 cases a year. In the years 1989-1992, 28 cases involving 49 appellants have been referred, including a number of cases stemming from the terrorist incidents of the early 1970s and inquiries into the activities of the West Midlands serious crimes squad. We were told by the Home Office that it receives between 700 and 800 cases a year which are no longer before the courts and where it is claimed that there has been a wrongful conviction. (The figure for 1992 was 790 of which 634 involved a custodial sentence.) Plainly, therefore, a rigorous sifting process is applied, and only a small percentage of cases end in a reference to the Court of Appeal under section 17.'

Year	No. of cases referred	No. of appellants	Results
1989	3	6	6 convictions quashed
1990	7	20	19 convictions quashed 1 retrial
1991	10	12	10 convictions quashed 1 retrial 1 appeal pending
1992	8	11	10 appellants pending 1 appeal dismissed

Both the retrials resulted in the defendant's acquittal.

Section 17 of the Criminal Appeal Act 1968 has been repealed and ss. 8-12 of the Criminal Appeal Act 1995 replaces the s. 17 procedure with a new statutory body, independent of the Government, called the Criminal Cases Review Commission.

The role of the CCRC is, *inter alia*, to review and investigate cases of suspected wrongful convictions and/or sentence in England and Wales and refer cases to the appropriate court whenever it feels that there is a real possibility that the conviction, verdict, finding or sentence will not be upheld. Cases originally heard at the Crown Court are referred to the Court of Appeal. Cases originally heard at the magistrates' court are referred to the Crown, so the new system includes summary convictions. To establish that there is a real possibility of an appeal succeeding regarding a conviction, there has to be an argument or evidence which has not been raised during the trial, or exceptional circumstances. To establish that there is a real possibility of an appeal succeeding against sentence, there has to be a legal argument or information about the individual or the offence which was not raised in court during the trial or at appeal.

The Commission is not a court and does not decide the appeal. It refers cases to the appropriate court. References by the CCRC take effect as if they were appeals by the convicted person under s. 1 of the Criminal Appeal Act 1968, and once the reference has been made, the CCRC has no further involvement. The CCRC may investigate cases of its own accord, or individuals may ask the Commission to investigate, but in either event, normal rights of appeal must ordinarily have been exhausted before the Commission can intervene (although failure to do this is not an absolute bar).

The first case referred to the Court of Appeal by the Commission was *R* v *Mattan, The Times,* 5 March 1998, where the conviction of a Somali Seaman was overturned, over 20 years after the Home Secretary had failed to see any reason to reopen the case under s. 17 as originally enacted. In *Mattan*, Rose LJ specifically recognised the role of the CCRC as: 'a necessary and welcome body without which the injustice in this case might never have been identified'.

On 30 July 1998, the Court of Appeal famously allowed the appeal and quashed the conviction of Derek Bentley who was hanged on 28 January 1953.

SAQ 4

A friend has been convicted of a criminal offence and asks you to which court or courts he will have to appeal in order to challenge the conviction. What is the first question you will have to ask him before you can give your reply to this question?

It will have become apparent to you in your study of the criminal justice system that cases which have been tried summarily, and cases which have been tried on indictment, are dealt with in very different ways by the courts. Your first question, therefore, to any person intending to appeal against the decision of a trial court would concern the place of original trial. As you may remember from the beginning of this section, it is the place of original trial which determines the mode of appeal, and therefore once this is ascertained, you will be able to advise your friend as to the appropriate route for the appeal.

7.5   Summary

Now that you have studied **Chapters 1** to **6**, together with the relevant sections of the *Cases and Materials,* you should be well acquainted with the different courts which make up the English legal system and with the ways in which these courts deal with different types of cases. In particular from this chapter you should be able to:

*   distinguish between the courts which deal with appeals in civil cases and those which deal with appeals in criminal cases;

*   comment on the availability of access to the appeal courts in different cases;

*   discuss the reasons for the preconditions which exist to determine whether a case may proceed to appeal stage;

*   chart the progress of a case through the appeal system.

7.6   Further Reading

Ingman, T., *The English Legal Process,* 8th edn, London: Blackstone Press, 2000, Chapter 6.

Bailey, S. and Gunn, M., *Smith & Bailey on the English Legal System,* 3rd edn, London: Sweet and Maxwell, 1996, Chapter 17.

www.open.gov.uk/lcd/consult/civ-just/appeal/appintro.htm
www.open.gov.uk/lawcomm/homepage.htm

7.7   End of Chapter Assessment Question

Turn to *Cases and Materials* (7.3) where you will find extracts from the following two cases:

(1) *Pepper* v *Hart* [1993] 1 All ER 42; and
(2) *R* v *R* [1991] 4 All ER 481.

For both of these cases, describe the route by which these cases progressed through the court system, from the first hearing to the final appeal. Include as much relevant information as possible from the report, i.e., dates and places of hearings and names of judges.

See *Cases and Materials* (7.4) for a specimen answer.

CHAPTER EIGHT

LEGAL SERVICES

8.1   Objectives

By the end of this chapter you should be able to:

*   describe the methods of funding services by private means;

*   discuss the provision of legal services from public funds;

*   appreciate the need for arbitration and other methods of alternative dispute resolution, particularly in the light of the Woolf reforms;

*   identify some of the causes of the unmet legal need and suggest solutions.

8.2   Introduction

A legal system should be accessible to all those who require it. You have come across the aims of the civil justice system in your study of the Woolf Report in **Chapter 5**. What was not discussed there, however, that will be considered here, is how legal services can be funded. The personnel involved in the provision of legal services will be considered in **Chapter 9**.

The means by which legal work has been funded have been in a constant state of flux for decades. Government proposals have recently been put into a legislative framework in the Access to Justice Act 1999. This Act is a broadly drafted statute and will require numerous regulations for it to be fully implemented.

Legal services can be costly and time consuming. One of the current approaches to these difficulties has been the development of alternative, preferably cheaper and quicker, methods of resolving disputes. Such methods will be discussed later in this chapter.

We begin by looking at the history of the legal aid system.

8.3   The History of Legal Aid

The Rushcliffe Report of 1948, which led to the Legal Aid and Advice Act 1949, clearly stated that there should be a State funded system for people 'of small *and moderate* means' (emphasis added) to enable them to pursue legal cases and for the providers of services to be paid as if their clients were paying privately. Further the system should be 'demand-led and never cash limited'. The aim of the system was, therefore, to put people who could not afford legal fees, for the first time, on the same footing as those who could. People who had the money to pay privately therefore would; others (assessed by a means test) who had a worthy case (assessed by a merits test) would benefit from State support. The two tests (means and merits) were designed to make sure that the system was fair but not a charity nor a bottomless pit of money. When it was introduced 80% of the population was eligible for some form of legal aid. Originally, the scheme was run by the Law Society.

Legal aid was not a unitary entity. There were a number of overlapping, but quite distinct schemes under which an individual may have received legal aid in both civil and criminal matters; from assistance with a divorce, to representation in a personal injury case and from the police station to a plea in mitigation before sentence.

A incredibly brief summary of the schemes that were operating at December 1999 is:

1.   Duty solicitor advice at the police station (obviously for criminal cases), available under the Police and Criminal Evidence Act 1984 and also at the magistrates' court for a first appearance on a charge where a defendant was unrepresented.

2.   Green Form (also referred to as form 10); covering a basic two hour's worth of advice and assistance, but not representation, in certain civil and criminal cases; means tested but not formally merits tested (legal providers would nonetheless give advice on the worth of the case - the chances of success).

3.   Assistance by Way of Representation, commonly referred to as ABWOR, available in some civil and criminal cases, generally for pre-trial matters where representation was required but not available under the Green Form Scheme; both means and merits tested.

4.   Full legal aid for civil cases, both means and merits tested.

5.   Full legal aid for criminal cases, again both means and merits tested.

For further information on the legal aid systems available before January 2000, see Further Reading below.

The 1970's saw a huge increase in the number of people involved in court cases and as a corollary, there was a rapid spiralling of the legal aid budget. As a result, the last two decades have seen increasingly strict conditions imposed on the eligibility for legal aid. This was generally achieved by setting the means test at a level at which only the very poor were eligible. By 1998, less than 40% of the population was entitled to legal aid. This meant that there was a considerable number of people who may have had a genuine legal claim which they were unable to pursue. These people were neither eligible for legal aid nor rich enough to pay the potential legal costs themselves from their own resources. The plight of people in this 'middle income gap' is discussed in more detail below.

SAQ 1

What factors do you think contributed to the legal aid budget spiralling over the past 20 years?

LEGAL SERVICES

Your answers may have included some of the following points. There has been an increase in the divorce rate (parties might have been eligible for up to three hours' assistance under the Green Form Scheme, or even eligible for full civil legal aid where the divorce was defended). There has also been an increase in consumer awareness, aided perhaps by the media focus on this issue. Economic factors also play an important role, especially when a recession has hit the country, as these bring about legal problems in areas such as unemployment, welfare and housing. You may have thought of other equally valid reasons, but it is clear that we have been living in an increasingly litigious country. Such litigation needs to be paid for, either privately or from public funds.

In 1988, the administration of the legal aid scheme was taken out of the hands of the Law Society and given to the newly created Legal Aid Board (LAB). In general terms, civil legal aid was granted by the LAB. Criminal legal aid was administered by local social security offices (means test) and the magistrates' courts or Crown Court where necessary (merits test).

During the mid-1980s, the previous Lord Chancellor was engaged in a series of measures designed to stem the increase in the legal aid bill. The Conservative Government suggested, and in the early 1990s started implementing, radical proposals in relation to the legal aid system. The two most controversial were franchising and block contracting. Franchising is essentially where a legal services provider (mainly, but not exclusively solicitors' firms) can establish and evidence certain quality assurance and management criteria to the Legal Aid Board. The LAB, if satisfied, would grant the provider a franchise and then devolve certain powers to the provider. The benefits of being a franchisee would be administrative convenience and a quicker service for the customer. Franchised firms would be financially rewarded too. Legal aid would not be restricted to franchised firms in the first instance, but is was clear that a franchised firm would have a 'competitive advantage' according to Slapper and Kelly (*English Legal System*, 4th edn, Cavendish: London, 1999, p. 453).

It was felt that the only way to keep a rein on the legal aid bill was to set the amount of money available in advance, making the system supply rather than demand led. Block contracting was the system where each regional Legal Aid Board received a single lump sum at the start of each financial year. Providers of legal services (originally not restricted to franchise holders) then bid to their regional LAB for part of that fixed, pre-set budget and supplied the relevant legal aid work under an annual contract. When the money was spent, no more would be available from central funds.

Hopes were high that the new Labour Government would abolish the franchising and contracting systems. These hopes were understandable, fuelled as they were by the denunciation of the schemes by the Labour Party when it was in opposition. In March 1998, however, Lord Irvine of Lairg, the Lord Chancellor, in an oral statement to the House of Lords, declared:

> 'At present the legal aid system is failing us all. It is failing the many millions of people on modest incomes who do not qualify for legal aid and who simply cannot contemplate going to law because of the potential legal costs if they lose. It is failing people on legal aid, because the Government cannot direct money to those who need it most and to those cases where there is a public interest in seeing justice done. Finally, it is failing the taxpayer who year on year is being asked to pay more and more, and yet can rarely get help from legal aid when it is actually needed.
>
> But even though legal aid is costing us more and more with costs running away ahead of inflation, it is helping fewer and fewer people each year. It is, therefore, our intention to modernise the way in which civil cases are paid for. We want a system of civil justice which is there for everyone when they need it, not just for the rich or for the very poor. We intend to transform the legal aid scheme so that we ensure we get good value for money from those

lawyers who are paid from legal aid; and so that we spend taxpayer's money on those who need it most and on those areas where it can do most good.'

Perhaps this stance is not surprising however, when one looks at the finances involved.

Criminal legal aid cost the taxpayer £733m in 1997-1998, a rise of 44% since 1992-1993, but the number of criminal legal aid orders (i.e. cases) rose by only 10%. This indicates the system was helping proportionately fewer people but was almost double the cost. Further, approximately 94% of defendants obtained criminal legal aid without making a contribution. This indicated that the means assessment was a waste of time and resources. In some cases (usually high profile), a defendant's assets were frozen for the duration of a case, so an apparently wealthy defendant was able to receive legal aid. This adversely affected public confidence in the system.

Civil and family legal aid cost £793m in 1997-1998, a rise of 35% since 1992-1993.

8.4 Public Funding Today

On 27 July 1999, the Access to Justice Act 1999 (AJA 1999) was given Royal Assent. Section 1 establishes the Legal Services Commission (LSC) which replaces the Legal Aid Board and takes over an estimated £1.6b annual budget. The LSC consists of between seven and twelve members appointed by the Lord Chancellor.

ACTIVITY 1

Read s. 2 of the AJA 1999 in *Cases and Materials* (8.1). Section 1 of the AJA 1999 establishes the LSC. What does s. 2 do?

The LSC's initial responsibility was to set up, oversee and manage two further bodies; the Community Legal Service (CLS) and the Community Defence Service (CDS). The former has a much more major role in civil cases than the Legal Aid Board enjoyed. The latter will have a major role in criminal cases. Because it is envisaged that, in the longer term, there may be advantages in administering the two services separately, s. 2(1) of the AJA 1999 allows for the replacement of the LSC by these two bodies by the Lord Chancellor.

It is fair to say that by the end of 2000, legal aid as Rushcliffe foresaw had been abolished. Instead, the CLS took over the administration of the existing civil legal aid system and overhauled the way the system operates. It has a duty to investigate where advice and assistance for civil matters is needed and provide a comprehensive service where such need is identified. It will enter into a number of partnerships continuing New Labour's aim to involve the private sector in public services. It will be funded, but not exclusively, by the Government. Other regional or local providers, such as local authorities, are expected to assist, but have not been put under a statutory duty to do so. Where a person is unable to pay for legal services, some financial assistance may be available in the form of the CLS Fund. The fund provides financial assistance in cases where a Conditional Fee Agreement (CFA, see below) cannot be used. If a conditional fee agreement *can* be used, no State representation is available. This is especially controversial as personal injury cases *may* be funded by CFAs. Certain types of case will be prioritised (subject to the availability of finances), however, such as those involving welfare, children and protecting people from violence.

New ways to deliver legal information and advice are being developed, such as through the Internet, digital television, telephone information and advice lines and so on. The Lord Chancellor's Department, in a press release in May 1999, foresaw a 'virtual legal advice arcade' on-line. Two important web sites that have started the ball rolling are at www.lawcentres.org.uk (the Law Centres site) and www.adviceguide.org.uk (the site for the National Association of Citizen's Advice Bureaux). The LSC is also expected to be innovative in this area.

Both the CLS and the CDS will purchase legal services from franchised providers. This means that public legal services will be available on an exclusive basis from franchise holders. Legal aid operated on a non-exclusive contracting basis which meant any lawyer could take on a legal aid case. There was no way of controlling quality. An exclusive contracting system means firms have to be able to evidence quality standards and the public will be assured of this by way of a CLS kitemark.

Before the enactment of the AJA 1999, the Law Society's *Gazette* Editorial (24/4/99) commented:

> 'The prospect that in the future the number of outlets providing publicly-funded legal services will be radically reduced is one of the most insidious aspects of the government's flagship Access to Justice Bill. The government's legal aid contracting proposals will inevitably lead to fewer providers, and the logical consequence of this is that access to legal advice will be reduced for perhaps some of the most needy citizens.'

You can see, therefore, that the new system is not without controversy and most legal commentators regard the short title of the Access to Justice Act 1999 as an ironic misnomer.

Exclusive block contracting operates on the basis of fixed fees especially in criminal cases. In the White Paper released in December 1998, the Lord Chancellor stated:

> 'Fixed prices create an incentive to avoid delay, and reward efficient practice.
>
> Contracts would be developed and implemented gradually in the light of experience. Subject to this, the long term aim is to establish contracts with solicitor's firms to cover the full range of defence services, from advice at the police station to representation in court; but where the case requires the services of a specialist advocate in the Crown Court, to provide this through a separate contract. Defendants would in practice enjoy a wide choice of representation of assured good quality. The CDS would also be able to employ lawyers directly to offer services to the public, as well as contracting with lawyers in private practice.'

By 2003, the CDS will be able to employ lawyers as employees rather than by having a contract with a private firm. This would, in all likelihood, parallel the operation of the Crown Prosecution Service (CPS). The Lord Chancellor believes that operating a system of salaried defenders will provide a competitive spur for the private sector.

SAQ 2

How can a salaried defence lawyer, a public servant, be free from the influences of the prosecution if he or she is paid by the Government, who also pays the prosecutor? What issues arise in your opinion?

At least two issues arise here. The first is the extent to which a person has the right to choose their own legal adviser even if they need State assistance to pay his or her fees. The second is the extent to which a fair trial can be ensured when it is the State that is both prosecuting (CPS) and defending (CDS).

ACTIVITY 2

Read s. 58(1) of the Police and Criminal Evidence Act 1984 and Article 6(3) of the European Convention on Human Rights in *Cases and Materials* (8.1). Tackle the SAQ above again in the light of these two sources. Do they change your opinion at all?

The Government accepts that exclusive contracting inevitably involves some restriction on the unfettered choice of lawyer that clients have previously enjoyed. Bearing Article 6(3) of the ECHR and s. 58(1) of the PACE 1984 in mind, the Lord Chancellor will make regulations about the extent to which defendants can choose their own representation and a literal reading of the two sources above certainly indicates that the provision of a 'State' defender is *not* contrary to existing law. That the CPS and CDS are both State funded may be a different matter that is yet to be tackled now that the Human Rights Act 1998 is in force. For further 'fair trial' issues under Article 6, see **Chapter 9**.

The means test for criminal cases will be abolished. Instead, judges will be able to order wealthy defendants to repay the costs of their representation at the end of the case. It may be that during the course of a trial, assets of a defendant come to light, or frozen assets are 'defrosted' and the judge can order costs against these. However, CDS Fund availability will be subject to the same merits test as was full criminal legal aid; that is whether it is in the interests of justice. Briefly, the court has to examine the effect a conviction would have on the defendant's reputation, livelihood or liberty, whether the defendant is facing a prison sentence, the complexity of the case, whether the defendant is capable of understanding the proceedings and whether it would be in the interests of another person, for example the alleged victim or a child, for the defendant to be represented.

It is expected that contracting with solicitors' firms will in time lead to a full range of defence services, from advice at the police station to representation in court, to be covered.

A party applying to the CLS Fund in a civil case will be subject to a Funding Assessment of their case, judged within Government-set priorities. Such an assessment would take into account, *inter alia*, whether the case could be resolved in another way (e.g. mediation, see below); whether the case could be funded in another way (e.g. conditional fee agreement, see below); and how the case fits into the identified priorities and available resources of the region. The legal strength of the case will be examined, the prospects of success, the ratio of potential benefit to the likely costs and the wider public interest. The Government has made it very clear that there is no automatic right to public funding. The resources are most definitely finite.

However, one weakness of the new scheme is that civil cases can never be prioritised over criminal cases.

SAQ 3

Why not?

Our obligations under the ECHR and the Human Rights Act 1998 prevent the State limiting access to criminal advice and representation. Accordingly, criminal cases must be prioritised. It is a shame, however, that certain funds have not been ringfenced for civil group actions or high profile civil test cases. The amount of money available for civil cases is likely to be reduce in any event. The criminal legal aid bill has increased by 44% in five years. Now that the Human Rights Act 1998 is in force, it is anticipated that there will be even more demand on funds for criminal work. Civil work, unless privately funded, could be squeezed out.

The new civil cases provisions came into force in April 2000 and the criminal provisions are expected to start in April 2001. From January 2000, however, only contract holders have been able to provide publicly funded advise and assistance, albeit under the old legal aid schemes for a few months.

SAQ 4

Exclusive contracting has consequences for the consumer of legal services. Can you suggest what these consequences might be?

Firms which do not have a franchise, or which have elected not to apply for a franchise, are not able to give State funded advice or provide State funded representation. Non-franchised firms who have relied in the past on legal aid may go under if they cannot find other sources of funding. Consumers will inevitably lose the right to choose to go to these firms if they don't exist! However, consumers (*when* they find a firm) will know that the firm has proven quality standards and the Government will be able to control quality and the budget.

SAQ 5

What were Lord Rushcliffe's original aims for legal aid? Make a list of how these aims have not, and perhaps could not, be met in today's society.

On the one hand, a legal aid system that was demand led and never cash limited would provide a comprehensive scheme ensuring anyone who could not afford to pursue a legal case privately could do so with public assistance. However, with spiralling costs, increased litigation and an inability to control the legal aid expenditure when lawyers accept legal aid work and then sent their bill the State, retrospectively as it were, for work done, put impossible demands on the taxpayer. The AJA 1999 changes (according to the Lord Chancellor) should target 'legal aid' under the two new funds on real needs within a pre-set budget that the taxpayer can afford, with fixed fees. A supply led budget benefits the consumer; a demand led budget only benefits the lawyer, says the Government.

8.5   The Unmet Legal Need

The unmet need for legal services has been mentioned briefly above. It is the situation where lawyers are used by a narrow social group for a narrow range of services. It is where an identifiable majority, or at least a very large minority, of citizens have a legal need which, for one reason or another is unmet.

The unmet need first attracted attention in the 1970s following Zander's article 'Who goes to Solicitors?' (1969) 66 LS Gaz 174, and again in 1988 when the Marre Committee, in its report 'A Time for Change: Report of the Committee on the Future of the Legal Profession' suggested several reasons why a person may be (or feel) excluded from access to legal services.

SAQ 6

From your reading so far, can you suggest at least a couple of reasons why there is an unmet legal need? Do not try to suggest solutions to the problem yet.

The Marre Committee suggested a range of reasons why the unmet legal need exists. First, a person may fail to see a problem as being a legal problem. This could arise, for example, in family or employment disputes. The committee also identified barriers within the legal profession; lawyers may be perceived as being inaccessible and elitist. You may also have identified cost as being a (or the) major barrier to achieving access to legal services. Geographical issues may also be identified as the urban population has undoubtedly easier access than the rural population to solicitors and other legal advisers. We have also already identified a large category of person who knows the problem is a legal one and wishes to pursue a case, but cannot do so as they fall into the 'middle income gap'.

The unmet legal need debate is far from over.

ACTIVITY 3

Read the article by Anne Johnson 'Paths to justice - going to law' ([1999] NLJ 1756) in *Cases and Materials* (8.2). Are there any factors identified that would indicate a change to the unmet needs mentioned by the Marre Committee over a decade ago?

Sadly it seems little has changed since the 1980s, except, perhaps the positive feelings expressed at the end of the article. However, in this article, you will have come across a number of suggested solutions to the unmet legal need which you can now use in SAQ 7 below.

SAQ 7

What are the solutions to the unmet legal need? Make a list of those which you know to exist from your general knowledge and reading so far. You may also wish to make a separate list of those solutions you would like to see in place but which are not.

Once you start to think about this question, you will probably find you know more about schemes that can solve the unmet need than you thought you did. For example, help with legal matters is often offered by trades unions and some legal commentators predict the role of the trades unions will be pivotal to many otherwise unrepresented parties now that the Human Rights Act 1998 is in force. Motoring associations also offer assistance with legal matters to their members. It is also possible to obtain insurance to cover legal expenses. Policies are available which enable the insured person to insure against legal costs up to a certain limit in prescribed categories of cases.

In addition, members of the public are able to get legal advice from Citizens' Advice Bureaux, Law Centres, Libraries, on the Internet or legal advice clinics run by local councils, MPs or Law Schools within Universities.

SAQ 8

Consider the changes made to legal services over the past year. Do you think the unmet legal need will now be met?

In 1990, the restrictions placed on solicitors' advertising were lifted. This started to empower people to take legal action as they became aware a problem they had was a legal one. We have also seen an increase in televised consumer programmes and even dramatisations are becoming more realistic allowing people to identify their legal issues. Such programmes may make lawyers seem less isolated from society (but see **Chapter 9**). On the other hand, the AJA 1999 changes may make lawyers geographically less accessible particularly in rural areas. The merging and other growth of legal firms (with the possible widespread introduction of multi-disciplinary partnerships, see **Chapter 9**) will reduce the total number of firms in the country and therefore inevitably the consumer's choice of firms. The failure of the Government to impose a statutory duty on local authorities to provide CLS funding will mean that the availability of legal services will be a matter of geographical pot lock.

The Government is aware of the unmet legal need and has attempted to placate the critics of the new system by extending the use of conditional fee agreements. These are the arrangements which it is possible for clients to make with their solicitors, sometimes referred to as 'no win no fee' arrangements, which are designed for use in contentious cases; that is, legal disputes between parties, which may lead to court proceedings.

8.6 Conditional Fee Agreements

The terms *conditional fee agreements* and *contingency fee agreements* are sometimes used interchangeably in textbooks, but there were some historically subtle and important differences between the two and the legal profession treated them differently in practice. The underlying theory was the same, however; that the solicitor undertook legal work for a client on the basis that no fee was payable if the case was lost, but if the client was successful in litigation, then the solicitor obtained his or her costs.

Until recently, both types of agreements were regarded as being against public policy because, in effect, they gave the lawyers a financial stake in his or her client's case. This would increase the risk of there being a conflict of interest for the solicitor. However, towards the end of the 1980s, the rising costs of litigation and the increasing difficulty of obtaining legal aid led to a recognition that agreements of this nature enabled clients to pursue legal claims for which they could not pay by any other means. This would provide access to justice which would otherwise be denied.

Section 58 of the Courts and Legal Services Act 1990 (CLSA) first sanctioned the use of **conditional fee agreements**. The Access to Justice Act 1999 has extended their availability.

ACTIVITY 4

In *Cases and Materials* (8.3), you will find an extract from s. 58 of the CLSA 1990. Read the section provided then answer the following questions.

(a) In what type of case can conditional fee agreements *not* be made?

(b) What format do the parties have to use for such an agreement?

(c) How does the client know how much money the solicitor will be allowed to claim if the conditions for payment are satisfied?

Section of the 58A CLSA 1990 as amended expressly excludes a number of cases from the operation of such agreements. These are concerned with divorce and other matrimonial matters, domestic violence cases and cases involving children such as adoption. You may have noticed from s. 58(3)(c) as amended that before conditional fee agreements could be used by the legal profession, it was possible for the Lord Chancellor to prescribe certain rules which were to be observed in all cases. Originally, the rules issued by the Lord Chancellor under the CLSA 1990 as originally enacted (Conditional Fee Regulations 1995 (S.I. 1995 No. 1675)) permitted conditional fee agreements to be used only in personal injury cases, insolvency cases and matters involving the European Court of Human Rights. As part of the overhaul of the civil legal aid system, most personal injury and non-family cases are no longer eligible for 'legal aid' or the new CLS fund. As a result, the use of conditional fee agreements has been extended under the Conditional Fee Agreement Regulations 2000 (SI 2000 No 692) by the Lord Chancellor, Lord Irvine, under the AJA Act 1999. Essentially, no win no fee agreements may be used in all except certain family and all criminal cases.

Conditional fee agreements also have to comply with the requirements of s. 58(3)(a) as amended by being in written form, and s. 58(4), stating the circumstances in which the legal fees would be payable, and specifying the percentage by which the standard fees would be increased in the event of successful litigation. This is called the 'success fee'. This latter point is a significant feature of this type of arrangement, and the percentage uplift on the fees has to be stated in this way so the client is aware of how much more money they will be required to pay as a result of using this method. The Lord Chancellor has provided that the allowable uplift on *fees* is 100% (although this is currently under review), and thus solicitors agree with their clients that the client will pay no fee to the solicitor if the case is lost (except the costs of disbursements), but could be liable to pay *double* the standard fee if the litigation was successful.

The uplift has generally been limited, however, to no more than 25% *of the total award of damages*. This is not a legal limit, but a voluntary limit suggested by the Law Society.

EXAMPLE
A sues B and wins.
A is awarded £2,000 damages.
A's solicitor's standard costs are £1,000.
A has an agreement with his solicitor for a 75% uplift, so the uplift should be £750.
However, as £750 is more than 25% of the damages, the uplift is limited to £500.

Under the CLSA 1990 as originally enacted, the lawyer's costs were paid by B as the loser of the case (this is a doctrine called 'costs follow the event'). *The uplift in fees was paid by the winner, i.e. A.*

This is not precisely the same under the AJA 1999, however. As the White Paper to the AJA 1999 *Modernising Justice* (December 1998) stated:

> 'The Bill would reform the law relating to conditional fees by allowing the court to order that a successful litigant should recover the success fee payable under the conditional fee agreement, and any related insurance premium, from the other side in costs; and by removing the statutory bar on conditional fees in cases relating to the division of matrimonial property. This would extend access to justice by making conditional fees fairer and more attractive by extending their use by defendants and non-money-claimants and in certain family cases; by ensuring that the costs of legal proceedings fall on those who cause the need for litigation; by ensuring that the value of any award by the court is preserved for the person it is awarded to; and by providing better regulation of the level of uplifts and premiums.'

SAQ 9

How does this change the example above?

The AJA 1999 means that the winner (A) would *not* have to pay the success fee out of his damages, but the loser (B) could be ordered to pay the uplift in addition to the normal costs and the cost of any insurance premium A had taken out (in the event that he lost and had to pay B's costs).

A further change made by the AJA 1999 is that it is now easier for membership organisations, such as trade unions or motoring organisations, to underwrite litigation on behalf of their members.

One issue that has received some academic commentary, but as yet appears to be unresolved, is how a *whole* case can be funded on a conditional fee agreement where experts are called as witnesses. The debate is raging.

ACTIVITY 5

In *Cases and Materials* (8.3) you will find an article by Brian McConnell 'No Win, No Fee, No Way' [1999] NLJ 1760 which is based on an exchange of letters published in *Litigation Funding*, a magazine devoted to helping firms survive conditional fees.

What issues arise? Can experts work within CPR, Part 35 *and* operate on a conditional fee basis?

CPR, Part 35 imposes a primary and overriding duty to the court. A CFA results in an expert taking a financial interest in the outcome of the case. His fees depend on the success of the litigation. On the one hand, experts are professional and can keep these two issues (duties, responsibilities?) separate just as solicitors and barristers working under a CFA do. A corollary of prohibiting CFAs for experts would be a drastic reduction in the number of litigants going to court as they would not be able to afford to pay expert fees in advance. CFAs would certainly stop being any sort of solution to the unmet legal need in these circumstances.

The other side of the argument is that a court is entitled to know if an expert is being paid as a result of a CFA. The weight of his evidence may be adversely affected as a result and the litigant would be the loser in this event.

A further issue with the use of CFAs is the extent to which clients appear not to understand them.

ACTIVITY 6

Turn to *Cases and Materials* (8.3) and read the article by F. Bawdon, 'Nothing to lose?' [1999] NLJ 1890. Why does the author prefer contingency fee agreements?

Contingency fee agreements are more understandable to the client. Perhaps this is a result of the inordinate amount of televised lawyer dramatisations from the USA where fee payment often attracts at least passing attention. There are a number of problems identified that are associated with the complexity of the current provisions governing CFAs and with their expansion, things are unlikely to get any easier. And if CFAs are inherently confusing, it does not make them easier if rogue members of the legal profession fail to work within s. 58 of the CLSA 1990 as amended. Michael Gould, a solicitor and legal academic, wrote to *The Times* in 1999 (*The Times*, 23 November 1999):

'I was recently asked for advice by a student on behalf of a friend who was being asked to enter [a no-win, no-fee] agreement. The friend had been injured in an accident while a passenger in a car. The agreement provided for a charging rate of £165 per hour, whatever level of fee earner handled the case, and that the client would be responsible for the payment of the fees if he ended the agreement early. It authorised the solicitors to retain one quarter of the damages recovered.

The implication of these provisions appeared to me to be that if the client became dissatisfied with the way the office cleaner was handling his claim and took his business elsewhere he would pay at the rate referred to above. If he waited until damages were recovered (as they almost inevitably would be in these circumstances), he would hand over a quarter of his damages to his solicitors in addition to the costs they would recover from the defendant.'

SAQ 10

What part of the above CFA falls outside the requirements of s. 58 CLSA as amended?

If the student who related the information to Michael Gould had correctly understood the terms of the agreement, then under s. 58(4)(b) of the CLSA 1990 as amended, a CFA must state the percentage by which the *fees* are to be increased in the event of success. A CFA phrased in terms of a percentage share of *damages* is a *contingency* fee agreement and is thus unenforceable under the CLSA 1990 as amended.

One of the barriers to obtaining a CFA is insurance.

ACTIVITY 7

Read 'Toon fans hurt in an expensive game of two trials' (*The Times*, 16 January 2001) in *Cases and Materials* (8.3). From the article, can you state the advantages and disadvantages insurance had on this case?

Without insurance, there would have been no case. With insurance, the case could have cost the fans far more than they could afford. Luckily, this story has a happy ending. In a letter to *The Times* (30 January 2001), Julian Harris, the solicitor mentioned in the article, revealed that Newcastle United Football club had agreed in November 2000 'to retain the legal expenses indemnity moneys and . . . not pursue any claim for costs against individual claimants beyond their insurance cover'.

The moral of the story is, however, important and one wonders how many litigants who have taken out AEI have been left in this situation.

8.7 Alternative Means of Resolving Disputes

Alternative dispute resolution (ADR) is any way of resolving a dispute without going to court. Broadly speaking, there are four identifiable methods of ADR.

SAQ 11

What do you understand by the following terms? Do they differ at all, and if so, how?

1. **Negotiation**

2. **Mediation**

3. **Conciliation**

4. **Arbitration**

The new Woolfian landscape encourages out of court settlements. One of the best ways to achieve dispute resolution is to negotiate a settlement. This may be the most informal of methods of resolving problems. It includes everything from having a chat with a neighbour about noise or parking; to tense discussions between partners about contact with children. Wherever the two conflicting parties try to resolve their dispute without any help or assistance from a third party, it is negotiation.

Traditionally, the term mediation was where the two conflicting parties were joined by a neutral third party (the mediator). The mediator's role is to help parties find a solution. In conciliation, the conciliator takes a more active role, suggesting the solution. You will find that the term 'conciliation' is gradually falling into disuse and the process is now regarded as a form of mediation.

ACTIVITY 8

Read in *Cases and Materials* (8.4) 'The lawyer as adviser and advocate' [1997] NLJ 1686 and 'How to settle disputes - without a legal punch up' (*The Times*, 3 August 1999). Compile a list of the skills a lawyer needs to be an effective mediator.

Surely we are all superb communicators, with the ability and flexibility to facilitate agreements between conflicting parties, whilst maintaining their professional or personal relationships and our calm. With experience, we can learn how to identify the real issues in any given debate and focus on them to the exclusion of extraneous arguments, whilst keeping an open mind. We are, naturally, diplomatic and trustworthy. We might not be neutral and objective in our own matters, but find it easy to be so when working as an independent third party, respecting the confidences of the warring factions. Yes, we could all be excellent mediators. Couldn't we?

Joking aside, a trainee solicitor or barrister may well be advised that if he or she does not have the above skills either to find a new vocation, or develop them quickly. If a lawyer does not recognise and practice these skills, he or she could be running the risk of being sued for professional negligence.

Mediation is set to become an even more important feature of the legal system as the Family Law Act 1996 makes provision for the court to direct the parties to a divorce to take advantage of mediation services.

The problem with negotiation, mediation and conciliation is that they can be time-consuming and a satisfactory conclusion may not be reached so the parties may in the end have to resort to court hearings. In this unfortunate event, ADR has merely postponed the court hearing, not been an *alternative* to it.

In the last decade there has been an accelerated development of ADR schemes of different kinds, in different areas, for different purposes. ADR service providers can apply to the Legal Services Commission (previously the Legal Aid Board) to be a franchise holder and to be able to provide State funded services. In addition, the Commercial Court (part of the High Court) runs an in-house ADR scheme under the provisions of the 1996 Practice Statement called ENE (early neutral evaluation). Using ENE, a neutral professional, a lawyer or a judge, hears a summary of each party's case and gives a non-binding assessment of the merits. So far, the Commercial Court has conducted ENE in only a handful of cases, but since Woolf, there is evidence to suggest that the number of parties settling is increasing.

Arbitration is a procedure which has found particular favour between parties to commercial contracts. When the contract is drawn up, the parties agree a form of arbitration clause which provides that if a dispute occurs concerning the performance of the contract, then instead of commencing a court action, the parties will take the dispute to an independent arbitrator. This avoids the cost, delay and publicity involved in court appearances.

An example of a typical arbitration clause is:

'In the event of disputes arising over questions of interpretation of this agreement, they shall be referred to arbitration. Each party shall nominate an arbitrator who together will adjudicate any disagreement. Should the arbitrators fail to agree they shall together appoint a referee who shall adjudicate. Decisions shall be binding on both parties. Costs of arbitration shall be shared equally between the parties.'

ACTIVITY 9

A recent statute has consolidated the law in this area. In *Cases and Materials* (8.4) you will find extracts from the Arbitration Act 1996. Study the sections set out and then answer the following questions.

(a) What is the underlying philosophy of the process of arbitration?

(b) In order for the agreement to be covered by the Act, what format must be adopted for it?

(c) Who chooses the persons who will act as arbitrators?

(d) What happens if one of the parties thinks that the arbitrator is acting unfairly and is biased against him or her?

(e) What sort of remedies can be awarded to a party to arbitration?

(f) If one of the parties to the original contract begins court proceedings instead of going to arbitration, what will happen?

Section 1 of the Arbitration Act 1996 sets out the purpose of arbitration, which is to ensure that parties can choose how to settle their legal disputes fairly and without unnecessary delay or expense. In order for the Act to apply, the arbitration agreement must be in writing, although it need not necessarily be signed by the parties (s. 5). Section 16 allows the parties to agree a method for the appointment of the arbitrator, and the Act itself provides a procedure to be followed if the parties' own arrangements fail for some reason. The arbitrator selected by the parties does not have to be a person with legal qualifications. The parties may prefer to select someone who has technical knowledge relating to their business.

If in the course of the arbitration one of the parties has reason to believe that the arbitrator is not acting impartially, then under s. 24 of the Act, that party can apply to the court to have the arbitrator removed. Under normal circumstances, however, after the parties have made representations to the arbitrator, he or she will make a decision which is binding on the parties. The parties cannot seek to overturn the arbitrator's decision through the courts unless there has been a clear denial of justice.

The parties can specify in the original agreement the types of remedy which the arbitrator may award (s. 48), including the types of award normally made by a court. The aim of the exercise is to avoid court proceedings, and thus if one of the parties breaches the arbitration agreement by starting a court action, s. 9 of the Act provides that the other party can apply to have the proceedings stayed. The court is under a duty to stop the proceedings unless it appears that the arbitration agreement is invalid. The Act therefore recognises that this method of dispute resolution takes priority over court proceedings where the agreement has been validly made.

8.8   Summary

As you will realise from this chapter, the law relating to legal services is in a state of flux at the moment and for the foreseeable future. The replacement of the Legal Aid Board with the Legal Services Commission, the abolition of legal aid and the increasingly restricted scope of State funding for legal services mean that litigants musk seek other methods of funding their legal actions or find other ways in which to resolve their legal conflicts.

So after reading this chapter, you should be able to:

- discuss the changes taking place in State provision of funding for legal services;

- appreciate the mechanisms for franchising and block contracting;

- give examples of ways in which litigation may be privately funded;

- give an account of the developments in the field of alternative dispute resolution.

8.9   Further Reading

Slapper, G. and Kelly, D., *The English Legal System*, 4th edn, London: Cavendish, 1999, Chapter 8, 12.

Centre for ADR: www.cedr.co.uk

ADR Group: www.adrgroup.co.uk

Chartered Institute of Arbitrators: www.arbitrators.org

Speaight, A., 'Acting as an expert', [1997] NLJ 1116

Sampson, T., 'Arbitration Act 1996 - a fresh start?', [1997] NLJ 261

8.10 End of Chapter Assessment Question

Consider the extent to which conditional fee arrangements provide greater access to legal advice and assistance to those who would not otherwise be able to afford it.

Turn to *Cases and Materials* (8.6) for a suggested answer.

CHAPTER NINE

PERSONNEL

9.1 Objectives

By the end of this chapter you should be able to:

- analyse the contribution lay people make to the legal system;

- compare and contrast the two branches of the legal profession;

- discuss the role played by the Crown Prosecution Service;

- comment on the nature of judicial appointments and further analyse the concept of conflict of interests.

9.2 Introduction

You already know a great deal about lay people in the English legal system. In **Chapter 1,** you may have noticed that all of the Activities designed to introduce you to the law were based on the jury system. There is no need to add to the topic as studied there.

In **Chapters 5** and **6**, we also made passing reference to magistrates and we will be making a more extensive examination of their role and the composition of the magistracy hereafter.

During the last few years, significant changes have taken place in the organisation, function and funding of the legal profession. These changes have been particularly noticeable in the nature of the work undertaken by solicitors and barristers. For example, 20 years ago, the demarcation between the role of the barrister and that of the solicitor was clear, with solicitors rarely undertaking advocacy work outside the magistrates' courts. The code of professional conduct for solicitors prohibited them from advertising, and solicitors enjoyed a monopoly in conveyancing, that is, the legal work associated with the buying and selling of property.

All this has changed in the intervening period of time, and as you read this chapter you will discover how much these aspects of the profession have altered.

Since the Crown Prosecution Service (CPS) was established in 1986, it has been the subject of numerous investigations and a Royal Commission Report. It has been restructured twice. You will be considering three main aspects of the CPS: first, its pivotal role in bringing prosecutions;

secondly, the recent restructuring as a result of the Glidewell Report; and thirdly, the future for the lawyers employed by the CPS under the Access to Justice Act 1999.

The nature of judicial appointments is currently the subject of widespread debate. You will examine the 'secret soundings' system and you will consider this and other aspects of the judiciary in the light of the Human Rights Act 1998.

We begin this final chapter by completing your understanding of the system of lay participation in the court process.

9.3   Lay People

'Lay' in this context means not legally qualified or 'of the people'. Laws in this country are made and enforced on behalf *of the people*. It is a tradition that ordinary people, untrained in the law, should take part in the legal process - either as member of a jury panel or as magistrates.

As was stated above, there will be no further study of the jury system. Refer to **Chapter 1**.

9.3.1   MAGISTRATES

9.3.1.1   Introduction

The question of guilt and sentence is dealt with by magistrates in approximately 98% of all criminal cases. Strictly, however, only one of the two types of magistrate is defined as a lay person in the legal system, and even then, a legal qualification is not a bar. The two types of magistrate are:

1. Lay Magistrates, or Justices of the Peace, and;

2. Stipendiary Magistrates, who are in fact members of the judiciary.

If the English legal system had to depend on judges alone for the administration of justice, the system would grind to a halt. So, in addition to judges, there are approximately 30,000 Justices of the Peace (JPs) who are part-time, unpaid, amateur volunteers who live within 15 miles of the court area in which they work. They generally sit in benches of three. They are also not without legal guidance as they are assisted by a Bench Legal Adviser (court clerk). From 1 January 1999, all court clerks had to be legally qualified.

Section 78 of the Access to Justice Act 1999 changed the title of Stipendiary Magistrate to District Judge (Magistrates' Court) (DJ(MC)). A DJ(MC) must be a qualified solicitor or barrister of at least seven years, who works as a full-time judge in receipt of a stipend (a wage). DJ(MC)s sit alone (except in the Youth Court). The AJA 1999 merged the then separate Metropolitan and Provincial Stipendiary Magistracy.

9.3.1.2 Work

ACTIVITY 1

If necessary, refer back to Chapters 5 and 6 and remind yourself of the jurisdiction of the magistrates' court. Make a list of the work of the magistracy. You should find that it is extensive.

In criminal cases (adult and youth), the magistracy deal with remand and bail, the adjournment of cases, the determination of the guilt or innocence of the accused, passing sentence or committing for sentence where relevant. They may have to enforce financial penalties and, as examining justices, they have to determine venue for trial. They may be required to hear appeals against conviction or sentence in the Crown Court (where they sit with a judge). In civil cases, they have an important role in the Family Proceedings Court and they also deal with licensing and the non-payment of household bills.

DJ(MC)s are expected to deal with the full range of business falling to be dealt with by the lay magistracy but they may be expected to hear the lengthier and more complex matters coming before the magistrates' court.

SAQ 1

Why?

As they sit alone, they are able to hear the whole of a long case without having unnecessarily lengthy adjournments. As JPs sit in three and often have commitments outside the magistrates' court (such as employment), it can be difficult to ensure the same lay bench throughout a trial. Secondly, DJ(MC)s are qualified and are generally regarded as a great deal quicker than their lay colleagues.

9.3.1.3 Appointment

JPs are appointed by the Lord Chancellor on behalf of and in the name of the Queen under s. 5(1) of the Justice of the Peace Act 1997.

Under the Access to Justice Act 1999, the Magistrates' Courts' Committees (MCC) who have responsibility for the organisation and management of the magistrates' courts, were amalgamated to improve efficiency. The MCCs are also now required to produce Charters and Annual Reports.

The AJA 1999 established a single authority to manage the magistrates' courts service in Greater London.

Local Advisory Committees, who work under the MCCs, are required to have regard to the need to ensure that the composition of the Bench reflects the community which it serves in terms of gender, ethnic origin, occupation and political affiliation (evidence of the latter is obtained by the voting pattern in the last two elections in the relevant constituency).

New directions on the appointment of magistrates were issued to the Advisory Committees in August 1998. These include a clear job description and key qualities defining the personal suitability of candidates (good character, understanding and communication, social awareness, maturity and sound temperament, sound judgment, commitment and reliability). The new directions also include the following requirement:

> 'The political views of a candidate are neither a qualification nor a disqualification for appointment. However, the Lord Chancellor requires, in the interests of balance, that the voting pattern for the area . . . should be broadly reflected in the composition of the bench.'

Applicants go through a two stage interview process after which the Advisory Committees must consider the extent to which an applicant who is personally suitable will comply with the requirements of a balanced bench (gender etc., as listed above). It may be that an otherwise suitable candidate is disqualified on the ground that their appointment would lead to a politically unbalanced bench.

District Judges (Magistrates' Court) are appointed by The Queen on the recommendation of the Lord Chancellor. The Lord Chancellor normally only considers applicants aged 40-55. They are generally appointed from the ranks of Acting Stipendiary Magistrates (now referred to as *Deputy DJ(MC)s*) who have made it clear they would be interested in a full-time position.

9.3.1.4 Merits of the Lay Magistracy

It is seen as a fundamental right within our legal system that we are tried by our peers. Many people say the foundations of this right can be traced back to the Magna Carta 1215. This is, however, a basic misunderstanding of the Magna Carta, which, in ensuring trial by one's peers was ensuring peer trial only for *peers*, i.e. Lords. It did not include the concept of lay participation, but it is also fair to say that juries and magistrates do have a traditionally important role to play in the criminal justice system. Their contribution may help the public to have confidence in the court system; although this point is generally associated more with juries than magistrates. There is an argument, however, that the better the balance of the lay magistracy, the better public confidence is.

Statistics published by the Lord Chancellor's Department in October 1998 indicate that a national gender balance has almost been achieved. At 1 January 1998, there were 15,713 male JPs and 14,648 female. These magistrates are able to bring their local knowledge to the cases they try and sentence. They do not sit alone and they are able to deal effectively with the more straightforward cases.

9.3.1.5 Criticisms of the Lay Magistracy

ACTIVITY 2

Turn to *Cases and Materials* (9.1.1) and read 'Time to lay off lay magistrates?' (*The Times*, 9 November 1999). The author calls for the replacement of lay magistrates with DJ(MC)s. You may wish to make notes on why. What the article does not mention is the new role of lay prosecutors (designated case workers). What comments could you add to the article in view of the use of lay case workers in a court run by lay people?

An apparently straightforward case can include complex legal issues that may *not* be apparent to a lay person. We have already noted that under the Narey system, lay case workers may not, for example, be able to grasp a key, but perhaps obscure, legal point. They are unlikely to receive assistance from the bench as, although trained in legal terminology and procedure, JPs will similarly be unable to identify when a issue has become a point of law. The Bench Legal Adviser, who is legally qualified, may assist, but his or her role is to assist the bench, not the prosecutor.

At the turn of the last century, appointment to the lay magistracy was based entirely on a property qualification and on a recommendation to the Lord Chancellor by Lord Lieutenants and MPs, who were often motivated by the wishes of the local political parties. The Royal Commission on Justices of the Peace (1946-1948) chaired by Baron du Parcq, expressed a minority view (3 from 16) that so long as JPs were drawn from every social class, no regard should be had to political affiliation.

In October 1998, the Lord Chancellor's Department Consultation Paper *Political Balance in the Lay Magistracy* pointed out that in 1997 the Labour Party saw its share of the vote increase from 34.4% to 43.2% - a 10% swing from Conservative to Labour.

SAQ 2

How quickly does this have to be reflected in the Magistracy?

Do you think it should it be?

Are you aware of any other member of the legal system who has to declare political affiliation?

If the need for political balance is to achieve a balance of the classes, do you agree that political affiliation is determined by social class?

If political affiliation were to be abolished as a criteria for selection, would it be replaced and if so, with what?

Political affiliation should be reflected on a local, constituency basis, using data from the previous two elections. No other public appointment is subject to political screening in this way and a number of investigations and reports show that there is very little to link political views and social class. You may or may not agree.

The LCD Report (above) suggested that if the current tests were to be abolished, they could be replaced with the geodemographic classification scheme. This would incorporate a wide range of socio-economic factors, but the most recent national study was completed in 1991.

The Lord Chancellor has temporarily abandoned the search for alternative criteria upon which to appoint lay magistrates and for now the political affiliation of the bench is to be a factor for appointment. Lord Irvine reluctantly concluded that political affiliation appears to be the most practical method of obtaining a balance in the social classes of the bench.

9.4   The Legal Profession

Legal work as a whole involves a great many different personnel, who perform widely varying roles. Thus in the course of your involvement with the law you may encounter 'paralegal' workers, such as qualified Legal Executives, licensed conveyancers, and different types of legal clerks. However, the terms 'lawyer' and 'legal profession' are generally understood to describe those who belong to the two branches of the profession, that is, solicitors and barristers.

9.4.1 SOLICITORS

9.4.1.1 Organisation

The Law Society of England and Wales is the governing body for solicitors, influencing all aspects of training, professional conduct and the organisation of the profession. Numerically solicitors form a much larger body than barristers and are more accessible to the public, solicitors' firms being found in the high streets of every town. Clients can employ the services of a solicitor directly which is not always the case with barristers.

SAQ 3

Estimate the number of solicitors and barristers in the country. Do you think the profession has grown or diminished in size over the last 30 years? What percentage of each profession is female? Compare your answer with the figures in *Cases and Materials* (9.2.1).

Solicitors are able to advertise their services (within the limits of the professional rules), and this enables potential clients to select a practitioner with experience of their particular legal problem. We have discussed this already in the context of the unmet legal need (**8.5** above).

A solicitor can choose to work alone as a sole practitioner in his or her own firm, but most work in partnerships with each other in private practice, offering their services to the public in general. A smaller number are employed in industry or in local or central government or for the Crown Prosecution Service (see **9.4.4** below).

9.4.1.2 Training

Most solicitors (approx. 60%) are law graduates. The remainder are either graduates of another discipline who have undertaken a conversion course in law (the Common Professional Examination or the Post Graduate Diploma in Law) or have qualified though the Institute of Legal Executives route (ILEX). ILEX is a body that allows a person to qualify whilst working in a law firm and taking a part time course of study. All potential solicitors must complete a professional course, the Legal Practice Course, which prepares them for the practical aspects of the work and then serve a prescribed period of 'articles' (usually two years) attached to a practising solicitor. At this stage, the trainee solicitor is in effect serving an apprenticeship. The trainee will be salaried during the term of articles. Obtaining training contracts is not easy, but as there are far more solicitors' firms than barristers' chambers, more places are available for trainee solicitors than budding barristers.

9.4.1.3 Work

Solicitors are largely occupied in providing legal services to clients on a face-to-face basis, or by telephone or letter. They have direct personal contact with clients and therefore need to employ personnel to assist in proving this service.

Increasingly, solicitors tend to specialise in their work in order to gain expertise in particular areas of the law. Within a firm in private practice, therefore, you may find different departments specialising in, for example, criminal matters, family law, probate (i.e. dealing with the property of those who have died), land law matters, and civil cases such as personal injuries. In the past, solicitors enjoyed a complete monopoly in matters of conveyancing (i.e. transferring ownership in land from one person to another), but in 1985, the first significant change in the work of solicitors occurred. The Administration of Justice Act 1985 (Part II) introduced a system of licensed conveyancers which allowed non-solicitors to carry out work for members of the public, for a fee.

SAQ 4

Consider who would have been eager for the solicitors' monopoly on conveyancing to be broken? Which other type of service provider would take advantage of the new licensed conveyancing system?

Estate agents wanted to be able to enter competition with solicitors. There is a growing culture in this country and elsewhere for what is often referred to as a 'one-stop-shop'. This means *one* professional service provider who is able to provide all of the relevant services for a particular range or type of transaction(s). Consumers are believed to want access to one professional; for example, an estate agent to show them properties, advise them on finance and mortgages, and convey the relevant land, without having to use, unless they wish, three different advisers.

In addition to the traditional conveyancing monopoly enjoyed by solicitors, practice rules of the court and tribunals ensured that only barristers had the right of advocacy in the House of Lords, Court of Appeal and High Court. Barristers also had a virtual monopoly in the Crown Court. As long ago as 1979, the exclusivity of the work of solicitors and barristers had been questioned by the Benson Commission on Legal Services.

The next significant change in the work of solicitors occurred in the Courts and Legal Services Act 1990.

ACTIVITY 3

Turn to *Cases and Materials* (9.2) and read ss. 17 and 37 of the Courts and Legal Services Act 1990, and then consider the following questions.

(a) What was the purpose of this part of the legislation?

(b) What were the implications for the legal profession?

(c) In authorising persons to provide conveyancing services, what does it appear were the concerns of the Authorised Conveyancing Practitioners Board (referred to in s. 37(1))?

The solicitors' monopoly over conveyancing had already been broken in 1985. Section 37 of the CLSA 1990 ensured that non-solicitors involved in conveyancing work would be suitably qualified, accountable and insured against the risk of loss to the client.

The CLSA 1990 was introduced with the specific aim of developing and improving the way in which legal services were offered to the public. Section 17(1) made it clear that the Act was an attempt to strike a balance between the desire to ensure that justice was administered properly and the wish to allow people other than members of the two professions to carry out some of the work which had hitherto been reserved for barristers and solicitors alone. This meant for the first time, the profession was faced with competition for its clients. The hope of those drafting the legislation was that this element of competition would lead to better services being offered to the public, for realistic fees.

Despite that fact that the Benson Commission recommended that no change should be made in the rights of audience in the courts, solicitors challenged the position whereby they enjoyed advocacy in the magistrates' and county courts only. Solicitors who, for example, had carefully prepared a case for Crown Court trial were frustrated that they had to hand over the case to a barrister (who would be less acquainted with it) for presentation at court.

Section 27 of the CLSA 1990 established a new system for authorising professional bodies to grant rights of audience and rights to conduct litigation to their members. Thus, for example, since 1993, the Law Society has been able to grant a Certificate of Advocacy to those solicitors who met the necessary training requirements, but it has become clear that at least some of the hopes for the new scheme have not been met. It was too complex and slow a system. Approximately 1,000 solicitors have applied for higher rights, and those that have, rarely get the opportunity to exercise them. Further, it was not until 1997 that employed solicitors (see in particular the CPS at **9.4.4** below) gained any new rights and even then, they were very limited. It was not until April 1998 that the Institute of Legal Executives was able to grants rights of audience in lower courts to its Fellows.

ACTIVITY 4

Read ss. 36, 39, 40 and 42 of the Access to Justice Act 1999 in *Cases and Materials* (9.2.1). Briefly explain the effect of each section.

Section 36 provides that all suitably qualified advocates should enjoy full rights of audience before the courts subject to the requirements of the authorised bodies. This section came into force on 27 September 1999. The higher courts did not, however, see a mass of solicitors running in on that day to present cases, as the Law Society will continue to require solicitors to apply for a higher courts qualification.

Section 39 allows for a person with rights of audience to change profession and for those rights of audience to follow him. Once a person is an authorised advocate, a change of employment from barrister to solicitor, say, will not result in a loss of advocacy rights. They are portable.

Section 40 specifically identifies the authorised bodies as the Law Society, the Bar Council and the Institute of Legal Executives.

Section 42 imposes a statutory, ethical, primary and overriding duty to the court to act with independence in the interests of justice. This duty overrides any other obligations, including contractual obligations to an employer.

9.4.1.4 Complaints

There are a number of issues with which you need to be familiar here. Many of the points made below apply equally to solicitors and barristers.

The first issue for examination is the nature of self regulation. The Law Society expects a solicitors' firm to be able to deal with a complaint internally. Failure to do so can lead to the firm being fined. The Access to Justice Act 1999 extends the power of the Law Society to investigate and discipline solicitors who break professional rules or provide an inadequate standard of service.

The Office for the Supervision of Solicitors (the OSS) was set up by the Law Society in 1996 following concerns about how its predecessor (the Solicitors Complaints Bureau) operated. The OSS has not faired any better. The Law Society in general and the OSS in particular are in trouble. The Legal Services Ombudsman (below) is currently satisfied with only 67% of complaints dealt with by the OSS (a decrease from the 70% with which she was satisfied in 1997). To put the role of the OSS in context, however, during 1996/7, the number of complaints against solicitors was rising at 39% per month whilst 950 firms generated 80% of the total number. In the same period, the OSS has added only 4% more staff and a 10% increase in its budget. As a result, the second annual report of the OSS (December 1998) warned that the average delay of six months before a complaint was allocated to a case worker would increase to 12 months by the end of 1999. It did not help the situation, however, that the OSS failed to meet many of the targets it set itself.

In fact, during 1999, the Law Society had to allocate a further £10m to the OSS which has allowed the OSS to employ an additional 150 staff, 100 of them as case workers.

The next issue is the role of the Legal Services Ombudsman. The post was originally established by the Courts and Legal Services Act 1990 to be a further level to which a dissatisfied customer could take a complaint. For example, in 1997, the Ombudsman dealt with one complaint for every three solicitors, one for every 21 practising barristers and one for every six licensed conveyancers. In 1998, the complaints were one in 2.4, one in 18 and one in six respectively. The current Legal Services Ombudsman is Ann Abraham. The AJA 1999 widens the powers of Ombudsman including granting her the power to make a *binding* award of compensation for the first time.

The AJA 1999 has provided for a further level of supervision of the self regulation of the professions. It has given the Lord Chancellor the power to appoint a Legal Services Complaints

Commissioner (LSCC) to oversee the handling of all complaints. The new LSCC is not expected to be appointed until mid-2001 at the earliest.

The final issue is the controversial immunity that lawyers in certain situations enjoyed. Refer to Activity 5 below (**9.4.2.4** complaints).

9.4.2   BARRISTERS

You have already examined much of the work of barristers indirectly as a result of the activities above. What we have not considered, however, is why there is a divided profession in England and Wales. This division has its roots in history and although critics point out that the system can result in duplication of effort, increased costs and sometimes confusion for the public, suggestions that there should be fusion (i.e. one single profession of 'lawyer') have never been accepted by either branch of the profession. Perhaps in view of the changes in the work done by each branch, fusion is no longer the issue it once was. The abolition of the traditional monopolies has blurred the line of demarcation between solicitors and barristers.

9.4.2.1 Organisation

From as early as the fourteenth century, the Bar has been organised around the four Inns. These are Inner and Middle Temple (taken over from the Order of Knights Templar), Lincoln's Inn (from the Earl of Lincoln) and Gray's Inn (from an association with the de Gray family). Since the seventeenth century, it was necessary to belong to one of the Inns to practice advocacy. The Inns are responsible for the 'call to the Bar', part of the procedure by which students become qualified barristers. The General Council of the Bar of England and Wales, commonly referred to as the Bar Council, is the governing body of the profession and is responsible for its Code of Conduct, complaints and disciplinary matters, standards, ethics and education and training. Its regulatory framework is provided for in the Courts and Legal Services Act 1990. The Council in fact operates on the basis of a series of committees, each with clear responsibility for different areas of professional work.

Barristers do not form (are somewhat controversially prohibited from forming) partnerships as solicitors do. Instead, they take tenancies in 'chambers', most of which are in London, which enables them to share office space, secretarial support, library resources, and most importantly, a clerk who acts a business manager. When a solicitor sends instructions (known as a 'brief to counsel') to chambers for the attention of a barrister, unless a particular barrister has been named on the brief, the clerk will allocate it to a member of the chambers and will also arrange the fee. The clerk is therefore able to control the amount of work which each barrister receives.

9.4.2.2 Training

Most barristers are graduates, but it is not necessary to have a degree in law to be called to the Bar, as conversion courses are available for graduates of other disciplines. A Bar student must become a member of one of the Inns of Court, eat a certain number of dinners there (known as 'keeping terms'), and complete a course of study leading to the Bar Finals Examination. Once the examination stage has been successfully completed, the student is called to the Bar and can then undertake the next stage in the process known as 'pupillage'.

This is the practical stage of training, and without it, a barrister is not able to practise. The newly called barrister has to find an established barrister who will take her or him as an 'apprentice' for one year. During that year, the pupil is not allowed to accept instructions until the second six months of the training. Once pupillage is completed, the barrister can look for a place in chambers from which to work. Competition for such places is extremely fierce.

SAQ 5

What sort of impression are you gaining about the conditions under which barristers work and the training which they undergo? Think about the following questions:

(a) Why is it beneficial to barristers to work in sets of chambers?

(b) What do you think is the point of the Bar student having to dine at the Inn to which he or she belongs?

(c) How do you suppose Bar students support themselves during the training period?

As you may have realised by now, barristers form a quite exclusive group, with their own rules of conduct and very ancient traditions, and to gain entry to this group is not easy. Their professional rules prohibit them from forming partnerships, but from an economic point of view, it obviously makes sense for them to share expensive resources, such as premises and library facilities – hence the formation of sets of chambers.

Because of the need for students to become acquainted with the customs and etiquette of the Bar, the requirement that they keep terms by dining at their chosen Inn for a specified number of times helps them to discover how the Inns work and the type of conduct which is expected. This does, however, involve a certain amount of expense in addition to the fees required for attending Bar School. Although a limited number of scholarships and bursaries are available, students generally have to support themselves, usually by means of loans, during their training period. This situation is aggravated by the fact that the newly qualified barrister is restricted in his or her earning capacity during the first six months of pupillage, so potential barristers require a great deal of determination and a reliable source of financial support if they are to survive their training.

9.4.2.3 Work

If asked to describe the work which a barrister does, most people would think of a man or woman in gown and wig, using their skills of advocacy in the courtroom. However, this is not their only work, for they also spend a lot of time researching points of law and giving advice to solicitors (known as 'counsel's opinion'). Historically, barristers have had a monopoly over rights of audience in the higher courts. This situation has been challenged repeatedly in recent years, by solicitors who feel that they have sufficient advocacy skills to represent their clients in court. See **9.4.1.3** above.

Another striking feature about the way in which they work is that with few exceptions, barristers are only permitted to take instruction from 'professional clients', a term which is carefully defined by the Bar Code of Conduct. In practice this means they receive instructions through the medium of a solicitor (or perhaps, for example, an accountant) and are not approached directly by the individual who needs their services. In June 1998, however, the Lord Chancellor published a consultation paper which suggested that the public should be allowed direct access to barristers in order to instruct them, without using a solicitor as an intermediary.

SAQ 6

What do you think might be the advantages and disadvantages of the public being able to make direct contact with barristers?

One of the great advantages from the point of view of the client in allowing immediate access to the barrister is that this might reduce the costs of litigation. Instead of having to pay a solicitor to instruct a barrister, the client can seek the advice of the barrister direct and cut out the 'middle man'. A disadvantage is that the client will not have the experience to select the most appropriate chambers from which to seek advice. From the barristers' point of view, such a change in their professional conduct would require them to make corresponding changes in the organisation of chambers in order to cope with the extra paperwork involved when clients are dealt with direct.

From April 2000, under the Access to Justice Act 1999, a barrister employed by a solicitor was able to provide legal services direct to the public. This is not an abolition of the rule we have just examined, but a reasonable middle way between the advantages and disadvantages listed above.

Barristers who achieve prominence through their success at the Bar are eligible to 'take silk', that is to become a Queen's Counsel. All barristers who are not 'silks' are known as junior barristers, and a number of them apply each year to be made QC. Once a barrister has taken silk, he or she will probably be instructed for more weighty cases, and will usually appear accompanied by a junior barrister who will share the work of the case. It is from the ranks of the QCs that most High Court judges are appointed, and so further promotion is possible for those who take silk.

The appointment of QCs is itself controversial, based as it is on a system of 'secret soundings'. We will come back to this point at **9.5.2** below.

9.4.2.4 Complaints

We have covered complaints against solicitors at **9.4.1.4** above. As regards barristers, first a couple of minor points need briefly to be added. Self regulation applies equally to the Bar as to solicitors. Within the Bar Council, there are five committees that work in standards and complaints and they are also able to provide arbitration services in appropriate cases. There is also a disciplinary staff handling approximately 400 complaints per year. The Legal Services Ombudsman is currently satisfied with the way 90% of complaints against barristers are dealt with by the Bar Council committees.

The controversial immunity mentioned briefly at **9.4.1.4** above needs to be examined in detail here.

ACTIVITY 5

Read the extracts from the speeches of Lords Steyn and Hope in *Arthur JS Hall* v *Simons* [2000] 3 All ER 673 in *Cases and Materials* (9.2.2).

1. Explain the nature, scope and reasons for advocates' immunity before this case.

2. Outline some of the arguments against the immunity.

3. Explain the grounds on which Lord Hope dissented (note that their Lordships unanimously dismissed the appeals as they related to civil proceedings. Lords Hope, Hutton and Hobhouse dissented from the majority as regards criminal proceedings).

There was an ancient immunity from actions in negligence given, for a variety of reasons, to barristers for acts concerned with the conduct of litigation. The dignity of the bar ceased to be recognised as a reason for the immunity in *Rondel* v *Worsley* [1967] 3 All ER 993. That a barrister does not enter into a contract with his solicitor or client ceased to be recognised as a reason in *Hedley Byrne* v *Heller* [1963] 2 All ER 575. However, it was made clear in *Rondel* that as the primary duty of the barrister is to the court, it would make barristers unwilling or even unable to carry out that duty properly if clients were allowed to sue in negligence. In addition, the reluctance of the courts to allow a client to relitigate cases and the 'cab rank' rule were reasons for the immunity.

In *Saif Ali* v *Sydney Mitchell & Co. (a firm)* [1978] 3 All ER 1033, Lord Diplock further recognised that it was not in the public interest to allow a court decision to be challenged by collateral (second) proceedings (i.e. a negligence suit against the barrister). The scope of the immunity was extended by s. 62 of the Courts and Legal Services Act 1990. Section 62 provided solicitor advocates with the same immunity as barristers.

However, despite the fact that barristers and solicitors are professional, no other profession has ever been granted such immunity. Accordingly, the immunity was seen to be an anomaly. Even though barristers are bound by the cab rank rule; solicitors are not. Immunity could therefore not be justified on the ground that an advocate must have immunity in a situation where he cannot choose whether to accept his client or not. Other professionals are not shielded from 'tiresome or disgusting [or] . . . vexatious [clients]' (*per* Lord Hoffmann), so there is no valid argument for protecting barristers. The advocate's overriding duty to the court, far from providing a reason for the immunity, provides a strong reason against it – if an advocate carries out his duty to the court, he has nothing to fear from a negligence action, because he will not have been negligent. It could be argued that the immunity actually harmed the profession and that actions against negligent advocates would help the public have more faith.

Whilst immunity from suit in a civil case could not be justified on the grounds of limiting a person's 'right' to relitigate, their Lordships had some difficulty in deciding whether or not to lift the immunity in criminal cases on this point. The problem lies permitting a civil court to review the conviction of a defendant passed in an earlier criminal case in an action by the defendant against his advocate. It is clear that a convicted person who is able to establish, on a balance of probabilities, that he was wrongly convicted (beyond reasonable doubt) as a result of counsel's negligence would cause untold damage to the legal system as a whole. Unless the conviction was quashed, the defendant would be entitled to damages, but not his freedom. To prevent this situation, Lord Hope felt it wise to continue the immunity in criminal cases as, he felt, abolishing it would damage the advocate's independence. Nevertheless, the majority of their Lordships recognised that a civil action against an advocate, which was in fact an appeal against conviction by another name, would be struck out as an abuse of process anyway (and it would further by highly unlikely that such a case would receive State funding under the Access to Justice Act 1999).

9.4.3   THE LEGAL PROFESSION - THE FUTURE?

A typical examination question on the legal profession is to consider the nature of a divided profession and the question of fusion. It may be that this type of question has had its day since the theoretical approval of the Multi Disciplinary Partnership or MDP.

An MDP is where professionals of other disciplines, notably accountants, enter into partnership agreements with law firms. This is part of the one-stop-shop culture mentioned above.

SAQ 7

Traditionally, MDPs have been criticised. What is the problem?

Much of our study on the workings of the legal profession has concentrated on the regulations and ethical standards of those professions. When professions are allowed to join together, the unanswered question is whose standards prevail? There are further issues of conflicts of interest, and the size of the partnerships.

ACTIVITY 6

Read 'Are MDPs the way forward?' (*The Times*, 30 November 1999) **and** the extract from 'Defiance or Alliance?' (*The Lawyer* 10 January 2000) in *Cases and Materials* (9.2.3) and 9.2.6. What points can be made in favour of and against MDPs?

It would seem that MDPs are not necessarily inevitable and whilst some of the larger firms are getting on the band wagon; not all are. Despite the opinion that MDPs are an effective way for consumers to obtain all their professional services from a single world-wide provider, there are serious concerns about the role the accountancy branch of a multi-disciplinary partnership would have in auditing a company when the legal branch has advised the same company. This could amount to a conflict of interest and would put at risk the independence of the firm.

9.4.4   THE CROWN PROSECUTION SERVICE

The post of the Director of Public Prosecutions (the DPP), now head of the Crown Prosecution Service (CPS), was created in 1880. Initially, the role now filled by David Calvert-Smith QC, was limited to responsibility for prosecutions in a very small number of difficult cases. During the 20th century, the majority of prosecutions were carried out by the police (either by in-house solicitors or by contract with local firms).

The Royal Commission on Criminal Procedure 1981 (the Philips Commission) concluded that it was inappropriate for the police, who investigated cases, to make the decision whether or not to prosecute as well, and then conduct the proceedings; that different police forces around the country used different guidelines to decide whether or not to prosecute and individual police forces were putting forward too many weak cases, sometimes against the advice of lawyers, resulting in a high percentage of judge-directed acquittals. There was a culture of prosecuting wherever an accused person had been charged irrespective of the strength of the evidence.

The Crown Prosecution Service was set up in 1986. It operated in 31 areas. In 1993, the then DPP, Dame Barbara Mills, reorganised the CPS into 13 areas with 93 branches, with the management based at a Headquarters in London. In hindsight, this resulted in an over-centralised and overly bureaucratic system of operation which has recently been reviewed and a further restructuring has taken place.

The Crown Prosecution Service's statutory responsibilities and duties are contained in the Prosecution of Offences Act 1985. Section 3(2) states its function is to provide an objective assessment of the results of police investigations and to prosecute cases. Section 10 provides for a Code of Practice.

ACTIVITY 7

In *Cases and Materials* (9.2.4), read the Code for Crown Prosecutors. What are the two tests used to decide whether to prosecute?

Under section 5 of the Code, there is an evidential test; that is whether there is a realistic prospect of conviction. Under section 6, the prosecution has to be in the public interest.

SAQ 8

In the first test, what standard of evidence is required? Think about the standard of proof in criminal cases.

As you know, the standard of proof in criminal cases is 'beyond reasonable doubt' so a prosecutor must bear this in mind. Looking at the case objectively, but not negatively, the prosecutor must be satisfied that it is more likely than not that that standard can be reached, seen as it is he or she that is under the burden of proof.

The Glidewell Commission was asked to review the second stage of the Code, especially where there was a nominal penalty or the loss involved was small. It expressed reservations about the discontinuance of cases on this basis but note that section 6.5(a) remains in place.

When the CPS took over prosecutions in 1986, the practice of discontinuing cases according to the Code, which before 1986 had been very rare, became more common. This is one of the reasons that the CPS did not enjoy particular popularity, especially within the police force. By 1988, two years after its inception, the general view was that the CPS had failed. Never had cases been discontinued or downgraded in this way and the number of trials had accordingly dropped.

Until 1999, it was the role of the police to compile the files for each investigated case and to arrange the date for the first appearance in court. The police *then* sent the file to the CPS. The CPS would review the evidence in the file and decide whether it justified the charge being laid by the police *after* the court date had been fixed. The CPS could discontinue the case, continue as per the charge, or could downgrade the charge which involves substituting it with a lesser offence.

In the Crown Court, the CPS then had to brief independent barristers because solicitors and *employed barristers* did not have the right of advocacy. Counsel employed by the CPS often worked against Counsel being paid a considerably higher fee under the legal aid scheme.

In 1998, the Glidewell Report into the CPS found that approximately 12% of cases were discontinued. It identified serious tension between the police and the CPS with a tendency for each party to blame the other if a case failed. Since 1986, Glidewell found, the CPS had become increasingly isolationist, and a rift in communication and co-operation had resulted.

The main recommendation of the Glidewell report, which has already been put into force, was to place CPS representatives into police stations to form a single integrated unit in charge of assembling and managing the case files, able to call on the police to obtain more evidence where necessary. To facilitate this partnership, the CPS has been restructured into 42 areas, removing an unnecessary layer of management, each area being coterminous with a police force.

ACTIVITY 8

Refer in *Cases and Materials* (9.2.4) to s. 37 of the Access to Justice Act 1999. What will this change for the CPS?

As part of the overhaul of the rights of audience of advocates, s. 37, which came into force in April 2000, provides that employed advocates will have the same rights of audience enjoyed by lawyers in private practice.

SAQ 9

Some critics have argued that CPS lawyers, even with the requisite qualifications, should not be permitted to conduct prosecutions in the Crown Court (see (1999) 26 SLR 33). What do you think such critics are concerned about?

There is a worry that an advocate under a contract of employment as a prosecutor will do anything to get a conviction. If teachers can be put on performance related pay contracts, why not prosecutors?

SAQ 10

How has the Access to Justice Act 1999 tried to deal with the concerns? Is this enough?

Section 42 of the AJA 1999 imposes a statutory, ethical, primary and overriding duty to the court to act with independence in the interests of justice. This duty overrides any other obligations, *including contractual obligations to an employer*. Whether this is enough when there is an incredible amount of pressure on Crown Prosecutors to succeed in terms of convictions rates remains to be seen.

9.5 The Judiciary

9.5.1 THE JUDICIAL HIERARCHY

Just as the court system is based on a hierarchy, so too is the judiciary. Judges are grouped into inferior and superior judges,

---

SAQ 11

Try to link the judge to the court. This is very approximate.

Judges	Courts
Law Lords	**Crown Court**
Recorders	**House of Lords**
Lords Justices of Appeal	**County Court**
High Court Judges	**Court of Appeal**
Circuit Judges	**High Court**
District Judges	

The maximum number of judges is subject to statutory maximums, any increases requiring the approval of Parliament and the Privy Council.

Judicial vacancies are now advertised. The first ever advert for the position of High Court Judge appeared in *The Times* on 24 February 1998. Previously, senior judges had been invited to their post. The topical issue is, therefore, no longer the invitation versus advertising debate, but the appointment system itself.

9.5.1.1 Inferior Judges

Eligibility for any judicial post is subject to the requirements of the Courts and Legal Services Act 1990. This governs eligibility in terms of qualifications based on rights of audience in the courts.

SAQ 12

From what you know of the CLSA 1990 already, what effect does the above statement have on solicitors?

As one of the Act's biggest effects was on rights of audience for solicitors who attained the certificate of advocacy, a corollary of this is that higher judicial posts were opened for all solicitors for the first time.

The first inferior judges for our consideration are District Judges (Magistrates' Court) which we examined above. At 1 May 1999, there were 93 DJ(MC)s, evenly split between London and the provinces. The statutory maximum number is 110. There are also 95 Deputy DJ(MC)s.

There is a larger number of District Judges who do not work in the magistrates' court than who do. District Judges, formally known as Registrars, have civil jurisdiction and work in the county court. In May 1999 there were 359 District Judges (a full complement would be 366) and 767 Deputy District Judges.

There are a number of inferior judges who are part-time judges. There are 875 Recorders who have mainly criminal jurisdiction in the Crown Courts, but under s. 5(3) of the County Courts Act 1984, they may also sit in the county courts. Of the 875,786 are barristers and 89 are solicitors. There are also 402 Assistant Recorders (85% barristers) and 112 Assistant Recorders in Training (95% barristers).

Circuit Judges are permanently assigned to a particular area, or circuit, on appointment. There are 361 Circuit Judges assigned in one of the six circuits: Midland and Oxford; North Eastern; Northern; South Eastern; Western and Wales and Chester. Each circuit also has two presiding judges who are High Court Judges.

Progress from inferior judicial status to superior is not an automatic promotion route. Only one Circuit Judge has ever been appointed directly to the High Court.

All inferior judges are appointed by The Queen on the advice of the Lord Chancellor.

9.5.1.2 Superior Judges

The first superior judge to be considered is a High Court Judge, but their title does not automatically denote the court(s) in which they preside. Obviously a High Court Judge does work in the High Court, but they also have important jurisdiction in the Crown Courts and may sit in the Court of Appeal if requested. High Court Judges, of which there are 98, are appointed by The Queen on the recommendation of the Lord Chancellor.

In practice, appointments are made from the ranks of Queen's Counsel, particularly from QCs who have sat as a Deputy High Court Judge and/or Recorder. Queen's Counsel, once the exclusive domain of the Bar, is no longer. Under the CLSA 1990, solicitors can also apply to be a solicitor QC, although only four have been appointed. QCs are appointed on an annual basis by the Lord Chancellor who carries out an extensive consultation process. It is this process that is currently so topical, and is referred to as the 'secret soundings system', although the Lord Chancellor has repeatedly pointed out that it is neither secret, as it is common knowledge that it takes place, nor a 'sounding', which has negative connotations, as it is more a consultation process. See further **9.5.2** below.

The Lord Chancellor has power under s. 9(4) of the Supreme Court Act 1981 to appoint persons qualified for appointment as a High Court Judge to be Deputy Judges of the High Court. A Deputy High Court Judge sits on a part-time basis.

High Court Judges are assigned on appointment to one of the three divisions of the High Court.

SAQ 13

Name the three divisions.

Refer to the end of the chapter for the answer.

There are 35 Lords Justices of Appeal who are appointed by The Queen, acting on the advice of the Prime Minister, who is in turn advised by the Lord Chancellor. Lords Justices of Appeal, broadly speaking, preside in the Court of Appeal. There is a statutory qualification which can be found in s. 10 of the Supreme Court Act 1981 as amended by s. 71 of the Courts and Legal Services Act 1990, but appointment is usually on promotion from the ranks of experienced High Court Judges.

In addition, with the same statutory qualification requirements as the Lords Justices of Appeal, there are four heads of divisions (five with the Lord Chancellor). The four are the Lord Chief Justice (currently Lord Woolf CJ), the Master of the Rolls (currently Lord Phillips MR), the President of the Family Division (currently Dame Elizabeth Butler Sloss P) and the Vice-Chancellor (Sir Andrew Morritt VC). The Heads of Divisions are appointed from among the Lords of Appeal in Ordinary (below) or Lords Justices of Appeal.

At the top of the judicial hierarchy are the twelve Lords of Appeal in Ordinary, commonly referred to as the Law Lords. They preside over the House of Lords, and you may recall that they also have an important role in the Judicial Committee of the Privy Council. The senior Law Lord is Lord Bingham. The statutory qualification for appointment as a Law Lord is to have been the holder for not less than two years of one or more of the high judicial offices described in the Appellate Jurisdiction Act 1876. In practice, Lords of Appeal in Ordinary are generally appointed from among the experienced judges of the Court of Appeal in England and Wales, the Court of Session in Scotland and the Court of Appeal in Northern Ireland. There are currently two Law Lords from Scotland (Lords Hope and Clyde) and one from Northern Ireland (Lord Hutton). On appointment, Law Lords are made life peers.

Appointments to the House of Lords are made by The Queen, acting on the advice of the Prime Minister, but the effective voice is, again, that of the Lord Chancellor.

The Lord Chancellor holds an office which is part political and part judicial. He has a role in all three branches of the State: the executive (as a Minister of State and member of the cabinet); the legislature (as Speaker in the House of Lords, he introduced the Access to Justice Bill); and he is head of the judicial system.

He is appointed by The Queen on the advice of the Prime Minister and his term of office ends when there is a change of Government.

The composition of the judiciary has been criticised. Some of the common criticisms are that the judiciary is predominantly elderly and male. The average age in the House of Lords in May 1999 was 65.4. Lord Denning was 83 when he retired, although as he was appointed before the Judicial Pensions Act 1959, he has been the exception rather than the rule in the last 20 years. There are no female Law 'Lords'.

Research carried out by University College London and the National Centre for Social Research 'The Paths to Justice' in November 1999 found that two out of every three people think judges are out of touch with ordinary people's lives. They are also seen as anachronistic, inconsistent in the sentences they hand down, and given to inexplicable utterances on rape and other subjects (*Guardian* 22 November 1999).

Further:

> 'The intellectual isolation of appellate judges who resolve "hard cases" with reference to notions of social justice and public policy which they are singularly (and collectively) ill-equipped to understand . . . remains a deeply worrying feature of our judicial process' (G Drewry [1984] 47 MLR 380).

Mr Justice Harman, who retired in February 1998, said in three different cases that he had not heard of the footballer Paul Gascoigne, the rock band Oasis nor the singer Bruce Springsteen. Make of that what you will.

9.5.2 'SECRET SOUNDINGS'

> 'There were sheaves of cuttings from the trials I had done. There were press cuttings from the Evening Standard about an actress I had been to a first night with. There was even an advertisement in the Times offering the charter of a yacht I had in the Mediterranean. But what really finished me off were getting on for a hundred scrappy notes addressed to the Lord Chancellor, many of them from one particular judge I had crossed swords with. Some of then were downright bloody lies. The most damning one was from this judge saying : "Sleeps with his divorce clients". It was totally untrue.'

(*Guardian*, 28 June 1986)

ACTIVITY 9

In *Cases and Materials* (9.3.1) read 'Judging the judicial selection process' (*The Lawyer*, 4 October 1999) and then answer these questions:

(a) What are 'secret soundings'?

(b) Why has the Law Society abandoned the practice?

(c) Why does the Law Society feel that barristers are also discriminated against by the use of this system?

The consultation process to discover factors that may influence the Lord Chancellor's advice to the Queen on judicial appointment is seen by the Law Society as being objectionable because it is neither open nor can the applicant have a chance to counter any allegations made. Of course, added weight is given to the unseen faces of the Bar more than the executive of the Law Society as the majority of applicant are barristers (remember also that the same system is used for appointing QCs), but the Law Society alleges discrimination against barristers too. This is because more than 50% of the judicial appointments come from seven sets of chambers.

In October, the Association of Personal Injury Lawyers (APIL), the Commission for Racial Equality and the Equal Opportunities Commission openly expressed support of the Law Society's campaign. Both APIL and the Law Society informed the Lord Chancellor that they will not be taking part in 'secret soundings' in the future. The EOC and CRE have also pointed out that the dramatic increase in the number of women and ethnic minority lawyers has not been reflected in the judiciary. The relevant statistics are available at the end of the article.

In December 1999, Sir Leonard Peach published his report into the Scrutiny of Judicial Appointments and Queen's Counsel Selection Procedures.

ACTIVITY 10

Part of the report's Introduction has been reproduced for you in *Cases and Materials* (9.3.1). What evidence is there that the concerns of the Law Society, APIL, the EOC and the CRE (above) are justified?

Despite the Lord Chancellor's affirmation that he will recommend for appointment the candidates who appear to him to be best qualified regardless of ethnic origin, gender, marital status, sexual orientation, political affiliation, religion or (subject to the physical requirements of the office) disability, it would appear that the biggest hurdle is getting women and ethnic minority lawyers to apply for judicial appointment. Perhaps the 'secret soundings' system puts them off.

ACTIVITY 11

Read 'The Peach report on Silk and judicial appointments' [2000] NLJ 8 in *Cases and Materials* (9.3.1). Answer the questions below:

(a)   What role will the JAC have?

(b)   What further role could it have fulfilled?

(c)   Why didn't Sir Leonard Peach propose a body with the power to appoint judges?

> **(d)   How does he, however, try to limit the role played by the secret soundings system?**

The JAC, to which the Lord Chancellor began appointing members in October 2000, will deal with grievances and complaints, it will audit the appointment processes and it will have a potentially pivotal role in recommending change to the Lord Chancellor. It will not have the power to appoint, because Sir Leonard Peach was asked to review how appointments are made, not by whom. In opposition, the Labour Party advocated a JAC to appoint, train and appraise judges. The 1997 Labour Party Policy Handbook for candidates said that the judicial selection process is 'too important to be conducted in secret in the Lord Chancellor's Department'. The Lord Chancellor may agree with Sir Leonard, therefore, that if the consultation process does not obtain sufficient information on a candidate, 'referees' may be named and asked for references, like any normal job. The Peach Report also recommends a hierarchical promotion system.

9.5.3   HUMAN RIGHTS ACT 1998

> 'One moment, there they were, more than 100 part-time Scottish judges, temporary sheriffs they're known as, happily doing their job of finding defendants guilty and sending them to prison, when -KAPOW! - suddenly. There they weren't . . .
> The magician in this case was Scotland's highest criminal appeal court, which decided that all those judges had no right to be there, and had to be abolished immediately. Just like that. The reason was that their existence offended against Article 6 of the European Convention on Human Rights (which is part of Scottish . . . law), which guarantees people a fair trial by an independent tribunal.'

(*Guardian*, 27 November 1999)

You may be wondering why. The judges in question were appointed by the Lord Advocate, Lord Hardie, on 12 month fixed term contracts. Since devolution, Lord Hardie has an executive role as he is ultimately responsible for prosecutions in Scotland, a role similar to that of the Attorney-General in England and Wales. The temporary sheriffs dealt with 25% of criminal cases in Scotland.

The judges were appointed at the beginning of each year and could be 'recalled' by the Lord Advocate without reason. They were paid by the day. They qualified for a pension only if they were promoted to the permanent bench. Guess who has the effective voice for appointment to the permanent bench? The Lord Advocate.

European human rights law indicates that judges *can* be appointed by the executive without contravention of the Convention, provided there is security of tenure. As you can see from the information above, the temporary sheriffs in this case did not have any.

SAQ 14

Who could this ruling have affected in England, why and when?

This judgment boded ill for any part-time English judge on 12-month fixed term contracts after 2 October 2000, when the Human Rights Act 1998 came into effect. Accordingly, in April 2000, the Lord Chancellor changed the relevant contracts (e.g. Assistant Recorders, tribunal members and Deputy High Court Judges) to 5-year fixed terms to provide extra security of tenure and so not offend the HRA 1998. Nevertheless, the Lord Chancellor is a political figure and a member of the executive, and thus appointments, discipline and removal of inferior judges, in his hands, surely continue to fail at least the spirit of the Article 6 obligations.

9.5.4 DISMISSAL AND JUDICIAL INDEPENDENCE

Superior judges (with the exception of the Lord Chancellor) hold office on a bond of good behaviour subject to a power to remove by both Houses of Parliament. This 'security of tenure' derives from the Act of Settlement 1701, but is now governed by the Supreme Court Act 1981. Inferior judges may be dismissed on the grounds of incapacity or misbehaviour.

The rules governing judicial pensions have recently been changed. To qualify for a full pension, a judge has to have served 20 years on the bench instead of 15.

SAQ 15

What effect will this change have on the average age of the judiciary?

Younger lawyers who wish to become judges will be going to the bench earlier than perhaps they would have done.

Judicial independence is the doctrine that judges should be free from improper pressure by the executive, litigants or by particular pressure groups. Judicial independence is said to ensure impartiality and therefore leads to fairer trials and supports the separation of powers in that the judiciary is able to act as a check on the branches of government.

ACTIVITY 12

Refer to 'Judicial training and autonomy' [1999] NLJ 1120 in *Cases and Materials* (9.3.2). Consider the role of the Judicial Studies Board. Why can training judges be seen to conflict with the concept of judicial independence?

If the paymaster of the judges and the body to train judges is the Government, it is at least arguable that the Government is able to dictate the tone of the training and the preferred interpretation of legislation and so on. So how is this risk of conflict resolved? The JSB prides itself on providing training *by judges, for judges.*

9.5.5 CONFLICTS OF INTEREST

We have examined the concept of a fair trial on numerous occasions throughout this *Learning Text*, in *Gregory* v *UK* (1998) 25 EHRR 577, *R* v *Gough* [1993] AC 646 and then of immediate relevance to this chapter is the recent case of *R* v *Bow Street Metropolitan Stipendiary Magistrate and Others, ex parte Pinochet Ugarte (No. 2)* [1999] WLR 272, which you considered in **Chapter 3**. One interesting point about the latter case is raised below:

'Whatever one's views about the merits, sagacity or neutrality of the current judiciary, there is significant evidence to support the proposition that, historically, judges have often been biased towards certain causes and social classes. For example, the book *The Politics of the Judiciary* (JAG Griffith, 5th edn, London: Fontana, 1997) is brimming with concrete examples of judges who have shown a noted leaning towards one side of the debate in cases involving workers, trade unions, civil liberties, Northern Ireland, police powers, religion and other matters. Lord Hoffman was wrong because he was a director of an organisation which was represented in the case before him. Nonetheless, it is ironic that while for centuries judges have been permitted to preside in cases where their highly contentious political views have quite evidently affected their decisions (sexist, racist, anti-union, etc.), the first senior judge actually to be successfully acted against for bias is someone whose agenda was nothing more than being against torture and government killings.'

(G. Slapper (1999) 27 SLR 30)

The key case is now of *Locabail (UK) Ltd* v *Bayfield Properties Ltd & another* [2000] 1 All ER 65 which you will consider in full in the End of Chapter Assessment Question.

Hot on the heals of the *Locabail* applications, Sion Jenkins, the former deputy headmaster convicted of murdering his foster daughter, Billie-Jo, also applied to the Court of Appeal. He applied for leave to appeal to the House of Lords on the basis that Mr Justice Penry-Davey was a inappropriate person to hear his previous appeal against conviction (which was dismissed) because the judge had connections with the school were Mr Jenkins had taught.

The *Locabail* and *Jenkins* cases are not going to be the end of the matter however.

SAQ 16

What is the likely effect of the Human Rights Act 1998 on these conflict of interest cases?

The role of the judge changed from 2 October 2000. Judges have been given legitimate power to declare executive decisions and actions as violating the ECHR. If judges enter the political arena, Parliament having given judges power to threaten its own sovereignty, the potential for allegations of bias will be even greater.

In a recent ruling, *R* v *DPP ex parte Kebilene and others* [1999] 4 All ER 801 the speech of Lord Steyn makes it clear that while Parliamentary sovereignty has been preserved, it has been drastically curtailed (*The Lawyer*, 15 November 1999).

9.6   Summary

Lay people are of fundamental importance within a legal system in a democratic State. There may be some valid criticisms of the composition of the lay bench, but a call for the abolition of JPs is likely to be regarded as an attack on one of the cornerstones of a free trial - trial by one's peers.

The Access to Justice Act 1999, in addition to introducing wide sweeping changes in the way in which legal services are funded, has evolved the way legal services are provided. Fusion of the professions is not necessary and finally there are no restrictions on employed solicitors and barristers enjoying the same rights of audience as their colleagues in private practice or chambers.

Something needs to change in the judiciary. Since 2 October 2000, it has certainly been possible for a judge to decide whether his or her own appointment contravenes the Human Rights Act 1998 and, as a result, force themselves to step down.

By the end of this, the final chapter, you should be able to:

- state and analyse the composition and contribution of the lay magistracy;

- trace and evaluate the recent developments in the work of solicitors and barristers, and include a commentary on the role of those employed by the Crown Prosecution Service;

- provide a balanced debate on the judiciary, the Human Rights Act 1998 and the conflicts of interest cases.

9.7   Further Reading

Griffith, JAG., *The Politics of the Judiciary*, 5th edn, London: Fontana, 1997.

Ingman. T., *The English Legal process*, 8th edn, London: Blackstone Press, 2000, Chapter 1.

www.lawsociety.org.uk

www.barcouncil.org.uk

9.8   End of Chapter Assessment Question

In *Cases and Materials* (9.4), read the cases of *Locabail (UK) Ltd* v *Bayfield Properties Ltd & another* [2000] 1 All ER 65 and answer the following questions:

1.   What are the central facts of each case?

2.   What is the key legal issue in each case?

3.   In which case(s) was the appeal allowed and why?

4.   How did the Lord Chief Justice distinguish *Dimes* and *Pinochet (No. 2)* in these cases?

5.   What guidelines were issued by the Lord Chief Justice on challenging a judge's impartiality?

Compare your answers with those at **9.5**.

9.9 Answer to SAQ 14

(a) Chancery,

(b) Queens Bench, and

(c) Family Divisions.

INDEX

INDEX

INDEX

INDEX

INDEX

INDEX